Global Human Resource Development

❧ ❧

MICHAEL J. MARQUARDT
DEAN W. ENGEL

PRENTICE HALL, Englewood Cliffs, New Jersey 07632

Library of Congress Cataloging-in-Publication Data

Marquardt, Michael J.
  Global human resource development / Michael J. Marquardt, Dean W.
Engel
    p. cm.—(Prentice Hall series on human resource development)
  Includes bibliographical references and index.
  ISBN 0-13-357930-1
    1. International business enterprises—Personnel management.
  2. Personnel management. I. Engel, Dean W. II. Title.
  III. Series.
  HF5549.5.E45M37 1993
  658.3'124—dc20
                                                              92-17719
                                                              CIP

Production Editor: *Kerry Reardon*
Acquisitions Editor: *Alison Reeves*
Cover Designer: *Mike Fender*
Prepress Buyer: *Kelly Behr*
Manufacturing Buyer: *Mary Ann Gloriande*
Production Assistant: *Joh Lisa*

©1993 by Prentice-Hall, Inc.
A Simon & Schuster Company
Englewood Cliffs, New Jersey 07632

Printed in the United States of America

10 9 8 7 6 5 4 3 2 1

ISBN   0-13-357930-1

Prentice-Hall International (UK) Limited, *London*
Prentice-Hall of Australia Pty. Limited, *Sydney*
Prentice-Hall Canada Inc., *Toronto*
Prentice-Hall Hispanoamericana, S.A., *Mexico*
Prentice-Hall of India Private Limited, *New Delhi*
Prentice-Hall of Japan, Inc., *Tokyo*
Simon & Schuster Asia Pte. Ltd., *Singapore*
Editora Prentice-Hall do Brasil, Ltda., *Rio de Janeiro*

Contents

Preface

At no other epoch in the history of business and industry has there been such an awareness of the critical importance of human resources. The industrialized world is becoming daily more global, with a number of countries moving away from traditional manufacturing and distribution activities and into the businesses of providing information and service. At the same time, the industrializing world is moving from agrarian and local business concerns that focused only on local markets to larger enterprises marketing on a worldwide basis. Finally, the world, itself, along with many of our assumptions about it, is changing. The "laws" of economics and nature, of international politics and human relations, are all being amended by people, events, and forces that are increasingly difficult to predict. The single necessary component in a successful response to all of these situations is people...ourselves and others.

Of some things we can be certain: in order to meet the global challenges of the twenty-first century, we need to be educated and trained. We need to be informed, flexible, and updated. We need to possess skills and vision, develop strategies, and effect change. In other words, we need to be prepared. Prepared for the enormous transformations that are taking place in our social, political, economic, and educational structures. Prepared for the evolution of our businesses into multibased global organizations capable of rapid change at both the global/strategic and local/market levels. Prepared for the elimination and obsolescence of traditional jobs and time-tested means of getting things done. Prepared for the emergence of areas of information, expertise, skill, and knowledge that we can hardly imagine today. Prepared, in brief, for almost anything.

And we need to be willing. Willing to adopt new cooperative strategies for getting the work done. Willing to give up some of the attitudes and postures that have characterized our thinking, informed our education, and been the basis of much of our training. Willing to change not only jobs, but careers, a number of times in our lives. Willing to be involved in a continual learning process that quickly outstrips and dates previously acquired degrees, certificates, and licenses. Willing to take pride in our work, and that of our colleagues. Willing to see value in a job well done and demand nothing less. Willing to take the time and care necessary to see that customers are well served.

We are talking here of enormous demands being placed on each of us and on our organizations and institutions. Increasingly, as these demands are recognized in the realms of business, government, and nonprofit development, organizations are turning to human resource professionals for advice, counsel, and collaboration. As a result, human resource development, *the art and science of empowering people and organizations to create maximum productivity, quality, opportunity, and fulfillment as they work to achieve common goals,* is rapidly developing as the principal means of responding to the demands of this new, global world of work.

As large corporations struggle to become or remain competitive globally, strategic planners and human resource professionals must collaborate more frequently in designing and developing strategies that are at once competitive, responsible, and comprehensive. Bren White characterizes this link between globalization and HRD, in his recent book, *World Class Training:*

> Rite-of-Passage into the globalized world system of the 21st century will be granted only to those organizations that adopt a focused and integrated learning process based on new world business strategies and encompassing new world skills (p.3).

International HRD practitioners must be able not only to operate on a global scale but also to work effectively in the myriad of distinct local cultures they encounter. They need to learn from the best of each nation's HRD programs as well as from the best of the global HRD technologies, ideas, and visions. In short, the successful HRD professionals of the nineties and beyond must be able to integrate globally what they practice locally.

It is with this focus in mind that we've written this book for practicing HRD professionals, managers who have global HRD responsibilities, and students in higher education who are considering a career in global human resource development. It is organized to provide the reader with an overview of global HRD as well as specific information about its various areas of concern, competencies, best practices, programs, and opportunities. The book is divided into the following six sections:

- **Foundations for Global HRD** considers in detail how globalization and culture affect the workplace and the profession of human resource development.

- **Roles and Practices of Global HRD** identifies and describes the four major roles of the HRD practitioner: developing learning activities, conducting training programs, consulting, and administering programs.

- **HRD in Global Organizations** examines the critical importance of HRD in enabling global corporations, public agencies, nonprofit organizations, and worldwide associations to become and remain successful.

- **HRD Practices and Programs around the World** surveys eleven regions of the world in terms of their cultural, economic, and HRD environment and profiles more than forty HRD programs around the world that have received national and global acclaim and recognition.

- **Entering the Global HRD Field** surveys career opportunities in five organizational categories (corporations, consulting firms, public international, government, and private nonprofit agencies) and then details the sixteen competencies most frequently mentioned by global employers as being essential for success in global human resource development.

- **The Future of Global HRD** identifies fourteen global HRD megatrends that will have an impact on human resource development around the world and describes how leading-edge organizations and HRD professionals are already incorporating these trends in their strategic planning.

It is our hope that the information contained in this book will in some small way encourage its readers in their contributions to the massive human effort that will be required in meeting the HRD challenges of the twenty-first century.

Michael J. Marquardt
Reston, Virginia

Dean W. Engel
Lafayette, California

Acknowledgments

The writing of a book on human resource development around the globe has required the assistance and encouragement of hundreds of people in the more than eighty countries we have worked in and explored during our combined fifty years in this exciting field of training and learning.

Our interest in, and dedication to, global human resource development began with Leonard Nadler, for many years professor of Human Resource Development at George Washington University, who pioneered the field of human resource development in the United States and in many countries around the world. Michael studied under his guidance, and Dean learned from his works. Thanks, Len, for the foundation and for the pushes.

Wayne Pace, the editor of this series, gave us the opportunity to write this book and then patiently waited for us to gain the confidence and time necessary to produce it. We hope he is pleased about this addition to the *Prentice Hall Series on Human Resource Development.*

Many others provided information, insights, and advice. Fred Ricci gathered information on major corporations from all corners of the world. Bruce Calvin of ASTD quickly did computer searches on HRD in whatever country or region we needed. Bren White and Quentin Englerth shared their tremendous knowledge on globalization, global leaders, and world-class training. The library staff at the Singapore Institute of Management allowed us full access to their resources.

We owe a special debt of gratitude to Victoria Bunney who prepared the manuscript, accurately and astutely, incorporating notes and data not only from California and Virginia but occasionally by fax and phone from 10,000 miles away in Southeast Asia.

Finally, we want to thank our wives, Eveline and Elianny, who gave us the time, space, encouragement, and, most importantly, love to carry us through this most challenging endeavor.

Michael J. Marquardt
Reston, Virginia

Dean W. Engel
Lafayette, California

Foundations for Global HRD

In the age of globalization, two apparently conflicting forces are at work—global vision and thinking versus local, culturally specific action and productivity; global integration versus local differentiation. As the workplace becomes more global, we also see a powerful countertrend to assert the uniqueness of individual cultures and customs.

Corporations realize the reality of these two dynamics as they seek at once to become competitive globally as well as to be successful in each locality in which they operate. They also realize that human resource development is the critical element in synergizing these dynamic forces and leading the work force and the organization toward both global and local success.

In Section I, we will explore how *globalization* and *culture* affect the workplace and the human resource development profession. Chapter 1 will first describe the general foundations of HRD—the practice areas, the roles and competencies, programs and activities—and then distinguish how global HRD differs from HRD as practiced in a single home country.

In Chapter 2, we will describe the factors that create cultures and the impact of culture on every aspect of HRD implementation and practice. To illustrate the powerful influence of culture, we will examine HRD practices in four regions of the world—(1) the United States and Canada, (2) East Asia, (3) the Arab region, and (4) Latin America.

1

CHAPTER 1

❦ ❦

GLOBALIZATION AND HRD

INTRODUCTION

> It is time for people to move beyond an awareness of the urgency of global competition and begin to develop skills for success in the global arena.

Nancy J. Adler

We have entered the Age of Globalization, where a single marketplace has been created by a combination of factors, including global telecommunications, growing free trade among nations, abundant energy sources, and worldwide financial services. The signs of this emerging era are all around us as companies, investment capital, information, and people travel the world with increasing speed and ease.

As the world's companies, large and small, adapt to the demands of global competition, they are finding that HRD is the lever for strategic success in the global marketplace. Although global HRD involves many of the same components, roles, functions, and activities as domestic HRD, there are at least ten factors that differentiate the two practices.

For the thousands of global HRD professionals working around the world, new competencies are needed to meet the challenges, responsibilities, and requirements of the emerging global business environment.

2

❦ *Value*

An understanding of globalization as it applies to the field of HRD will enable you to develop competencies and skills to respond to emerging challenges faced by global and soon-to-be global organizations. A recognition of the differences between domestic and global HRD practices will ensure appropriate response to training, organization, and career development needs.

❦ *Learning Objectives*

After studying this chapter, you should be able to:

1. Describe the critical role of HRD in the globalization process
2. Define Human Resource Development and identify the key roles and competencies associated with it
3. Outline the key factors that differentiate global from domestic HRD
4. Identify the organizational roles, approaches, and challenges involved in delivering global HRD programs

AGE OF GLOBALIZATION AND IMPORTANCE OF GLOBAL HRD

❦ *Signs of Globalization*

We have entered the Age of Globalization. A single marketplace has been created by (a) the competitiveness of global corporations, (b) global telecommunications enhanced by fiber optics, satellites, and computer technology, (c) growing free trade among nations, (d) abundant energy sources, and (e) worldwide accessible financial services. Organizations now "shop the world" for human resources, technology, markets, and business partners. Globalization will be the major cause for change for the remainder of this decade and well into the twenty-first century.

What are some of the rapidly emerging signs of this globalization?

- Giant multinational corporations and even small businesses are beginning to lose their national identities and are becoming global; product design, manufacturing, sales, and services are integrated and coordinated on a worldwide basis.
- In over 100 countries, English is either the primary or the common second language; one billion people speak English.
- In 1991, more than one billion passengers flew the world's airways.

- U.S. corporations have invested $400 billion abroad and employ over sixty million overseas workers; over 100,000 U.S. firms are engaged in global ventures valued at over $1 trillion. On the other hand, 10 percent of U.S. manufacturing is foreign owned and employs three million Americans.
- McDonald's operates more than 10,500 restaurants in fifty countries and is adding 600 new restaurants per year.
- Foreign investment in the United States has now surpassed the $2 trillion mark.
- Many Gulf countries have more foreign-born workers than native population.
- Financial markets are open twenty-four hours a day around the world.
- Global standards and regulations for trade and commerce, finance, products, and services are emerging.

❦ HRD as the Lever for Strategic Success in the Global Marketplace

In every industry and sector throughout the world, success and, in some cases, survival will depend upon the ability of organizations to compete globally. Even the largest companies in the biggest markets will not be able to survive on their domestic markets alone. They will have to be in all major markets, especially North America, Western Europe, and the Pacific Rim. Thinking and operating globally will be essential if an organization is to survive and adapt in the twenty-first century.

The ability to compete globally will be very dependent on the quality and level of HRD in the organization. For organizations seeking to compete in globalized markets, world-class global HRD can make the critical difference. HRD is the ultimate key to executing the bold vision and strategies needed for global success.

Bartlett and Ghoshal note how organizations that compete globally must now compete for the most important resource of all—talent. In a recent issue of *Fortune* magazine, Stewart reports how intellectual capital can become America's most valuable asset. The difference between failure and success will depend on how well organizations select, train, and manage their employees.

White notes that training must be the locus through which the "nutrients" enter into the organizational system. Training can provide "translocation" for the whole system.

COMSAT, for example, clearly sees training as the key lever toward global success. Its corporate training charter reads:

> The mission of the training function at COMSAT is to support the organization's strategic direction by providing effective training opportunities for all employees. The efforts will help us develop the perspective, knowledge, competencies and behaviors that will further strengthen our position as a major player in the global telecommunications arena over the long term.

❧ U.S. HRD Preparation for Global Participation

While American companies spend $200 billion per year in HRD, very little of it has a global focus. In this respect, the United States is far behind Asia and Europe in preparing its employees for the global marketplace. Some facts:

- 70 percent of American business people who are sent abroad are given no cultural training or preparation.
- 59 percent of the HRD executives surveyed by ASTD said there was no international training for personnel taking assignments outside the United States, and another 5 percent didn't even know there was any such training!

The attitudes and actions of other countries are quite different:

- Japan takes up to three years to prepare managers for an overseas assignment.
- A June 1990 survey of 6,000 employers in France, Spain, UK, Sweden, and Germany found that global preparation was seen as critically important and spreading rapidly.

Why are Americans so far behind? Why is there such a large gap between recognized global business and the necessity for preparing staff for such assignments?

According to Black, who has surveyed American executives in Asia and Europe, the fundamental reason is that American businesses simply do not believe global training is necessary. The assumption is that American ways and business practices are the norm, and a manager or sales representative who is successful in Boston will be just as successful in Bangkok or in Buenos Aires. Furthermore, many American managers feel that foreign assignments are undesirable— a step off the career path.

By contrast, companies in Europe and Asia see global training and experience as an integral part of the employee's development and as mandatory for future senior executives. Therefore, these countries insist on more international experience and cross-cultural training.

❧ The Importance of Global HRD

Successful global corporations cite the critical need to train staff to work in an international environment. Global training and development have several benefits, including:

1. Improved ability to identify viable business opportunities
2. Reduced waste of resources on ill-conceived ventures

3. Increased competitiveness around the world
4. Improved job satisfaction and retention of overseas staff
5. Less business lost due to insensitivity to cultural norms
6. Improved effectiveness in diverse business environments

Before discussing what *Global* Human Resource Development is, it is necessary to first briefly define and examine the fundamental aspects of HRD itself.

HUMAN RESOURCE DEVELOPMENT—DEFINITIONS, ROLES, AND COMPETENCIES

❦ *Definitions*

Defining and determining exactly what constitutes "Human Resource Development" has been a long and difficult process for HRD professionals. In an attempt to identify a common vision and language for HRD, the American Society for Training and Development (ASTD) interviewed hundreds of HRD practitioners and arrived at the following definition: "HRD is the integrated use of a) training and development, b) organization development, and c) career development to improve *individual, group* and *organizational* effectiveness."

ASTD distinguished HRD from Human Resources Management (HRM) and other Human Resource (HR) functions, as pictured in the Human Resources Wheel (Figure 1.1).

As we can see in Figure 1.1, there are eight other human resource functions in addition to the three practice areas of HRD. These are:

1. Organization/Job Design
2. Human Resource Planning
3. Performance Management Systems
4. Selection and Staffing
5. Compensation/Benefits
6. Employee Assistance
7. Union/Labor Relations
8. HR Research and Information Systems

The first four of these human resource functions are closely related to HRD, but developing human resources is not their primary purpose. The

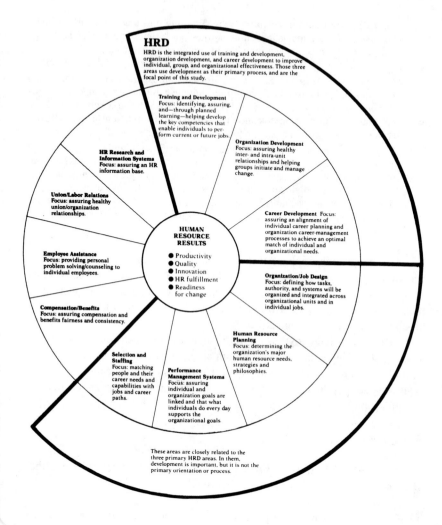

HRD is the integrated use of training and development, organization development, and career development to improve individual, group, and organizational effectiveness. Those three areas use development as their primary process, and are the focal point of this study.

Training and Development Focus: identifying, assuring, and—through planned learning—helping develop the key competencies that enable individuals to perform current or future jobs.

HR Research and Information Systems Focus: assuring an HR information base.

Organization Development Focus: assuring healthy inter- and intra-unit relationships and helping groups initiate and manage change.

Union/Labor Relations Focus: assuring healthy union/organization relationships.

Career Development Focus: assuring an alignment of individual career planning and organization career-management processes to achieve an optimal match of individual and organizational needs.

Employee Assistance Focus: providing personal problem solving/counseling to individual employees.

HUMAN RESOURCE RESULTS
- Productivity
- Quality
- Innovation
- HR fulfillment
- Readiness for change

Organization/Job Design Focus: defining how tasks, authority, and systems will be organized and integrated across organizational units and in individual jobs.

Compensation/Benefits Focus: assuring compensation and benefits fairness and consistency.

Human Resource Planning Focus: determining the organization's major human resource needs, strategies and philosophies.

Selection and Staffing Focus: matching people and their career needs and capabilities with jobs and career paths.

Performance Management Systems Focus: assuring individual and organization goals are linked and that what individuals do every day supports the organizational goals.

These areas are closely related to the three primary HRD areas. In them, development is important, but it is not the primary orientation or process.

FIGURE 1.1
Human Resource Wheel

other four contribute to human resource productivity but are even less focused on development.

Let us now examine more closely the three practice areas of HRD:

1. *Training and Development.* This area focuses on identifying, assuring, and helping develop, through *planned* learning, the key competencies that enable *individ-*

uals to perform current or future jobs. Training and development's primary *emphasis* is on individuals in their *work* roles. The primary training and development intervention is planned individual learning, whether accomplished through *training, on-the-job learning, coaching,* or other means of individual learning.

2. *Organization Development.* This area focuses on assuring healthy inter- and intraunit relationships and helping *groups* initiate and manage change. Its primary *emphasis* is on *relationships* and *processes* between and among individuals and groups. Its primary intervention is *influence* on the relationship of individuals and groups to effect impact on the *organization* as a system.

3. *Career Development.* This area focuses on assuring an alignment of *individual* career planning and *organizational* career management processes to achieve an optimal match of individual and organizational needs. Its primary *emphasis* is on the person as an individual who performs and shapes his or her various work roles. Its major interventions are influence on *self-knowledge* and on processes that affect individuals' and organizations' abilities to create optimal *matches* of people and work.

The integration of these three practice areas in HRD is necessary to accomplish the optimal level of individual and organizational effectiveness. It is important to recognize that everyone in an organization, not just HRD practitioners alone, must perform a role in the development of individual and group knowledge, skills, and attitudes.

HRD can include anything from a single training activity to entire systems for achieving strategic goals within an organization. It is a very dynamic, multidisciplined, and evolving field that draws upon education, management science, psychology, communication, economics, organization behavior, philosophy, and sociology.

❦ Roles

In the *ASTD Models of Excellence Study,* eleven major roles for the HRD professional are identified and described:

1. *Needs Analyst*—identifies gaps between ideal and actual performance as well as causes for these discrepancies.
2. *Program Designer*—prepares objectives, defines content, and selects and sequences activities for a specific HRD activity.
3. *Researcher*—identifies, develops, and tests new information for HRD utilization.
4. *Materials Developer*—produces and adapts written or electronically mediated instructional materials.
5. *Instructor/Facilitator*—presents information, directs structured learning experiences, and manages group discussions and group processes.

6. *Evaluator*— identifies the impact of the HRD intervention on individual or organizational effectiveness.
7. *Organization Change Agent (consultant)*—influences and supports changes in organizational behavior.
8. *Administrator*—provides coordination and support services for the delivery of HRD programs and services.
9. *Marketer*—markets and contracts for HRD programs and services.
10. *HRD Manager*—plans, staffs, leads, and supports the HRD function and links that work with the total organization.
11. *Career Development Adviser*—helps individuals to assess personal competencies, values, and goals and to identify, plan, and implement career and personal development actions.

It is important to realize that these eleven roles are not job titles. Rather they are a functional grouping of tasks that an HRD practitioner performs. Although occasionally a job title may be the same as an HRD role, typically an HRD position encompasses more than one role.

❦ HRD Competencies

The ASTD study also identified thirty-five key competencies that enable people to do HRD work and grouped them into four content categories as follows:

Technical Competencies

1. Adult learning theory
2. Career development theory
3. Competency identification skill
4. Computer competence
5. Electronic systems—computer, teleconferencing, etc.
6. Handling logistics
7. Setting objectives
8. Performance observation
9. Content competence
10. Training and development techniques and methods
11. Research skill

Business Competencies

12. Business work and economics
13. Cost-benefit analysis
14. Delegation
15. Industry or sector understanding
16. Organizational behavior
17. Organization development theories and techniques
18. Organizational systems
19. Project management
20. Records management

Interpersonal Competencies

21. Coaching skills
22. Feedback
23. Group process
24. Negotiation

25. Presentation
26. Questioning
27. Relationship building
28. Writing

Intellectual Competencies

29. Data synthesis and analysis
30. Information search
31. Intellectual versatility
32. Model building

33. Observation
34. Self-knowledge
35. Visioning

GLOBAL HUMAN RESOURCE DEVELOPMENT—HOW IT DIFFERS FROM DOMESTIC HRD

❧ Definition and Distinctions

Global Human Resource Development takes place across more than one culture or nation and may occur on an *international* (between nations), *multinational* (many nations), and *regional* (i.e., European, Pacific Rim, Latin America, etc.) scale.

Although global HRD involves the same practice areas (training and development, organization development, and career development), roles, functions, and activities of domestic HRD, it is shaped by factors outlined in the next section that differentiate and distinguish it from domestic HRD.

(The terms *global* and *international,* although carrying distinct connotations, are generally used interchangeably when referring to HRD.)

❧ Contrasting Global HRD with Domestic HRD

There are ten factors that differentiate global HRD from domestic HRD (see Figure 1.2) and make global HRD much more complex and challenging. Let us briefly examine each of these factors and illustrate how they affect the implementation of global HRD.

1. *Trainees.* In global HRD, the composition of the trainees may include one or more of the following categories:
   (a) Local/host country nationals (HCNs); e.g., Australians if you are training in Australia

(b) Expatriates/parent country nationals (PCNs); e.g., Americans who are also among the trainees in Australia

(c) Third country nationals (TCNs); e.g., Japanese who are among the trainees in Australia

Global HRD trainees in the United States can also include any or all of the above categories of trainees. For example, the Training Director of Subaru-Isuzu in Indiana trains Americans of various cultural groups as well as Japanese and, occasionally, Europeans.

2. *Culture*. Because the trainer(s) and trainees come from different cultures, an overriding dynamic of culture impacts every aspect of global HRD. (See Chapter 2 for a detailed analysis of how culture influences HRD programs and activities.) Culture, briefly defined, is comprised of the values and practices of a group of people. There may be several cultures within one nation; for example, the United States has numerous cultural groups. On the other hand, one culture may dominate over many national borders (Hispanic, Arab, Indian, Chinese). Global HRD may be *intercultural* (interaction between two or more cultures within or outside a nation), *cross cultural* (crossing cultures and national borders), and/or *multicultural* (involving many cultures in the HRD activity).

3. *Administration*. The coordination and management of global HRD programs involves numerous administrative issues such as transportation, relocation, cultural orientation, language translation, host government relations, housing, facilities, and support services. Chapter 6, Administration of Global HRD Programs, discusses these factors in greater detail.

4. *Learning Styles*. The trainees will, in most cases, have developed a different learning approach from that of the trainer. This learning style is based upon their educational system at the formal and nonformal levels, the cultural influences on learning, and their reasons for, and expectations in, learning. For example, they may be accustomed to a philosophical, didactic, deductive, collaborative, rote style while your approach as a learner has been practical, individualized, inductive, and questioning.

FIGURE 1.2
Factors Impacting Global HRD

5. *Physical and Financial Resources.* The resources available to the global HRD practitioner may vary from luxurious, large facilities equipped with the best learning technologies to an outdoor classroom with no flipcharts and handouts which could not be read anyway by the illiterate trainees. In situations where there is equipment, it may no longer function or require parts that are not obtainable or affordable. Trainees may be seated at executive tables, crowded in child-sized desks, or seated on the floor. Typewriters and photocopiers may not be available, even though promised.

6. *Environment.* The training may take place in a country whose government may be democratic or totalitarian, military or civilian-controlled. The economy may be booming or experiencing negative growth. Labor may be well trained and paid above U.S. wage levels or paid less than $1/day. Terrorism and kidnapping may be a risk for the global HRD practitioner. There may be very little private enterprise, or industry may be concentrated in one sector such as mining (Zambia). The society may be highly agricultural (Nepal) or totally urban (Hong Kong, Singapore). Crime may be a serious concern, and bribery may be necessary for government approvals. The people may be of numerous nationalities and very cosmopolitan or isolated and suspicious of outsiders. The weather may be extremely hot and humid or frigid and cold.

7. *Distance.* The fact that the global HRD practitioner may be thousands of miles away from his or her headquarters and cultural base adds a significant number of challenges. Communications to and from supervisors, peers, subordinates, colleagues, and vendors are of less frequency and quality. Supplies, equipment, materials, and even co-trainers may arrive late, or not at all. The support of family and friends, recreational opportunities, time and place to spend alone may all be absent. Distance also hinders and delays information, decisions, and resources. It may also lessen (or increase) the level of interest and commitment on the part of senior organizational staff regarding your work and your career.

8. *Roles of Trainers.* The roles and expectations of trainers in the United States are significantly different from those of trainers in most other cultures where the teacher/trainer is placed on a pedestal because of various cultural factors and customs (the writings of Muhammad and Confucius, few who are highly educated or have degrees, etc.). All trainers are expected to act and behave in an expert, disciplined, ethical, authoritative way.

   There are usually different expectations of the U.S. trainer; an American will be perceived as very individualistic, friendly but superficial, hardworking but selfish, honest but not very religious. The expectation of an American woman might be that of one possessing professional skills but probably lacking in morality.

9. *Language.* Language may be a factor in global HRD in at least three situations:
   (a) The HRD practitioner's language may be a nonnative language for trainees, co-trainers, and/or administrative staff in the country and at corporate headquarters.
   (b) The HRD practitioner may communicate in a second language that is the native language of some or all of the other parties.
   (c) The HRD practitioner and the other parties may all communicate in a nonnative language that is more or less understood by everyone. For example, a native English-speaking trainer working in French West African countries might train in French, which would be the second (or third or fourth) language of the trainees.

In any case, using a second language presents many difficulties to the HRD practitioner:
- Levels of fluency and comfort will affect interaction and tend to make it stiff and unnatural.
- Translation, if used, slows the process and the spontaneity of the learning.
- Certain words, meanings, connotations, and even feelings cannot be conveyed across languages.

10. *Co-HRD Practitioners.* The global trainer generally works with HRD staff from local or third-country cultures in the design, delivery, and/or administration of HRD activities. These co-workers will probably think differently, operate differently, and have different directives from their superiors. For example, they may believe that training should consist primarily of lectures, that more time should be set aside for religious ceremonies or official functions, that theory is more important than practice, that women should be separated from men, or that the foreign trainers should stay in the background.

Since each of these ten factors introduces significant difficulties and complexities into the practice of global HRD, being successful in domestic HRD does not necessarily guarantee success in global HRD activities.

ORGANIZATIONAL APPROACHES FOR DELIVERING GLOBAL HRD PROGRAMS

There are two basic approaches that a global organization can utilize to deliver its HRD programs—centralized and decentralized.

❦ *Centralized*

Many companies take a centralized approach to HRD programs, sending headquarters trainers around the world to deliver the training, although the training is adapted as much as possible to each locale.

For example, at McGraw-Hill, corporate headquarters trainers deliver training programs in their specialty area to their field offices throughout Europe and Asia. Likewise, the Corporate Director of Training for Johnson Wax designs and delivers training for forty-five subsidiaries around the world.

❦ *Decentralized*

The other approach is to have training developed and delivered regionally and/or locally. IBM, for example, organizes its education functions from 132 countries into five geographic units. Within each country, there is a training operation. Some countries have as few as five trainers, while the U.S. division contains some 2,000 people.

3M is even more decentralized in its approach to global training. Each of its subsidiaries in fifty-two countries is responsible for its own training. Often the subsidiaries develop and deliver their own courses. Sometimes, however, they will ask for consulting help from the headquarters training staff. This is also the case, for example, with Mobil Corporation in its worldwide language training programs.

CHALLENGES FOR GLOBAL HRD

The global economy, technological advancements, restructuring, evolving workplace, and changing cultural work force are creating tremendous challenges for the HRD profession. These include:

1. Preparing individuals and organizations to be both globally and locally focused
2. Providing a lifelong learning environment and support for employees to keep pace with the growing volume of global information
3. Demonstrating the power of global HRD in improved work force productivity, performance, cost effectiveness, and efficiency
4. Guiding the accelerated rate of change and the more uncertain business environment caused by the global economy
5. Recognizing the global customers' expectations in terms of quality, service, and product to determine needs and objectives for HRD programs
6. Identifying the culturally appropriate resources and methodologies among the vast and increasing array of tools, technologies, methods, theories, and packaged programs in HRD
7. Responding to the increased diversity (demographics, values, experience) of all levels of the work force, both in the United States and throughout the world
8. Developing higher capability and flexibility for managers as they work internationally
9. Involving HRD in the strategic levels of the global corporation
10. Adapting the HRD roles and processes to fit the global and local environments
11. Guiding individuals into appropriate positions in the global HRD arena
12. Building upon HRD knowledge, experience, and successes around the world

These challenges will be explored in the pages that follow.

SUMMARY

Globalization has significantly impacted the world of work and the work of HRD. HRD is being seen by more and more leaders as the key lever for corporate success in the global arena. HRD, whether global or domestic, involves the use of (1) training and development, (2) organization development, and (3) career development to improve individual, group, and organization effectiveness. There are eleven major HRD roles and thirty-five key competencies.

Global HRD is distinguished from domestic HRD in the manner in which the following ten elements are considered—trainees, culture, administration, learning styles, physical and financial resources, environment, distance, roles and expectations of trainers, language, and co-HRD practitioners.

A global organization can choose to deliver its HRD programs in a centralized, headquarters-based approach or in a decentralized, field-based approach. Twelve significant challenges are faced by the global HRD professionals due to the global economy, technological advancements, corporate restructuring, evolving workplace dynamics, and the changing cultural work force.

REFERENCES

ADLER, NANCY. *International Dimensions of Organizational Behavior.* Belmont, Calif.:Kent Press, 1986.

AMERICAN SOCIETY FOR TRAINING AND DEVELOPMENT. *Models for HRD Practice.* Alexandria, Va.: ASTD Press, 1988.

BARTLETT, CHRISTOPHER, AND SUMANTRA GHOSHAL. *Managing across Borders.* Cambridge: Harvard Business School Press, 1987.

CHANG, RICHARD. *An Introduction to Human Resource Development Careers.* Alexandria, Va.: ASTD Press, 1990.

GEBER, BEVERLY. "A Global Approach to Training." *Training* (September 1989), pp. 42-47.

KIRKPATRICK, MARCIA. "Why Aren't American Firms Training for Global Participation." *Management Development Report* (Summer 1990), pp. 1-6.

STEWART, THOMAS A. "Brainpower." *Fortune* (June 3, 1991), pp. 44-60.

WHITE, BREN. *World Class Training.* Dallas: Odenwald Press, 1992.

❦ ❦

CHAPTER 2

Culture and HRD

INTRODUCTION

"A slow sort of country," said the Queen. "Now, here, you see, it takes all the running you can do, to keep in the same place. If you want to get somewhere else, you must run at least twice as fast as that!"

Lewis Carroll
Through the Looking-Glass

Culture can be defined in many ways, but no matter the definition, a global HRD program cannot succeed if cultural factors are ignored. Experienced global trainers categorically state that diagnosing and understanding trainees' *cultural values* is as important as recognizing their *training needs*.

In this chapter, nine components of culture are identified and each is explored in detail with regard to its impact on HRD practices. The roles of trainer and learners as well as the processes of program analysis, design, development, delivery, and administration are analyzed in terms of cultural environment. Finally, the cultures of four regions of the world are examined to see how HRD can be culturally adapted and implemented.

❧ Value

A recognition of the importance of culture in HRD will enable you to more effectively design and deliver training programs in an international environment. Familiarity with the nine aspects of culture prepares you to systematically address new cultures to gain as much understanding as possible of the characteristics, beliefs, values, and attitudes of the learners.

❧ Learning Objectives

After studying this chapter, you should be able to:

1. Explain the impact of culture on HRD practices and programs
2. Describe the components and characteristics of culture
3. Identify and discuss the factors that influence cultural environment
4. Recognize the impact of regional cultural values on HRD practice and provide specific examples for four regions of the world

THE IMPORTANCE OF CULTURE IN HRD

Roger Dixon, a trainer with a record of success in cities throughout the United States, has just completed his first day of management training in Thailand, and he's not feeling very good about it. His style and techniques, which worked so well from Boston to Los Angeles, appear to be less effective here in Bangkok.

From the moment he entered the training room, Roger sensed a difference in the environment. Normally, he likes to put the trainees at ease by being very informal, encouraging them to address him as Roger, to raise questions and even challenge his concepts. This group, however, remained aloof and distant and obviously preferred to call him Mr. Dixon.

Believing in the importance of practicing the skills of management, Roger had, early in the day, described a typical management/subordinate situation and then asked for two volunteers to role play the scene. No one volunteered! Finally, Roger selected two older men who were, to say the least, uncomfortable and embarrassed by the activity.

Sensing that things were not going as well as planned, Roger thought that it would be appropriate to get some feedback and evaluation from the group regarding their perception and feelings about the workshop. He encouraged everyone to feel free to make either negative or positive comments about the training program thus far. The few who spoke said that the training was fine. Roger was now totally confused. These trainees sure had a strange way of learning. Why couldn't they be trained like Americans?

Roger had obviously failed because he had not accounted for the impact of culture on his training. Cultural gaffes of this sort are committed daily in global human resource development. The trainer's lack of knowledge and insensitivity to a particular people's religion, history, sense of space and time, communication patterns, and so on, have led to training ineffectiveness and cancellations and sometimes to resentment and anger for years after.

Experienced global trainers categorically state that, in the design and implementation of training programs, the diagnosis and understanding of the trainees, *cultural values* is as important as that of their *training needs*. If training across cultures is to be effective, it must not offend cultural values or it will be rejected.

Hofstede (1980), who studied thousands of employees in over forty countries for the past twenty years, believes that national culture explains over 50 percent of the differences in the behavior and attitude of employees—more than the differences in professional roles, age, gender, or race.

And these differences do not go away if one is employed in a global corporation. Laurant discovered that the impact of culture was greater in multinational corporations than in domestic ones. As a matter of fact, Laurant noted, a multinational environment causes people to *cling* to their own cultural values.

COMPONENTS AND CHARACTERISTICS OF CULTURE

Culture can be described in many ways. Most definitions contain three elements; (1) it is a way of life shared by all or almost all members of some social group, (2) that older members of the group pass on to younger members, and (3) shapes behavior and structures perception of the world.

Bierstadt describes culture as consisting of a system of explicit and implicit guidelines for *thinking, doing,* and *living. Thinking* (ideas) encompasses values, beliefs, myths, and folklore. *Doing* (norms) includes laws, statutes, customs, regulations, ceremonies, fashions, and etiquette. *Living* (materials) refers to the use of machines, tools, natural resources, food, clothing, etc. Pace *et al.* also include ideology (the combination of ideas and norms), technology (combination of ideas and norms and materials), and communication and language in the description of culture.

Hofstede (1991) defines culture as "a collective programming of the mind....It is learned, not inherited. It derives from one's social environment, not from one's genes" (p. 5). Culture is different from human nature in general and from individual personalities as can be seen by Figure 2.1.

FIGURE 2.1
Culture as Distinguished from Personality and Human Nature

For Hofstede, *human nature* is what all human beings have in common and is inherited with one's genes. The human ability to feel anger, fear, love, joy, sadness, the need to associate with others, to play and exercise are all part of this level of human programming. However, *what* one does with these feelings, how one expresses fear, joy, observations, and so on, is modified by *culture.* The top part of the triangle, *personality,* is the individual's unique human program which is not shared with any other human being. It is based partly on heredity and is partly learned, that is, modified both by the influence of culture and unique personal experiences. For example, all human beings eat. Different cultural groups eat different foods and in different ways. In turn, each individual has unique ways of eating.

Finally, it is important to realize that culture is multilayered (see Figure 2.2). *Practices,* including behaviors, symbols, rituals, and artifacts, are more visible to an outside observer. They are also more easily influenced and changed than the core of culture which is formed by *values* and underlying assumptions not easily recognized or understood by outsiders. These values are among the first things children learn—not consciously, but implicitly. Most children have their basic value system firmly in place by the age of ten. Teachers, leaders, managers, friends, and others of influence may be able to change practices in adults, but changing values is much more difficult.

FACTORS INFLUENCING THE CULTURAL ENVIRONMENT

There are nine interacting factors that create the various cultures (Figure 2.3). What distinguishes one culture from another is not the presence or absence of these factors, but rather the patterns and practices found within and between these factors. And each of these factors has a significant impact on HRD practice as we will see later in this chapter.

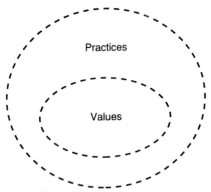

FIGURE 2.2
Layers of Depth of Culture

☙ *Religion*

Religion, the belief in a particular view of the supernatural with accompanying rituals and rules, is probably the single most influential factor in cultural thinking, living, and doing. Religion helps to establish the beliefs and norms, determines whether a people see themselves as basically good or evil, in control of or controlled by the environment, and defines what is truly important in life. Many religious writings even describe how one should eat, dress, relate to others, and work.

☙ *Education*

Education determines a society's means of transmitting the knowledge, skills, and attitudes necessary to live in that society. Education may be formal (primary, secondary, higher, and vocational), nonformal (structured

FIGURE 2.3
Nine Factors of Culture

1. Religion
2. Education
3. Economics
4. Politics
5. Family
6. Class Structure
7. Language
8. History
9. Natural Resources/Geography

learning outside the academic system; e.g., workplace learning), or informal (unstructured such as learning from one's parents).

Some cultures encourage inductive learning (open-ended, case-by-case) while others are more deductive (general to specific). Many societies encourage rote learning in an environment with complete, absolute respect and obedience to the instructor, while other societies support open, participative learning with a more egalitarian relationship between teacher and student.

❧ Economics

Economics are the activities concerned with the production and distribution. Societies may be (a) free-market, capitalistic, (b) centrally planned, government-controlled, or (c) a mixture of the two. Approximately half the world's population lives under a centrally planned, government-controlled economic system although recent events in Eastern Europe, Asia, and Africa show a rapid movement toward a more capitalistic free-market economy. Nevertheless, the impact of Marxist economics will influence the cultural behavior of these societies for many years.

❧ Politics

The political factor encompasses structures and activities related to the allocation and use of power as well as the regulation of access to resources and opportunities. Political systems may range from totalitarian to democratic and may exclude specific groups on the basis of ethnicity, gender, age, or economic status.

❧ Family

The concept of family in a culture may range from nuclear (immediate parents and children) to extended (including grandparents, cousins, aunts, and uncles). The nuclear family has limited interaction outside the immediate family, and family members are more free to ignore expectations of the extended family, or even the nuclear family, in choosing one's marriage partner, profession, home, etc.

In the extended family, the obligation to family members overrides the desires and wishes of the individual. The son, especially, is expected to remain with the family to support it in whatever way he can. Most of Asia, Africa, and Latin America place a high emphasis on the extended family structure.

❦ Class Structure

Class structures range from open to closed. In open class structures, individuals have the ability to choose and to move up, down, or laterally in the system without major difficulty. *What you do* is the important criterion.

In a closed society, one's position is determined and limited by *who you are*, that is, by birth rather than by individual achievement. The United States, for example, has a very open class structure compared to rural India, where the class system is very closed.

❦ Language

Language is the carrier and conditioner of all cultures. The words and structures available in a language strongly influence a speaker's values, beliefs, relationships, and concepts.

English, for example, is a very direct and active language. If I read a new book and enjoy it, in English I might say, "I think it's a good book," clearly defining myself as a person entitled to, and capable of, making such a judgment. In Japanese, a less direct language, I would say the equivalent of, "With regard to me, the book is good." The assumption of authority and objectivity is less present.

English is also a less formal language than many. For example, there is only one form of the second person for both singular and plural, "you." In Vietnamese, by contrast, there are many counterparts of "you," and their use is dependent upon age, gender, relationship, number, status, and so on. Thus it is easy to see how much more natural it is for an American to be informal and egalitarian than for a Vietnamese.

❦ History

A society's history has a significant impact on the culture. China's long, glorious history has created a culture where one's perspective of time is very different than it would be in a newly formed nation in Africa. (A Chinese trainer once stated that China would soon be an economic power, meaning within the next 100 or 200 years.) Colonized countries of Africa and Asia have many values derived from, and/or in contradiction to, their colonizers. The Arab world identifies with the military achievements of Muhammad and his successors. The United States's brief history includes the rugged frontiersmen, rapid industrialization and expansion, and pride, possibly arrogance, in being the "last, best hope of mankind."

❦ *Natural Resources/Geography*

Obviously, the land in which a society lives influences the culture. Hofstede (1991), for example, positively correlates a country's attitude toward equality with a country's latitude and observes that colder climates require smaller power distances between people. The vast spaces, minerals, forests, and farmlands of the United States helped form a culture based upon optimism, materialism, and confidence. On the other hand, societies regularly faced with hurricanes, flooding, drought, lack of minerals or scarcity of arable land tend to be more fatalistic. The oil and sand of Saudi Arabia have certainly had an impact on Arab culture as have the rain and forests of Liberia on Liberian culture.

LEVELS OF CULTURE

When we hear the word *culture*, we usually think only of a nation's culture. However, the definitions and characteristics discussed in the previous section can relate to five levels or types of culture—corporate, ethnic, regional, national, and global.

❦ *Corporate Culture*

Each organization also has a distinct culture that is passed on from the older to the newer members and determines their way of thinking, doing, and living. Deal and Kennedy, in their bestseller *Corporate Culture: The Rites and Rituals of Corporate Life*, noted how every organization functions in a way that is distinct from every other organization. The customs, language, folklore, and way of living at IBM, for example, are unique and different from those in all other corporations.

❦ *Ethnic Culture*

Most nations have many ethnic cultures within their borders Sri Lanka has two distinct ethnic groups; Cameroon has over 100. Los Angeles County has 150 cultural groups! The same ethnic group may also be found in many different countries as seen by the Chinese and Indians.

❦ *Regional Culture*

There are some cultural characteristics that are "many-nationed" since the cultural factors influencing the various national cultures are powerful and similar. For example, there are many common characteristics of the peoples throughout Latin America or the Middle East.

ẽ National Culture

National culture exists in countries that have within their national borders a distinct, discrete manner of thinking, doing, and living. This is the case in very few countries and usually reflects a history where other cultures have been driven out or destroyed.

ẽ Global Culture

The impact of global business and worldwide communications has resulted in a growing overlapping of values, norms, and beliefs around the world. More and more economists, anthropologists, and HRD professionals are referring to global culture. Ohmae identifies the economic characteristics of a borderless world. White describes the common characteristics of world leaders. Naisbitt sees a greater and greater global sharing of life style and behavior.

The HRD professional needs to be cognizant of all five of these levels of culture when conducting a training program. Each level has an impact on the design and delivery of the HRD activities.

THE IMPACT OF REGIONAL CULTURAL VALUES ON HRD PRACTICE

As discussed in Chapter 1, there are generally approved principles that can be applied to the sequencing and components of HRD design and delivery, the roles of the trainers and trainees, and the general administration and environment of the project or program. However, the implementation of these HRD principles is significantly affected by the cultural environment in which the activity occurs. Culture is like the filter through which training must pass as shown by Table 2.1.

As we can see, the factors of culture or cultural environment can have an impact on:

• Roles of the trainer and learners
• Program analysis and design
• Program development and delivery
• Program administration and environment

HRD PRINCIPLES	CULTURAL ENVIRONMENT	HRD IMPLEMENTATION
Roles of Trainers and Trainees		*Roles of Trainers and Trainees*
Analysis and Design	Factors and Characteristics	*Analysis and Design*
Development and Delivery		*Development and Delivery*
Administration and Environment		*Administration and Environment*

TABLE 2.1
Impact of Culture on HRD Practice

FOUR REGIONAL CASE STUDIES

We will now briefly review the cultures of four regions and then examine how Human Resource Development can be culturally adapted and implemented. The cultures we will explore are those found in:

1. The United States and Canada
2. East Asia
3. The Middle East and North Africa
4. Latin America

☜ *The United States and Canada*

Cultural Factors/Environment.

1. *Religion.* The dominant religious influence is that of Protestantism, with its emphasis on individualism, personal salvation, and the work ethic.
2. *Education.* Educational opportunities are universal with a strong public education system from kindergarten through graduate schools. Emphasis is on learning that is practical, utilitarian, and applicable. The inductive approach of thinking is encouraged. Experiences tend to be evaluated in terms of dichotomies (right/wrong, do/don't, successful/unsuccessful, good/evil, work/play, winner/loser, subjective/objective).
3. *Economics.* The economies of these countries are market driven and capitalistic. Competition is seen as healthy for economic development.
4. *Politics.* These countries believe in and practice democracy with universal suffrage. Government is seen as serving the people and should not be too powerful. Individual rights are legally protected.
5. *Family.* Families are nuclear, and children are responsible primarily to themselves for career choices and education.

6. *Class Structure.* These societies have an open class structure with opportunities for almost anyone to advance. Initiative is respected and rewarded, and equality of opportunity is the norm.

7. *Languages.* English is very active, direct, clear, and analytical, with a precise but abundant vocabulary. It is a language that patterns in linear structures and lends itself in support of detailed, observation-based analysis.

8. *History.* Compared to the cultures of Asia, the history of these countries is relatively short. They have generally been economically and militarily successful, especially over the past one hundred years.

9. *Natural Resources/Geography.* As a result of the arable lands and temperate climates, farmlands are abundant and fruitful. Canada and the United States enjoy vast frontiers and open spaces that encourage rugged individualism and independence.

Impact on HRD Implementation. Each of these nine factors of culture has an impact on the implementation of HRD in these countries. In the following section we will identify some of these HRD practices and what cultural factors account for them.

1. *HRD Roles.* The relationship between the trainer and the learner is much more equal in these societies than other cultures. Trainers must prove their competency. They can and will be challenged by the learners. Credibility must be earned. The trainers, however, are able to be informal and casual in working with the trainees. Such regional cultural factors as *class structure, politics,* and *language* support these roles and relationships between trainers and trainees.

2. *Analysis and Design.* In determining the objectives of a training program, the trainer, in collaboration with the trainees and their management, is expected to determine program objectives. Participants are expected to openly state their needs since there is an almost universal belief that everyone can improve and learn. Learners in these countries want to achieve success. The learners are also involved in setting objectives since they should have some awareness of what is best for them. Clear measurable objectives can be reached if the learners apply themselves. The teachings of *religion* and *history* encourage this approach to needs analyses and objective setting.

3. *Development and Delivery.* Training programs should be practical and relevant. Behavior can be changed and skills developed. A wide variety of methodologies are encouraged. Both inductive and deductive learning are desired. Methodologies based upon analysis, problem solving, learning from fellow trainees and by oneself are appropriate. Lecturing by the trainer is tolerated in short dosages. Cultural factors like *natural resources, education,* and *economics* favor this type of development and delivery.

4. *Administration and Environment.* The venue should be comfortable and economical. Fancy ceremonies and speeches from dignitaries are not necessary. Learners are selected based upon the needs of the organization and the perceived benefits of training the selected individuals, not because of their family name or class. Beliefs about *politics* and the *family* drive these approaches in Human Resource Development administration and environment.

❦ East Asia

Cultural Factors/Environment. Global HRD professionals who have worked in countries of East Asia—Burma, Malaysia, Thailand, Singapore, Korea, China, etc.—realize that they must significantly modify their training implementation if they wish to be successful (something Roger did not do at the beginning of this chapter). The cultural factors necessitating these changes are as follows:

1. *Religion.* Buddhism and Hinduism are the dominant religions. Both preach the importance of harmony with nature and one's fellow human beings, of accepting the world as it is, of seeking collaborative means to resolve problems. Humility is a valued virtue.

2. *Education.* The influence of Confucius with his high emphasis on education and respect for the educator permeates these cultures. It is thought that opportunities may be limited, so one seeks to learn what one can. In formal education, the teachers are highly respected and teach primarily by lecture while students learn primarily by rote.

3. *Economics.* The economies in these countries in recent years have been state-managed and centrally controlled but are now beginning to become more capitalistic. Small family businesses are numerous, with the government controlling most large-scale enterprises. Entrepreneurship and hard work emerges from Confucianism.

4. *Politics.* Although democracy is beginning to emerge in some countries, for the most part, power is still concentrated in the hands of a few, and the military often determines if an elected government may continue. Most of these countries have lived under European colonialism and the people have a love/hate relationship with those cultures.

5. *Family.* The family structure is strongly extended (again the Confucian influence). One is expected to respect and obey parents and grandparents in the selection of profession, domicile, and spouse. The needs of the extended family and even the village are more important than those of the individual. "Guanxi" (relationships) are needed to accomplish results.

6. *Class Structure.* Class structures have traditionally been closed and remain so in rural areas. However, there is a trend in the cities to be judged instead by one's achievement and hard work.

7. *Languages.* These societies are "high context," that is, the environment or context can influence what is being said as much or more than words themselves. The languages also have numerous forms of "you" to distinguish the myriad of relationships with others. Some languages, like Mandarin, are very rich and complex while others, like Bahasa Indonesian, are very simple and have a limited vocabulary.

8. *History.* The Chinese, Japanese, and Korean cultures and histories are thousands of years old with much past power and glory. Time frames are long term and there is an appreciation of the past.

9. *Natural Resources/Geography.* Huge populations strain the food and mineral resources of these societies. Numerous floods and earthquakes create a sense of the inevitability of nature's power.

Impact on HRD Implementation. Because of these cultural factors, the global trainer should adapt his training in East Asia the following ways:

1. *HRD Roles.* Learners have the utmost respect for all educators and treat them reverently. They expect the trainer to behave, dress, and relate in a highly professional, formal way. Learners may become uncomfortable with too much informality. They also hope to be treated with respect and sensitivity. The trainer is seen as knowing all, and it is believed that his assignments and expectations must be carried out without question or disagreement. *Religion, education, politics, family, class structure,* and *language* all contribute to this view of the roles of the trainer and trainees.

2. *Analysis and Design.* Since the trainer is omniscient and therefore should know what the trainees need to learn, it should not be necessary to undertake a needs analysis. And it would represent a loss of face or be embarrassing for learners to admit weaknesses to an outsider. Questioning of Asians can result in ritualized behavior, withdrawal, or even resentment of the trainer. Asking for self-analysis may be fine for Americans who value frankness and openness, but it is disastrous in East Asia, where a much higher value is placed on hiding one's own feelings and thoughts and not prying into the feelings and thoughts of others.

   Establishing objectives is also challenging. The concept of planning and goal setting has less impact on most East Asian philosophies and religions, which tend to be collective and fatalistic. Therefore, training that begins by asking for expectations, fears, and goals is "unlikely to meet with comfortable or coherent responses" (Rigby, p. 20).

3. *Development and Delivery.* East Asians, through their rigid education system, are accustomed to lectures, note taking, and limited and respectful questioning of the teacher. Trainees attempt to soak up information like a sponge and repeat it back verbatim. Learners from these societies also tend to place a high value on orderliness, conformity, and clear, specific instructions. Therefore, training materials should be orderly, well-organized, and unambiguous.

   Designing a workplace learning program that includes role plays and structured experiences will be painful because of various cultural factors. First, it is very uncomfortable for Asians to place themselves in the shoes of someone else because of their high respect for others. Role plays also generally include confrontation and/or innovation, both of which are hard to initiate in a culture whose *religion, education, politics, language,* and *history* value compromise, conformity, clear authority relationships, and conflict avoidance. Most learners believe that it is much better for the trainer, himself, to demonstrate what is the best knowledge, skill, and/or attitude.

   Mixing learners of different age, sex, professional rank, etc., and thereby ignoring their status differences may be seen as a means of undermining authority and power in the workplace. Exercises that strip the participants of status tend to cause embarrassment, confusion, and loss of face for all participants at the expense of learning.

4. *Administration and Environment.* A very high value is placed on visible signs of status and worth. An HRD professional's authority is determined to a great extent on the location and decor of the HRD office, how many people report to him, who they are, and so on. The quality of the training room, the training announcements, and the educational resources are indications of how important a training program is and greatly influence attendance.

Ceremonies with important dignitaries in attendance, certificates, plaques, and speeches are taken as signs of the value of the training program.

❧ The Middle East and North Africa (Arab World)

Cultural Factors/Environment. The Arab world, stretching from Morocco in North Africa to the Persian Gulf, includes more than 300 million people, bonded by a common religion (Islam) and language (Arabic), both powerful factors uniting the cultures of these different countries.

1. *Religion.* The Islamic religion permeates the daily life of the region. The five pillars of Islam—the one God (Allah), prayer, charity, Ramadan (holy month of fasting), and pilgrimage to Mecca—guide all, rich and poor, Egyptian and Iraqi, young and old. The teachings of Muhammad in the Koran regarding, for example, the brotherhood of all Muslims, the status of women, the rituals, and the mosques deeply affect the education, politics, and family life of these societies. Fatalism is so ingrained that the most common phrase in this region is "Insha'allah" (if God wills) since only that which Allah chooses will occur.

2. *Education.* The key learning experience for most Arabs involves the memorization of the Koran. The education system therefore emphasizes an imitative rather than a creative approach to learning. One learns from memorization rather than from independent research and original work. In most places, girls are educated separately from boys.

3. *Economics.* The region includes some of the richest countries in the world (Saudi Arabia, Bahrain, United Arab Emirates) and some of the poorest (Yemen, Egypt). Oil is the primary source of wealth, and foreign workers in the rich countries who send their remittances back to their families represent a major source of income for their own, poorer countries. Social relations are as important as getting the job done. Misfortune may be attributed to outside influence, i.e., what Allah wills.

4. *Politics.* Although democracy is being demanded by larger and larger numbers of people, most countries in the region are oligarchical, run by benevolent royal families and military dictators. The mullahs (church leaders) are very powerful and influential among the people and in some governments. Decisions are made by consensus, by ruling councils, and by families.

5. *Family.* The extended family is the foundation of Arab life with the Koran spelling out proper roles and relationships. There are formalized social distances between

persons differing in age and gender; men have a higher status than women, age is valued over youth, those who are married outrank those who are not. A parent's word is final, and great respect for one's elders is expected and given. The family is the primary determinant of individual behavior in such areas as choice of occupation, spouse, and living site, as well as numerous social obligations. Families are paternalistic and male-centered. Many homes will have a special meeting room, a "diwaniah," where neighboring men spend time socializing each evening.

6. *Class Structure.* Social organization is highly stratified; the division of labor is primarily on a class basis so that social mobility is difficult. Social morality prevails over individual morality. Thus, concepts of right or wrong, reward or shame derive not from an individual's determination of appropriate behavior, but from what society in general dictates as the social norm. People retain a formality of manner, particularly in initial social relationships.

7. *Language.* Arabic, the language of the Koran, is, for Arabs, a language to be spoken and heard. Arabs love to listen for hours to Arabic poetry, speeches, and songs. *How* one says something becomes almost as important as what one says. Arabs are generally much better at speaking their language and the languages of others than they are at writing them.

8. *History.* Within one hundred years of the death of Muhammad, the Arabs were masters of an empire extending from the shores of the Atlantic to the Chinese border. While the western world was experiencing the Dark Ages, Islamic culture was flourishing in the arts and sciences. More recent history, however, saw much of the Arab world colonized by the British, French, and Ottoman (Turkish) empires. Most Arab countries became independent in the twentieth century.

9. *Natural Resources/Geography.* Much of this region is desert with hot, dry weather. The Bedouin traditions of hospitality and generosity to people traveling from oasis to oasis remain strong. Elaborate greetings and close physical contact while communicating also derive from these traditions. The main natural resource has been the rich deposits of oil, but they have enriched relatively small segments of the population.

Impact on HRD Implementation

1. *HRD Roles.* Muhammad declared that education was the highest profession, and therefore, teachers and trainers must be granted high respect by Arab trainees. At the same time, the learners also want to be respected and will seek to develop a friendly relationship with the instructor.

   Formality is important, and even casual encounters with a colleague begin with traditional and elaborately formal words of greeting.

   In the more traditional societies, males (including trainers) are not to touch (for example, shake hands with) a female trainee. In some areas, men are not even allowed to be in the same room with women. *Religion, family,* and *class structure* are important cultural determinants for HRD roles.

2. *Analysis and Design.* Identifying needs and weaknesses in an individual or organization is difficult since people are not expected to speak negatively of others even if they dislike them. "God loveth not the speaking ill of anyone," according

to the Koran. The frankness of Americans regarding others' faults is regarded as highly improper.

The fatalism of the Arab culture may result in less motivation to totally achieve learning objectives since doing so would imply that one can control one's own future.

In designing the training program, it is important to allow considerable time for socializing and building relationships. Prayer time must also be built in. Things should not be rushed, for, as the Koran teaches, "haste is of the devil."

3. *Development and Delivery.* A number of strategies and structures, based on the factors of culture, can enhance the effective delivery of training programs in Arab societies.

• Provide ample opportunities for interactions between the trainer and learners and among the learners themselves.

• Rely more on oral rather than written demonstrations of knowledge acquired.

• Avoid paper exercises and role playing since they are thought to be games for school children.

4. *Administration and Environment.* The Arabs, reflecting their language, like the learning process to be permeated with flourishes and ceremonies. Training should not be scheduled during Ramadan, the month of fasting. Do not expect quick decisions from one person, since the culture is very consultative and time is flexible. (One of the authors was told that the definition of *bukra* "tomorrow" is similar to *mañana* but that it lacks the *urgency* of that Spanish word.)

❦ Latin America

Cultural Factors/Environment. The countries of South America and Central America share many cultural characteristics.

1. *Religion.* The Catholic religion with its historical emphasis on hierarchy, patriarchy, and fatalism permeates the Latin cultures. The Spanish missionaries established a highly structured social and economic system. Women are much more active in religion than men.

2. *Education.* The Latin education system tends to emphasize the theoretical and the humanities with less emphasis on the practical. Upper classes send children to private schools and universities, most of which are under the auspices of the Catholic Church. Illiteracy is high, and limited vocational education is available.

3. *Economics.* Free market capitalism is preached although economic power is primarily in the hands of small number of families in most countries. Societies are divided between the wealthy and poor with a small middle class.

4. *Politics.* The Spanish tradition of monarchy and authoritative government was continued in the Americas until independence from Spain was achieved in the nineteenth century. Most countries, however, maintained the tradition of the strong, decisive ruler and have had a succession of military dictatorships. (Bolivia has had over 150 coups in its 150 years of "independence.") The democratic form of government has begun to emerge throughout the Latin societies. People still elect charismatic, powerful, decisive leaders and like their strong individuality (personalismo).

5. *Family.* Latin culture has an extended family structure, and there is high respect for the family. Women are "placed on a pedestal," and a man's machismo protects and impresses them. Authority is centered in the father and is often extended to the " father of the nation," a strong dictator.

6. *Class Structure.* Latin culture is primarily a closed class structure where one is born high or low. Throughout Latin America, there are three distinct classes: (1) the rich Spanish families whose wealth was earned from the coffee plantations and haciendas as well as the new corporate leaders, (2) the workers, Latinos, who are mostly of mixed Spanish and Indian descent, and (3) the native Indians at the very bottom economically and politically.

7. *Language.* Spanish, a Romance language, is a rich language based upon Latin. It employs the passive voice more frequently than English, thereby implying less active control or responsibility for the world around it.

8. *History.* Many Latin American countries identify with the long and glorious history of Spain which colonized the region for over 300 years. The native Indian population has been decimated or assimilated except in Bolivia, Peru, and Guatemala. Rich today—gone tomorrow. Chance guides their destiny.

9. *Natural Resources/Geography.* When many of us think of Latin America, we think of the large cattle ranches and coffee plantations, the Andes, and the Amazon. However, Latin America has become the most urbanized society in the world. The two largest metropolitan areas in the world are São Paulo in Brazil and Mexico City.

Impact on HRD Implementation.

1. *HRD Roles.* As can be surmised from the cultural factors of *politics, economics, class structure,* and *family,* Latin American societies prefer a trainer who is a decisive, clear, and charismatic leader. They like to be identified with a successful trainer and will be loyal to him or her as a person.

2. *Analysis and Design.* In many ways, the Latin culture is similar to the Arabic (they did coexist for over five centuries in Spain during the Middle Ages); therefore, there are many similarities in conducting needs analyses and designing training programs. The macho and personalismo qualities make it difficult to expose one's weaknesses and faults in a needs analysis. Opportunities for affiliating and socializing are important. *Class structure* and *family* factors, however, can cause tensions if Latinos and Indians are trained together.

3. *Development and Delivery.* In developing the curriculum, the trainer needs to be aware of the Latin *education* tradition of lectures and more theoretical emphasis than in the United States. Unlike the Southeast Asian and Arabic cultures where English is the acceptable language for training, Latin American countries expect the training to be done in Spanish.

4. *Administration and Environment.* The value and importance of the training are determined to a large extent by venue, which dignitaries are invited for the ceremonies, and the academic affiliation of the trainer. Time is very flexible, and beginning or ending at a certain time is not important. Important decisions are often made by a single person at the top of the organization.

SUMMARY

Culture is a way of life shared by a social group which shapes the members' behavior and perception of the world. It is mental programming that is both learned and inherited. Culture is vitally important in the design, delivery, and administration of HRD programs. Simply put, HRD cannot succeed if cultural factors are ignored. Just as form (i.e., structure) impacts function (i.e., operations) in organizations, so does culture significantly influence training and learning.

There are nine interacting factors that create culture—religion, education, economics, politics, family, class structure, natural resources/geography, language, and history. In this chapter we examined how these nine factors affected the implementation of HRD in the four regions of the world— (1) the United States and Canada, (2) East Asia, (3) the Middle East and North Africa, and (4) Latin America.

REFERENCES

BIERSTADT, ROBERT. *The Social Order: An Introduction to Sociology.* New York: McGraw-Hill, 1963.

DEAL, TERRENCE, AND A. KENNEDY. *Corporate Culture: The Rites and Rituals of Corporate Life.* Reading, Mass.: Addison-Wesley, 1982.

HOFSTEDE, GEERT. *Cultures and Organizations: Software of the Mind.* London: McGraw-Hill, 1991.

HOFSTEDE, GEERT. *Culture's Consequences: International Differences in Work Related Values.* Beverly Hills: Sage Publications, 1980.

LAURANT, ANDRE. "The Cultural Diversity of Western Conceptions of Management." *International Studies of Management and Organization* (Spring-Summer 1983), pp. 75–96.

NAISBITT, JOHN, AND PATRICIA ABURDENE. *Megatrends 2000.* New York: Avon, 1990.

OHMAE, KENICHI. *The Borderless World.* New York: Harper Business, 1990.

PACE, WAYNE, PHILLIP SMITH, AND GORDON MILLS. *Human Resource Development.* Englewood Cliffs: Prentice Hall, 1991.

RIGBY, J. MALCOLM. "Culture and Design of Management Training Programs in Southeast Asia." In *International HRD Annual II.* Alexandria, Va.: ASTD Press, 1986.

WHITE, BREN. *World Class Training.* Dallas: Odenwald Press, 1992.

Roles and Practices of Global HRD

In the field of global human resource development, there are five major roles for the HRD practitioner— developing learning activities, conducting training programs, consulting, administration, and career counseling. The first four are examined in this section; the career development function is discussed in Section V.

In Chapter 3, the seven steps of the global training model are described with strategies and procedures to acculturize, that is, effectively implement each of the steps across cultural boundaries. Examples of successful acculturization strategies will be discussed.

In Chapter 4, the focus is on the actual delivery of training programs in various cultures. The impact of cultural differences on the setting, the role of trainers and trainees, language, learning styles, groupings, training methodologies, scheduling, and applications are some of the issues that will be explored.

Consulting within one's own culture is a tremendous task; to consult in a foreign environment is an even greater challenge. In Chapter 5, we will look at the eight roles of the global consultant and the five phases of organizational consulting. Following a review of the unique challenges of international consulting, we will investigate the key cross-cultural consulting skills.

A global HRD administrator has three primary administrative responsibilities: managing HRD staff and consultants, coordinating HRD programs, and marketing and negotiating HRD capabilities. Chapter 6 will examine how cultural customs and national regulations affect each of these responsibilities as they are implemented around the world.

❦ ❦

Developing Training Programs for International Settings

INTRODUCTION

Two roads diverge in a wood, and I—
I took the one less travelled by,
And that has made all the difference

Robert Frost

Like the traveler in the Robert Frost poem, global HRD practitioners could chose between (a) the easy road of simply transposing a successful domestic training program upon another cultural setting, or (b) the difficult, time-consuming road of "acculturizing" the design of the program to fit the culture of the learning group.

We strongly advocate the second path since it is critical that the HRD professional provide not only a learning environment but one that is culturally appropriate so that there are as few roadblocks to learning as possible. Each of the seven steps of the Global Training Model should be acculturized, that is, adapted and modified in terms of the culture of the target audience in order to ensure the likelihood of success in the foreign environment. Relevant cultural factors must be identified and then applied in synergy with the design and delivery of the training program. This is a time-consuming and difficult process and one that, in order to ensure maximum possibility for success, should include informants for whom the target culture is native.

❦ Value

The seven steps of the Global Training Model will give you a basis for comprehensive program design. And an appreciation and understanding of the need for acculturization of training programs should prepare you to successfully design, develop, and deliver such programs in international settings.

❦ *Learning Objectives*

After studying this chapter, you should be able to:

1. Outline the seven-step process for designing global training programs
2. Recognize the need for acculturization of methods and materials in designing international training programs
3. Identify the typical acculturization concerns at each design step
4. Apply the acculturization process to each step of the global training design process

GLOBAL TRAINING MODEL

The steps in developing global training programs are similar to those utilized in developing domestic training programs. The major difference, however, is that the elements of each step must be acculturized.

Figure 3-1 presents the Global Training Model with the seven steps in designing a training program plus the acculturization element which is applied after each step. The Global Training Model is a systems model. Following the final evaluation, new and changing needs of the organization and trainees are identified.

ACCULTURIZATION—DEFINITION AND IMPORTANCE

Before examining how acculturization works with each training step and the training program in general, let's first define what we mean by acculturization.

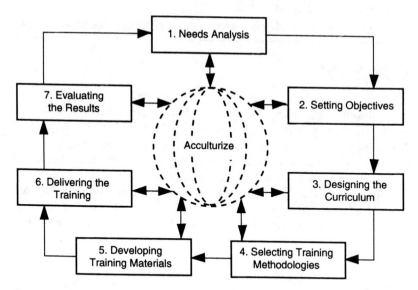

FIGURE 3.1
Global Training Model

Acculturization is the conveying of a program (including its ideas, content, and objectives) across cultural boundaries to assure that the training program is, to use a computer term, user-friendly.

An acculturized training program will include as few roadblocks to the learner as possible. The objective for the HRD practitioner is to ensure not only that learning occurs but that it is appropriate for the cultural milieu in which it takes place. The cultural adaptation is crucial. It is as important to success as is language translation (where that is necessary). Without it, little or no learning will occur.

In designing and delivering training programs in other countries, the HRD practitioners must factor the influence and impact of culture into their efforts. They must not only identify the relevant cultural factors but also synergistically involve the culture in the training design and delivery. Such efforts are difficult and time-consuming but obviously critical for training success.

Since an "outside" foreign person will have difficulty in fully understanding and applying another's culture, it is important and highly beneficial to involve local people in the acculturization aspect of each step in the Global Training Model, to test for cultural relevance and effectiveness.

GLOBAL TRAINING MODEL AND ACCULTURIZATION STRATEGIES

❦ *Needs Analysis*

Needs analysis is the collection, organization, and asessment of information pertinent to diagnosing the training and development needs of an organization. These needs are identified by finding the gaps between the desired capabilities of the organization and the present competencies of staff. A number of jobs exist within the organization that, when occupied by people with the requisite skills, can enable the organization to succeed. Typically, a job analysis is used to identify the duties, responsibilities, and tasks included in the job.

There are a number of methods which can be employed in gathering this data including:

- Observation
- Questionnaires
- Consultation
- Interviews

- Tests
- Analysis of reports and records
- Review of work samples

We can gather this information from present and former employees, supervisors, and managers, as well as outside people who provide services to the organization (e.g., vendors, consultants).

Acculturization. An important element of needs assessment is the identification of the gaps, weaknesses, and limitations of the individuals to be trained. In many cultures, it is difficult for the client to admit such a need or to allow the needs analyst access to such information. It may cause a person to "lose face" if he were to admit some degree of incompetence and weakness, especially in front of other people. In addition, the "expert" HRD professional should already have this information since that is presumed to be why he is in an authoritative position. It's taken as a sign of his incompetence that he has to ask you what he should already know.

Another difficulty is that in cultures that place a high value on agreement and politeness, the learners will attempt to guess what you are looking for and give you that response when you ask them what knowledge or skills they might need. The HRD practitioner must, accordingly, strike a delicate balance between discovering and predetermining the learning needs.

For these and other reasons (language, unfamiliar organizational environment, different educational system, cultural and corporate customs and rituals, etc.), it is critical to spend much more time and attention in conducting needs analyses when you are in other cultural settings. The use of local HRD staff can also be helpful in this stage of training design.

❦ Setting Objectives

In establishing training objectives, American trainers are encouraged to set clear-cut, competency-based objectives that the learner will be able to demonstrate at the end of the program. Objectives should include exactly what the person will do (performance), under what circumstance he will be able to do it (condition) and the degree of performance desired (quality).

Acculturization. For many cultural groups, such clearly defined objectives may be seen as:

* *Presumptuous*—The learners may wonder how the trainer can know beforehand what the learners will be able to do and/or what only God/Allah knows.
* *Threatening*—If the learners are unable to do this, they will have failed! Therefore training designs which begin by asking for expectations or personal goals are unlikely to be met with comfortable or enthusiastic responses.
* *Foreordained*—If God/Allah wills them to have these competencies, it will happen with or without their efforts.

Another cultural fact is that for many learners the primary and only objective is the acquisition of a certificate and not the learning since, in their culture, credentials are much more important than competency for career advancement.

For trainees in many cultures, the building of relationships and the development of friendship is of equal or higher importance than learning. A key training objective is the opportunity to practice and apply the learning together, both during or after the training.

Another factor when establishing goals in other countries is the importance of standards and testing requirements which have been established by labor ministries and the specific regulations which cover the various occupations and jobs.

❦ Designing the Curriculum

The most important part of designing the curriculum is to determine (1) the structure of the learning plan, and (2) the sequence of the training.

1. *Structure of the Learning Plan.* Structure refers to the relationships among skills and topics and is important because it provides a framework for learning. There are three types of structure that the curriculum developer may use to organize training programs:

   (a)Task-centered structure, which arranges the training topics to be learned by their relationships to job tasks

   (b)Topic-centered structure, which arranges the instruction simply by listing the topics to be covered

   (c)Problem-centered structure, which bases the training program around the problems the learners will face on the job

2. *Sequence of the Training.* There are two basic ways to design the training sequence:

   (a)Inductive—step-by-step, going from the specific to the general; from the known to the unknown, from the simple to the complex; generally more concrete and practical

   (b)Deductive—from the general to the specific; from an overview to the individual; generally more philosophical and generic

Based upon the training objectives, the interplay of the learning tasks, and the characteristics of the participants, the curriculum designer chooses the most appropriate training structure and sequence.

Acculturization. In developing the curriculum, it is important to study the cultural learning styles in order to determine how the trainees learn best and what structure and sequence they expect from the training. These styles are influenced by the cultural factors identified in Chapter 2 and differ from country to country and even from locality to locality.

There are, however, some fundamental differences between the learning style of Americans and that of the rest of the world.

Kohls, a leading anthropologist and cross-cultural specialist, notes that Americans (and northern Europeans) have a cultural system, learning style, and reasoning preference which tends toward the inductive task or problem-centered approach to learning. Most of the world, though, has a strong preference for deductive, topic-centered reasoning. Kohls suggests that these people rarely apply factual data in the multiple ways that people in inductive cultures do every day of their lives.

In developing a curriculum for deductive cultures, where trainees respond slowly to generalizing from specifics, Kohls suggests that a deductive approach and topic-centered structure should be initiated. After a period of time, an inductive, experiential approach can be used.

Another aspect of curriculum development is the scheduling of time allotted to various content areas and activities. Some useful suggestions:

- Do not schedule too tightly; most groups want considerable time for discussion and exploring.

- Take into account the values, styles, and attitudes of the learners; do not limit team activities to fifteen minutes when the cultural perception of agreement is harmony and consensus rather than majority rule.

- Bilingual programs need much more time than those that are monolingual.

- If English is the second language, schedule more frequent breaks to allow rest for the trainees, who are attempting to comprehend and speak in English.

- Allow time for socializing and building relationships.

Global trainers, in comparing curriculum designs, find that Germans feel comfortable with training developed in the United States since American curricula are highly structured, have a tight logical flow, and employ the rapid pace enjoyed by Germans. The French, on the other hand, prefer a slower pace and find American training lessons too cursory. The French enjoy discussing and arguing the merits of a subject. A one-day program in the United States would generally need to be designed to last two days in France.

☞ Selecting Training Methodologies

There are over 100 different training methodologies available to global HRD practitioners, ranging from the didactic, trainer-directed to the experiential, learner-centered. Figure 3.2 shows the relative degree of the most commonly used methodologies on this scale.

Acculturization. Many American trainers believe that experiential, process-oriented learning is more effective and enjoyable. For people of most cultures, however, these self-directed learning methodologies can be very uncomfortable and run counter to cultural norms. Participants from Asian and Arab cultures especially feel much more relaxed learning by rote and prefer to observe the instructor demonstrating a skill rather than risk being seen as foolish through risk taking and learn-by-doing methodologies.

Cultures which expect their instructors (a)to teach with authority and power, and (b)to be experts with absolute truths will obviously prefer the training methods which are more teacher-centered. Cultures which are more egalitarian, participative, and seek less structure will prefer training methods which are more learner-centered.

Global trainers have learned that certain methodologies may be effective or ineffective depending on the specific culture. Rigby, who has trained in Asia for many years, discourages the use of role playing and structured expe-

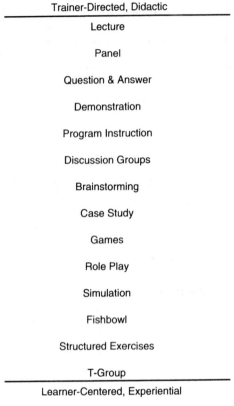

FIGURE 3.2
Training Methodologies

riences in these countries since learners find it difficult to place themselves in the shoes of others or to confront each other because of the high cultural value placed on conflict avoidance and authority relationships. In addition, risk taking through role playing, in countries like Japan and Korea, is taboo, since no one wants to be a fool or stand out.

Games, according to Rigby, can also be ineffective since Asians separate game playing from the serious business of learning. In Asia, the best participative training methodologies are small group discussions and case studies carried out among participants of similar age and status which should then be followed by a report of results presented to the total group by representatives of each group. This allows the representatives to discuss the process freely without any individual member having to take personal responsibility or receive accolades.

Rigby strongly discourages structured experiences or role plays that reverse the normal power positions held by participants. Asians attach great value to their positions and status differences. Exercises that strip them of these trappings tend to cause embarrassment, confusion, and loss of face for all participants and thus reduce learning.

The use of interactive video as a training strategy is not appreciated in countries like Japan (where it was invented) and other collectivist societies because it is a method that focuses on the individual. Japanese prefer to learn and work in teams.

Some global trainers discourage the use of debate or extensive verbal methodologies in China and Japan because they conflict with at least three cultural beliefs by:

1. Placing human-centered hierarchy over propositional truth
2. Over emphasizing definition and distinction in cultures where the languages create a world view more given toward imagery and ambiguity
3. Valuing oral communication over meditation, reflection, and thought

In a similar vein, the use of the case analysis in Arab countries may be ineffective since the Arab culture encourages verbal comments by only the leader or manager of the group and not the individual participants.

In Saudi Arabia and other Gulf countries, paper exercises and games are thought to be activities for school children; the preferred methodology for learning is group discussions.

Germans tend to prefer methodologies which are orderly, systematic, detailed, and analytical (case analysis), while the French seek lively, witty activities (e.g., brainstorming).

Since the eventual utilization of experimental methodologies is so critical to developing certain skills and competencies, Kohls and Wigglesworth recommend that the HRD practitioner should begin the training program more formally, through lecturing and modeling. Only after gaining the confidence and comfort of the trainees should he begin employing more learner-centered methodologies.

❦ Developing Training Materials

During this step of the training design, all the necessary training materials are written, adapted, and/or produced. This includes workbooks, handouts, instructor guides, audio- and videotapes, and computer software. These materials provide the content to enable the learners to achieve the training objectives.

Acculturization. The process of creating new materials or adapting already developed materials for export to other cultures is not a simple task. We must not only translate materials, but also be sure to transpose all that we have learned to a totally new environment in a way that gains acceptance in the local culture.

As materials developers, we should assume cultural differences rather than similarities. We should treat each cultural environment as different and requiring culturally appropriate learning materials that will not be seen as offensive to, or resisted by, the learners.

Sheehan has developed the following eight-step plan for creating training materials to use in another culture:

1. Local instructors and a translator, ideally someone who is bicultural, observe a pilot program and/or examine written training materials.
2. The educational designer then debriefs the observation with the translator, curriculum writer, and local instructors.
3. Together they examine the structure and sequence, ice breaker, and materials.
4. They identify stories, metaphors, experiences, and examples in this culture which might fit the new training program.
5. The educational designer and curriculum writer make changes in the training materials.
6. The local instructors are trained to use the materials.
7. Materials are printed only after the designer, translator, and native-language trainers are satisfied.
8. The language and content of the training materials are tested with a pilot group.

There are also a number of culturally specific guidelines to consider as you develop training materials:

- Avoid culturally inappropriate pictures or scenarios (e.g., women for Arab culture).
- Use plenty of graphics, visuals, and demonstrations if the trainees are learning in a second language.
- Provide many handouts and instructional materials; these are highly valued and even displayed in many cultures.
- Beware of corporate ethnocentrism in which the company wants to be presented exactly the same all over the world.

In many cultures, especially where a high value is placed on clear and specific instructions, training materials must be very well organized and unambiguous. The materials should include written examples for all worksheets required to be completed by participants, explicit written instructions for any exercise, and materials completely and accurately summarizing all lectures. Without these specific instructions, participants may become agitated by the lack of direction and, often covertly, blame the trainer for any negative outcomes resulting from the training experience.

Adaptation of Existing Training Materials. Several years ago, World Education, a literacy training organization, was working in India and using pictures of different objects—cattle, rice, insects, houses—to help the local village women learn words. The materials developer acculturized all the materials, but since the insect picture was the same size as the house, the villagers could not identify it—they had never seen such a gigantic insect!

In adapting training, one should avoid using training materials that represent American culture or imply that the American way is the best or only way. If too American-focused, these materials may not tell the trainees how to apply the knowledge and skills in their own environments.

Illustrating concepts with examples that are familiar and acceptable to the trainees makes learning much more productive and enjoyable. Exercises should be tailored to the local culture, for example, through the use of local names, titles, and situations whenever possible. One should modify the situations, change case studies, and rewrite applications when taking training materials to another culture.

The degree of adaptation required depends upon what is being taught. The more technical the topic, the less need for change. For example, if you want to teach someone to operate a particular machine, very little adaptation will be needed. On other topics, however, such as communication and supervisory skills, the amount of training material to be adapted will be considerable.

Translation. Translation is more than translating word for word the content from one language to another. Values and local applicability must also be translated. Translating instructional materials is a difficult process especially when it involves formulating new words to conform to good language usage, cultural meaning, and to the learning objectives of the training program.

It is important to remember that there are words that are not directly translatable into another language (e.g., "no" into Thai, the many "you's" of Thai into English). There is also not an automatic interchangeability of technical terms (e.g., there are no Arabic words for "metal tubing" or "jet propulsion").

It is important therefore to study the language—vocabulary and terminology. Gaining agreement with the local people on terminology and a glossary will help in preparing training manuals and workbooks. An excellent source for terminology is the International Labor Office which has published a series of glossaries for technical and vocational training in a number of different languages.

A final aspect of translation is the level of language skills, written and oral, of the trainees. Training materials should be prepared according to their language capabilities.

Computer Software. Computer-based learning (CBL) is increasingly being used in global training. Global CBL specialists realize that the necessity for computer courseware to be acculturized is even higher than other training materials because it is not an oral medium which can be acculturized "on the run" by an instructor. Learning through CBL systems depends on the written and graphic communications between a program and a learner.

Reynolds identifies a number of areas to consider in adapting computer programs to other cultures:

1. *Space.* Some languages require more printed space than others to convey the same information. For example, German requires approximately 30 percent more space than English. Extra space must therefore be reserved simply to provide sufficient room for the new language.

2. *Format.* When the target language does not lend itself to an acceptable presentation within the available space format, problems can arise. For example, Arabic is written from right to left, and therefore the graphic should go on the left of the text rather than the right as in English.

3. *Simplicity.* Although creativity is valuable for making a program which is interesting and effective, it is important to keep a lesson reasonably simple so that it can be more easily adaptable.

4. *Clarity.* An explanation or narrative that is obscure in English will be just as obscure in Indonesian or Swahili.

5. *Standardization.* Standards protect against practices that make adaptation difficult. Specify the size of the borders and locations where certain information will always appear on the learner's display.

6. *Cultural Relevance.* Use narratives and examples that fit the culture and environment. Reynolds relates how a HRD practitioner used snow skiing in Saudi Arabia! Baseball is not understood in most parts of the world.

7. *Jargon.* Jargon does not lend itself to translation, and employing current slang in training materials or presentation is usually neither necessary nor effective.

8. *Acronyms.* Acronyms create confusion. What is easily pronounced or understood in English may be unfathomable in another language.

9. *Humor.* Humor is always potentially dangerous since it can leave the learner wondering what the point is or, worse, feeling insulted. It is also difficult to translate.

Videotape. What do you do if you are producing a video that you plan on utilizing in two or more cultures? Do you dub in the local language, use subtitles, or reshoot all or part of the video? According to Murray, who has worked extensively in developing and adapting videos for other cultures, it depends on two factors: (a) the norm for the culture you are working in, and (b) the skills that you are trying to teach.

Based on the cultural norm, she suggests that in France you would generally dub (French are accustomed to watching American movies) while in Scandinavian countries you would use subtitles (that is the custom there).

If the topic you are developing is "interpersonal skills," you would reshoot the entire video since this skill is so very cultural. "Business etiquette" would also need to be reshot due to unique cultural differences. For example, Americans talk business during a coffee break while French are there to drink coffee.

The video content must fit the culture and be sensitive to local customs and behavior. Boston, a global trainer with McGraw-Hill, describes the time when he presented a videotape to show trainees how to sell. When it came time for them to role play the situation, there was an embarrassed silence. Why? Because the person demonstrating sales on the tape was a woman and in that culture women were not salespeople. It was obviously a serious faux pas to present her as a model to be emulated.

❦ Delivering the Training

The sixth step in the Global Training Model is the delivery of the training program itself in which the program is conducted and facilitated according to the previous five steps. The cultural impact on actual training delivery will be discussed in the following chapter.

❦ Evaluating the Results

The seventh step is evaluation, which includes both formative and summative evaluation. Formative evaluation is the data collection and analysis which is done *throughout* the training program and after each of the preceding steps that enables the trainer to modify and *reform* the content and process of the training program. A summative evaluation is completed at the *conclusion* of the training program to get a picture of the overall effectiveness of the course.

Evaluation seeks to measure the reactions and learning of the trainees and the quality of the training itself, including course design, the instructor, and materials. The evaluation should also identify ways of revising and improving the training program.

Acculturization. There are significant cultural differences as to who evaluates, what is evaluated, and how and when evaluation is done. In the United States, in addition to evaluating the learners' progress, the trainer generally seeks feedback from the trainees on how well he is doing. The trainees are encouraged to identify ways in which the learning can be improved as well as changes that might be made.

American trainees are generally comfortable in providing information about how they are doing and how the instructor is doing, particularly if it can be done anonymously. However, people from most other cultures would not be comfortable with such a process. Any suggestions or criticisms might imply a lack of confidence in the authority-expert trainer. Therefore they will respond with only positive comments. And if critical evaluation is offered by the trainer, there will often be a significant deterioration or even a cessation of performance by the trainees.

Our sense of evaluation is based upon U.S. values of frankness and openness, whereas many other cultures more highly value hiding one's feelings and thoughts and not prying into the feelings and thoughts of others.

Experienced global HRD practitioners suggest the following strategies in designing the evaluation component:

- Appoint a steering committee to meet at the end of each day. Trainees should be encouraged to give feedback and suggestions to this committee which would then forward these comments to the trainer.
- Designate a person (be sure the group sees him or her as a leader due to position, age, status, etc.) to whom individuals can provide feedback on the progress of the program at any time.
- Utilize the training team member(s) who are from the local culture in gathering the data.
- Design the evaluation instrument to focus more on the positive; ask for suggestions for improving what is going well.
- Plan to spend time following up with some trainees individually.
- Show that learning has indeed occurred by allowing participants to demonstrate the competencies they have developed.

In order to evaluate the competency attained by the trainee versus what is required for the position, it is necessary to develop a culturally reliable data base of norms for that position and culture. For example, let's consider measuring the warmth, approachability, and friendliness of a salesperson. If we were to measure an Italian salesperson against English norms, that person would be rated as uncontrollably emotional. A German salesperson measured against French norms might be judged humorless and cold.

In developing evaluation measures, Wilson Learning, for example, developed fifteen different data bases that enabled them to measure German behavior against German norms, French behavior against French norms, etc. These data bases take time to develop; Wilson Learning tests about 500 people in each culture to develop such a cultural data base.

Another aspect of evaluation which Wilson Learning has analyzed and developed is the comparative value of a culture's rating relative to other cultures. For example, there is a great reluctance among the Japanese to ever rate anyone at the top end of the scale since the Japanese simply do not deal in superlatives the way Americans do. To compensate, Wilson decided that a rating of "4" in Japan and a "10" in Indonesia equalled a "7" in the United States (Sheenan and Murray, p.18).

SUMMARY

Designing training programs for different cultural settings requires that the content and capabilities be acculturized—i.e., designed so as to be effectively conveyed across cultural barriers. Several acculturization strategies were identified for each of the seven steps of the Global Training Model: (1) needs analysis, (2) setting objectives, (3) designing the curriculum, (4) selecting training methodologies, (5) developing training materials, (6) delivering the training, and (7) evaluating the results. In the development of training materials, the HRD practitioner must differentiate between creating new materials, adapting existing materials, and translation of materials, as well as the design of computer software and videotape materials.

REFERENCES

KOHLS, ROBERT. "Square Pegs into Round Holes." Unpublished. Address at ASTD–World Bank Roundtable, Washington, D.C., 1986.

REYNOLDS, ANGUS. "Adapting Courseware for Technology Transfer." In *Technology Transfer*. Boston: IHRD Press, 1984.

RIGBY, J. MALCOLM. "Culture and Design of Management Training Programs in Southeast Asia." In *International HRD Annual II*. Alexandria, Va.: ASTD Press, 1986.

SHEEHAN, TRACEY AND KATE MURRAY. "The Art of Training Abroad." *Training and Development Journal*. (November 1990), pp. 15–18.

WIGGLESWORTH, DAVID. "Is OD Basically Anglo-Saxon." In *Corporate Cultures: International HRD Perspectives*. Alexandria, Va.: ASTD Press, 1987.

CHAPTER 4

ܟ ܟ

Delivery of Training Programs around the World

INTRODUCTION

Blessed are the flexible, for they shall not be bent out of shape.

Several years ago, one of the authors arrived in India to deliver a sales training course that had an enviable track record of success at client locations around the world. The sales model, one that is fairly common in the United States and Europe, involved identifying prospective clients' needs, describing the features of the product that would meet those needs, and then predicting benefits for the client.

The model came crashing down, however, when participants told the trainer that it would be, at best, rude to inquire about a client's needs and unthinkable to speculate about possible benefits. In the experience of the salespeople in the room, one of the most prized American benefits, better price, didn't play a very important role in client decisions. Established trust and friendship was much more important. Obviously, in cases like this, the flexibility and nimbleness of the trainer to adapt his delivery is put to the test.

In this chapter, we will focus on guidelines and strategies that can help to avoid scenarios of the sort described above. Designing an effective, culturally appropriate training program is only a beginning; applying the design and conducting the training program remain a formidable challenge. The trainer needs all of his creativity, sensitivity, and flexibility as well as extraordinary interpersonal and technical skills to make it a successful program. We will also examine the setting (environment, venue), the characters (trainers and trainees), and the play (actual delivery) of training.

❦ *Value*

Understanding all of the aspects of the training process and identifying strategies for adapting each of them to the cultural setting and audience will help ensure that you successfully structure and present training programs in an international environment. The culture-specific guidelines not only will help in the particular cultures discussed but also are illustrative of the sorts of issues that need to be considered whatever the target culture.

❦ *Learning Objectives*

After studying this chapter, you should be able to:

1. Identify the important factors in delivery of a training program in other cultures
2. Draw upon strategies and techniques for adapting program delivery to target cultures and audiences
3. Give examples of culture-specific training guidelines for a number of cultures and countries

TRAINERS

❦ *Role and Expectations*

In the American egalitarian culture, the trainer (even a college professor) is generally casual and informal with the learners. She may lean on the desk as she converses with the participants who are allowed to disagree and even contradict her.

How different this image of the trainer is from that found in most of the rest of the world. Most cultures perceive the teacher/trainer as an omniscient fountain of knowledge. The Koran, for example, calls teaching the noblest of all professions. In India, people have a tremendous reverence for teachers; standing at a lectern gives one instant credibility. The teacher or "guru" is perceived as someone who reveals God to you, even represents God to you, and therefore a respectful distance must be maintained. The teacher (and God) are responsible for the learning to be achieved.

Another aspect of perception and expectation of a global trainer is the fact that he brings the "baggage" that comes from being an outsider and from being identified as the representative of a particular culture. Although you are an individual and a trainer, you are also a German or a Nigerian or an American. If you are from the United States, you are seen as the "typical" American with the stereotypes associated with that culture. Americans, for example, are often thought of as being impatient, individualistic, hard-working, arrogant yet friendly. The learners expect you to act and teach in the "American" way.

As a trainer, be conscious of these expectations. Make no assumptions that foreign participants will see you as you are seen by trainees in your native country. Make additional, conscious efforts to show that you possess the best attitudes and competencies of a trainer; that you are interested in their country, language, and people; that you have respect for their culture and ways of learning.

❦ Working with Local HRD Practitioners

Since you are an outsider who can never fully grasp all the nuances of a local culture, it is extremely valuable to identify, develop, and utilize, when possible, the services of local HRD practitioners. Attempt to involve local staff in the design, delivery, and follow-up of the training program. Solicit their HRD expertise as well as their knowledge of the local cultural environment, traditions, and, very importantly, norms of behavior and learning.

Develop professional, collegial working relationships when possible so that progress and information on the training program can be shared and understood. And be sure that proper credit and recognition is given to local HRD professionals for their efforts.

Finally, it is important to develop the capabilities of the local trainers so that they can cotrain with you as well as be able to conduct the training programs on their own.

TRAINEES

❦ Learning Habits

Our learning habits are an ingrained part of our cultural heritage and are the result of our experiences at home, school, and work, the beliefs and behavior of our parents, the methods of our teachers, and the norms of our communities and businesses. These ways of learning vary from culture to culture, and even between regions in a country.

The American culture and educational system is inductive and practical and seeks not only to provide knowledge but to change attitudes and behaviors and develop skills. Our open, egalitarian values encourage students to speak up in front of large groups of fellow students and to challenge the trainer/teacher when we disagree.

For most other cultures, the role of the trainee is to listen to the lecture, take notes, soak up the information like a sponge, and return it back verbatim. Learners expect lectures. Contradicting or criticizing the instructor is not encouraged or, in some cultures, even tolerated. Silence is a sign of respect, not lack of interest or low motivation.

Learners are expected to stand up when the instructor enters the room and address him in a formal manner. A trainer who does not meet the exalted expectations will be seen as undermining accepted authority structures in the society. If this occurs, little of the course program is utilized, and the program will lose credibility and effectiveness.

DELIVERY AND PRESENTATION OF THE TRAINING PROGRAM

❦ *General Guidelines*

There are a number of do's and taboos when delivering a training program in another cultural setting.

1. Language
   (a) If you are unable to speak the local language, try to at least learn some of the basics phrases (good morning, thank you, etc.). The trainees will be pleased with your interest in their language.
   (b) Be sure to learn and use the culture's body language and nonverbal cues. For example, in India and some Arab countries, the shaking of the head from left to right does not mean "no," but rather, "keep talking, I'm listening to you." And the American gesture meaning "ok" has another, obscene meaning in Brazil and Greece.
   (c) If the training program is being conducted in English and English is not the first language of the participants, be sure to carefully assess their language ability and respond accordingly. Do not assume that they understand you or the training materials. Avoid colloquialisms or jargon unless you carefully define and explain them.
   (d) Concentrate on speaking slowly and clearly. Remember that the American accent may be very difficult to understand for Indians, East Africans, and others who speak British dialects.

(e) Use visuals as often as possible. Overhead transparencies, graphics, and pictures will make it easier for the learners to follow you.

(f) To ensure understanding, reinforce key points and ask the participants to restate them.

(g) Plan for the fact that the training program will take longer.

(h) Encourage participants to speak and give them reinforcement when they do. This will help them become more comfortable in using a foreign language.

(i) Distribute training materials in advance when appropriate. This will allow time to prepare and gain a better understanding if the materials are not in their local language.

(j) Be patient and listen carefully. Respect their efforts to convey learning and feelings in another language (and therefore in another cultural context).

2. Culture

(a) At the beginning, address the issue of cultural differences. Ask their indulgence for any blunders you might make. Encourage them to provide cultural feedback to you.

(b) Explain your expectations—of yourself as a trainer, of the trainees, and of the interactions between you and them. Try to be specific about behavior rules—how you wish to be addressed, how you will address them, and your expectations.

(c) Be sensitive to the local educational system and cultural habits for learning. Be careful in ascribing motivation or meaning to behavior even when it seems familiar. For example, behaviors that we associate with timidity might actually reflect assertiveness on the local cultural scale.

(d) Realize that the trainees in many cultures may be reluctant to raise questions. Therefore create a climate and expectation that trainees can ask questions without fear of offending the trainer or appearing foolish if they make mistakes.

(e) Remain comfortable with occasional silences. The silence may be related to the cultural behavior of learners or it may be that they are taking time to translate and/or think in English, two time-consuming processes.

(f) Recognize that participants may tend to base their response on what they think you want rather than what they actually believe or feel.

❦ *Culture-Specific Guidelines*

Each culture has some specific cultural expectations regarding the manner in which a trainer presents the training program. Let's look at a few cultural nuances:

1. *Japan.* The good trainer should begin in a humble vein and show his respect for the learners by honoring them in some small way. He must be dressed conservatively. Sincerity is important. Japanese prefer an indirect approach with a careful exploration of inner meanings. The trainer should avoid exaggerations and be prepared to give specific information. He should speak to the group as a group and not identify particular participants or subgroups.

2. *France.* In France, the trainer has to prove herself. Opinions have to be supported with facts and numbers. Since the French separate a person's public and pri-

vate life, the trainer should be reserved about mentioning the latter. Political jokes are widely used. The use of "hard sell" techniques will turn off French trainees. They prefer gentle persuasion.

3. *China.* Never acknowledge another person's emotions in China because you would be embarrassing that person with such a public acknowledgment of feelings.

4. *Britain.* The British see American trainers as being too forward, too informal, and too open. They, like many other groups, are often ill at ease with what they perceive as the premature informality and familiarity by Americans.

5. *Germany, Sweden, United States.*The types of questions the participants ask can often be predicted by different cultures. Germans, for example, focus on technical questions. Americans favor practical questions to explore how things work in practice. Swedish groups ask more theoretical questions that seek to define the implications of strategies.

ACTIVITIES AND METHODOLOGIES

In many cultures, the trainer should be prepared to begin training in a more didactic manner, with lectures and formal presentations. She can then gradually shift to more learner-centered strategies as the participants become more comfortable and willing to participate in inductive, experiential activities.

As you begin to use more experiential methodologies, search in advance for the participants who may be most comfortable and successful with them. For example, in looking for a volunteer to critique a role play, designate the most senior person as the observer because he or she may normally critique the performance of subordinates.

Allow flexibility and time. Distribute role-play materials in advance to allow the trainees time to become familiar with the roles and perhaps even rehearse the situation. Give them the option to role play or simply to discuss it if they are uncomfortable.

❦ Groupings

As you are conducting the training program, there will be a number of occasions on which you will need to put people into small groups. In the United States, you may do this solely at random (count off into groups of three, draw numbers, etc.). In other countries, this random approach could result in some very uncomfortable, ineffective, and even offensive groupings, especially at the early stages of the training program when cultural patterns are still strong and the participants have not yet become comfortable with foreign approaches.

In creating groups, be aware of the cultural significance, if any, of mixing by gender, status, age or ethnicity. In some cultures, for example, learning would be next to impossible with groups of mixed gender. In many places, a person's status in the community or group continues to determine the degree to which he can state his opinion. Throughout Asia, according to Rigby, young people in a group will hesitate to speak out if older people are in the group.Mixing people from cultures with a history of antipathy will usually be counterproductive, if not impossible.

Schedule frequent breaks, especially if participants are learning in a non-native language. Don't rush them or you will only wind up wasting time later restating and explaining information that you thought had been covered.

While working in small groups, participants might be allowed to discuss the case or problem in their own language and prepare a flipchart summary, also in their native language. In presenting to you and the whole group, the group spokesperson could then translate the summary into the common language.

❦ Distributing Materials and Returning Assignments

There is a much higher respect for written materials and one's own writings in other societies than in the United States. Therefore, when providing trainee materials and workbooks and returning assignments, handle them with care. Koreans, for example, expect that you will reverently return with both hands the manual or completed assignment to each person, not just leave them in a pile or toss the materials to them.

SCHEDULING

There are three aspects of scheduling that are extremely important for the trainer to take into account in determining the day-to-day activities—time, meals, and events.

❦ Time

Different cultures have widely differing perspectives regarding the use of time. In the United States, time is very important. "Time is money" and "don't waste time" are dictums we hear from early childhood onward. Time is seen by Americans as a precious resource they can and should control. This attitude is less prevalent in many other societies, especially in Latin America and the Middle East where time is not only not worshipped, it is downright ignored. In these regions of the world, relationships are more important than promptness; and fully understanding and discussing an interesting point is more important than staying on schedule.

If you are training in another culture, there may be a number of differing expectations regarding the 9:00 a.m. start. In some cultural settings, when the schedule indicates 9:00 a.m. as the starting time, it may mean that no one arrives until then, and the true starting time will be 10:00 a.m. Other cultures take the 9:00 a.m. as absolute and, if the instructor is a few minutes late, participants feel he is not taking them or his responsibilities seriously.

In these situations, it is critical for the instructor to determine and make clear to everyone which cultural definition of time will be employed—his or the group's—and then *stick* to it.

☙ Meals

In allocating time for meals, remember that different societies have different customs regarding the amount of time set aside. In most countries, it typically takes about one hour for lunch. However, in France, they expect two hours; in Spain, they take two to three hours but then are willing to work until 8:00 p.m. Remember the important social and group interaction values that eating provides for various cultures. If eating times cannot be compressed, try to build some learning activities into these longer eating times.

☙ Events

It is important to allow time for formal events in the training program. Ceremonial time for awarding certificates, listening to short speeches from outside dignitaries, and other such formalities show the importance of the program and encourage greater group motivation, participation, and learning.

TRANSFER AND APPLICATION

An effectively designed training program should include a variety of support systems that enable the learning to be transferred and applied to the workplace. There are a number of steps which the trainer, the learner, and his superior can take before, during and after the training program to transfer and apply the learning.

No matter how well a program is designed, however, it is incumbent on the instructor to sense if the designed application will indeed work and what modifications will need to be made. In many cultures, the learners expect the trainer to be specific, focused, directive, and knowledgeable about how the learning will apply in their organization.

An example of the importance of such knowledge on the part of the instructor can be seen in delivering sales training in Japan. In the United States, it is perfectly appropriate and recommended for salespeople to write introductory letters to high-level executives to gain entry to the company. In Japan, taking such a step would be highly inappropriate. The Japanese sales trainees, instead, should be taught that in Japan, the salesperson goes to the office every week for months to leave behind his business card. Only then will he be granted an interview.

EVALUATION AND FEEDBACK

In many cultures, the global trainer faces a double dilemma in evaluation and feedback. First, it is difficult for participants to be critical of the training designed and delivered by the trainer, whom they probably see as an expert, guru, authority figure. Second, it is difficult for the trainer to criticize the participants and, thereby, cause them to lose face.

Care must be taken that evaluation and feedback are based upon the culture in which the process is taking place. Using American norms to judge the success of training in India or France would not be appropriate or helpful.

One way to help the learners evaluate their learning progress is to provide some comparative analysis and assessment procedures so that the participants can do some self- or peer evaluation on the success of the program in increasing their knowledge or skills.

If a feedback/evaluation technique does not appear to be culturally satisfying and effective, invite the learners to suggest adjustments to the feedback process which may be less embarrassing to them.

SUMMARY

Once a training program has been designed and acculturized for presentation overseas, the trainer still faces the considerable challenge of delivering the program. In order to be effective, she has to consider a number of factors that might be taken for granted in a domestic program. The role and behavior of the trainer has to be seen in the light of participant expectations, which are culturally based; similarly, trainer expectations of the behavior of both trainees and local HRD practitioners need to be modified in light of the educational philosophy and practices of the target culture.

The target language and culture will determine some of the modifications that need to be made in delivery style. For example, even if the trainer doesn't speak the native language, she should be familiar with the body language of the culture so that she doesn't send incorrect or even offensive nonverbal signals. In this chapter, we presented culture-specific training guidelines for Japan, France, China, Britain, Germany, Sweden, and the United States.

The activities and methodologies that are employed in an international training session should also be modified in accordance with the target culture(s). Such matters as grouping of participants, distribution and return of materials, scheduling of the sessions, meals and special events, and transfer and application of the learning points need to be carefully considered.

Finally, the evaluation and feedback processes need to be modified to take into account local practices and beliefs about communication of "negative" information. In many cultures, getting objective feedback from the participants is a formidable task and providing constructive criticism even more so.

References

MARQUARDT, MICHAEL. "Planning in International Programs." In *Technology Transfer: A Project Guide for International HRD*. Boston: IHRD Press 1984.

RIGBY, J. MALCOLM. "Culture and Design of Management Training Programs in Southeast Asia." In *International HRD Annual II*. Alexandria, Va.: ASTD Press, 1986.

❦ ❦

CHAPTER 5

Consulting across Cultures

INTRODUCTION

Consultants should enable people and organizations to relish change and become leaders.

Jamaican Executive

A recent issue of the trade newsletter *Consultant News* estimates that there are over 100,000 consultants worldwide earning over $10 billion per year from corporations and government agencies. The consulting business has been growing at 20 percent to 25 percent per year and represents a growing portion of work for the international HRD practitioner. In this chapter, we will focus on the roles, challenges, and required cross-cultural skills of the global consultant.

❦ Value

An understanding of the roles of the global consultant as well as the challenges and limitations of the field will better prepare you to evaluate your interest in pursuing such a career. The required cross cultural-skills as well as the frustrations and joys of the work are considered in detail, enabling you to identify those traits in yourself that might make you a good candidate for global consulting.

❦ Learning Objectives

After studying this chapter, you should be able to:

1. Outline a number of different roles that the global consultant might play to transform organizations
2. Identify the five distinct phases of the consulting process
3. Recognize the common limitations and challenges faced by global consultants
4. Identify the cross-cultural skills required in global consulting
5. Cite culture-specific examples of the challenges facing the global consultant

THE GLOBAL CONSULTANT

❦ Growth of International Consulting

Consulting is experiencing a global boom. Several factors account for this significant worldwide increase in the utilization of consultants:

- The public sector is contracting out more and more of its responsibilities to consultants
- Corporations are downsizing and retaining fewer full-time staff
- The rapidly changing environment requires higher and higher specialization
- Global competitiveness among governments and corporations necessitates that the best talent from whatever country and culture be contracted to improve the competitiveness of the organization.

❦ Roles of the Global Consultant

According to noted international consultants Ronald and Gordon Lippitt, there are eight different roles for the HRD consultant, ranging in a continuum from directive to nondirective (see Figure 5-1). By directive, the Lippitts mean that the consultant's behavior assumes a leadership posture and that the consultant initiates and directs the activities. The nondirective consultant merely provides data which the client may or may not choose to use. These eight roles are not mutually exclusive since the consultant, for example, may serve as a technical specialist and advocate at the same time. Also, it is important to note that the level of client activity increases as the role of the consultant becomes less directive.

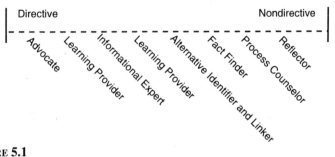

FIGURE 5.1
Consultant Roles

Let us briefly examine these eight consultant roles and provide cross-cultural examples of each.

Advocate. In this role, the consultant attempts to influence the client, often because the client is asking for a specific recommendation. The advocacy may be either in *content* (influencing the client to select certain goals or to subscribe to particular values) or in *methodology* (influencing the client to use certain methods of problem solving or change management). No skills or knowledge are being passed on to the client.

A consultant, after extensive research and data gathering, recommending that a corporation focus its marketing efforts in Eastern Europe, would be implementing this role.

Informational Expert. In this role, the consultant has been called upon because of his expertise and knowledge in a particular area that has been identified by the client. Examples of this role might be the systems analyst asked to write a computer program for an agricultural cooperative, or a World Bank trainer explaining the World Bank funding process.

Learning Provider. Innovative consultation requires the use of training and education within the client system. The HRD consultant advises what learning methodology or techniques can best be used in a particular situation. Assisting a client in the design and development of a globalized curriculum would be an example of this role.

Joint Problem Solver. This role utilizes the synergy of the client and the consultant in solving the problem. The consultant serves both to help the client maintain objectivity and to stimulate ideas. The consultant serves as a peer in the decision making. An example of this role would be the consultant and corporate client determining and agreeing that the company's distribution strategy in Japan was ineffective and that a new system was necessary.

Alternative Identifier and Linker. Here, the consultant helps to establish relevant criteria for assessing various alternatives for the client and develops cause-effect relationships for each alternative along with an appropriate set of strategies. A consultant who identifies the benefits, disadvantages, and consequences of several different training strategies for a Singapore management program would be employing this role.

Fact Finder. In this role, the consultant gathers data through interviews and observation and then analyzes and synthesizes it for the client. He functions basically as a researcher. A consultant who makes an evaluation of training programs in Africa would be carrying out this role.

Process Counselor. The focus for the global consultant is to enable the clients to perceive, understand, and act upon problems on their own. He provides feedback to help the client improve the working process and to tap the resources within and available to the client organization. Consultants who assist global organizations in developing and renewing themselves will generally employ this role.

Reflector. The reflector asks questions that will help clarify a situation. He serves as a facilitator or catalyst for action, but action is totally in the hands of the client. A consultant who assists a global corporation in the selection of new manufacturing sites by raising reflective questions would be operating in this very nondirective role.

❦ *Phases of International Consulting*

Consulting, whether in local or global circumstances, generally follows these five distinct but interrelated phases—entry, assessment, planning, implementation, and evaluation. In international settings, however, the cultural environment significantly impacts each phase.

Entry. Entry involves the establishing, developing, and contracting for an overview and scope of planned efforts, roles, and relations with the client system. In the United States and some other cultures, this phase may require a written contract which is often quickly achieved. In many cultures, such as the Arab, Chinese, or Japanese, this entry agreement can last months on end and require approvals from numerous levels and individuals within the organization. Global consultants must be patient—very, very patient. Allow plenty of time for laying the groundwork and be ready to jump through hoops of trust and acceptance.

Assessment. The second phase of the consulting process includes the assessing of the situation through the formal or informal gathering of information about or for the client in order to identify appropriate action steps to take. The methods one employs to gather necessary information will be affected by the cultural milieu. Cultures vary in their comfort in sharing data, being observed, admitting weaknesses, and stating strengths.

Planning. The planning phase involves the examination of the various means of accomplishing the goals of the intervention and developing possible strategies for action. This planning, depending upon which of the eight roles is being utilized by the consultant, involves varying levels of client input.

The consultant must be very conscious of cultural context in planning. Certain strategies may be inappropriate because of factors such as religion (too individualistic), class structure (violates status expectations), politics (not socialistic), or history (too identified with colonial ways).

Implementation. Once the actions have been planned, the consultant needs to coordinate or manage the implementation. Again, cultural characteristics such as time, space, values, thinking, and learning patterns will influence the how, when, who, and where of implementation. If, for example, the implementation involves the providing of negative information about another's behavior or actions, direct and frank feedback to that person in countries such as Indonesia or Thailand would be culturally inappropriate and therefore ineffective.

Evaluation. The final phase of the consulting process involves assessing the effects of the intervention. How effective is it? Will it continue after the consultant departs? What cultural factors will support or diminish the change? How could the intervention have been more effective in this culture?

Even the gathering of this information is much more difficult in some cultures than in others. Many cultures will be uncomfortable in telling an outsider that any part of the consulting has been done poorly.

CHALLENGES FACED BY GLOBAL CONSULTANTS

Consulting in one's own culture and country is a complex, complicated task. Attempting to provide assistance across cultures is even more difficult. Ramchandran has identified 12 major challenges that may arise when consulting in other cultures.

1. Work Ethic. Many cultures have a different attitude toward work within the organization than does the Western, Protestant culture. Motivation, daily attendance, and the identification of oneself with one's job vary considerably from country to country.

2. *Concept of Time.* The sense of punctuality and urgency, so important for Americans, is, according to Ramchandran, "a casualty...since everything can wait" (p. 73). In many countries, projects are delayed, plans are easily modified. Decisions must often await the personal review and approval of numerous senior and seemingly unnecessary officials.

3. *Acceptance of Criticism.* Criticism from the consultant can be taken personally in many cultures. Personal relationships can become strained. Organizational projects and programs in which a consultant recommends change may cause the manager to lose face, something which many societies wish to avoid at all costs.

4. *Expression of Agreement or Disagreement.* As we noted in Chapter 2, it is difficult in many cultures to directly say no whether in negotiations or in rejecting ideas and advice from a consultant. The desire to avoid direct refusal is a cultural trait rooted in courtesy and respect. The consultant needs to distinguish from a variety of contextual cues as to the level of agreement or disagreement felt by the clients.

5. *Problem-Solving Approach.* Since education in some societies is based upon rote learning, a consultative style involving mutual problem solving may be confusing and flustering. The rote learning approach added to the tradition of giving primacy to the viewpoints of the more educated outside expert results in expecting solutions rather than jointly working out the problem.

6. *Management Style Participation.* In many cultures, an autocratic management style is employed, and there is a clear hierarchy based upon status—age, sex, family, title, etc. This discourages lower-level managers from airing their views freely, lest they be construed as disrespectful. The frank discussion of problems by participants of differing status levels is rare.

7. *Efficiency vs. Employment.* In many cultures, particularly in government-controlled economies, both the public and private sector will make a commitment to retain high numbers of employees, even those who are incompetent or unnecessary to the organization. Workers have no pressure to increase productivity for their employment to continue. A consultant who suggests a reduction in the work force will be seen as culturally and/or politically insensitive.

8. *Role of Women.* Women are in different stages of emancipation around the world. Most countries place women at a lower status level. The consultant who ignores these cultural moves may be resented by both men and women.

9. *Bureaucracy.* Of course, there is bureaucracy everywhere, but in countries with a socialist pattern and centralized planning (i.e., Eastern Europe, much of Africa, China) there are mammoth governmental bureaucracies with their accompanying form completing and delay in decision making. Rules become ends in themselves, delays become interminable, and implementation may be subject to the whims of numerous bureaucrats.
10. *Limited Resources.* In many developing countries, there may be limited resources of such basic needs as flipchart paper, markers, and private meeting or working space. Telephones may be unavailable or, if available, not working.
11. *Organizational Structure and Staffing.* In many socialist and developing countries, the structure and staffing of an organization may have no relationship to the reality of products or services being rendered or to customer/client needs. The number of employees and their qualifications, or lack thereof, have been determined by various political forces. The authors recollect working with the Labor Ministry in one country where 200 workers were crowded into one large room with a few typewriters amid long tables. Most "workers" arrived at 9:00 A.M., talked among themselves for a couple hours, and left for the day at 11:00 A.M.
12. *Corruption.* Particularly in countries in which public salaries are extremely low, public officials expect payments to speed up or facilitate the approval of projects and funding. This may be seen as appropriate for service rendered or as a means to provide the income they need for their extended family.

COMMON LIMITATIONS OF GLOBAL CONSULTANTS

Roberts, who has hired numerous consultants for the World Bank, identifies four common pitfalls of consultants working abroad:

1. Inadequate flexibility in understanding the social, political, and cultural contexts in which the local organizations operate
2. Inadequate flexibility in adjusting to the learning style and preferences of country managers
3. Over-reliance on models, concepts, and materials derived from the consultants' own background that are inappropriate elsewhere
4. Lack of long-term commitment to providing adequate follow-through and reinforcement

CROSS-CULTURAL CONSULTING SKILLS

At a recent conference of the American Society for Training and Development, several noted global consultants met to identify the skills they felt were essential to be successful in consulting in other countries and cultures (Gormley). They selected the following nine skills:

1. *Cultural Self-Awareness*. This skill refers to the ability of the consultant to engage in an ongoing process of self-analysis as to what is happening within oneself in cross-cultural situations. The consultant must know and understand what factors about his own culture are an integral part of his thinking, values, behavior, etc.

   For example, a U.S. consultant might depend upon planning carefully and concentrating his energies on getting things done. The local client might want to spend more time conceptualizing and analyzing how and why things should be done. The consultant should be aware of his cultural tendency to become impatient with this "waste of time" and recognize it as a cultural perspective. He needs to somehow blend the two world views.

2. *Nonjudgmental Perspective*. Global consultants need the ability to remain nonjudgmental in intercultural situations. They must grasp what the other culture considers important as well as how organizations and individuals function in that culture. Unfamiliar perspectives, values, and behaviors should be examined within the context of the surrounding culture. Without a doubt, the ability to suspend judgment is one of the biggest challenges facing the cross-cultural consultant. Ideally, the consultant should be able to say, "This is my vision of what is desirable. You may have different values. Both are valid, and we need to find ways to build together."

3. *Empathic Information Gathering*. In order for cross-cultural consultants to be effective, they must develop empathic relationships with clients of the local culture. This requires that they are able to listen actively to the other culture, that they use observation skills to learn and understand, that they are descriptive rather than judgmental about events. Consultants must know how to ask questions appropriately and avoid questions which are too personal, embarrassing, or probing for the culture.

4. *Filtered Data Gathering and Interpretation*. Much of a consultant's work involves the gathering and utilization of information. Difficult enough in one's own culture, it is even more challenging to collect and validate in a different culture where the possibility of error is magnified.

   The consultant must be able to gather information and be sure that it is not filtered in such a way that one's own cultural biases affect the accuracy or interpretation. The successful consultant can blend two or more cultural perspectives and interpret them in a way that transcends any single one of them.

5. *Establishing of Interpersonal Relationships*. Consultants cannot be effective without being able to establish and maintain strong interpersonal relationships; this usually requires much more time and effort in another culture.

6. *Working in Ambiguous Situations*. In cross-cultural consulting, it is often difficult to interpret what is going on and what course of action one should take. This ambiguity could cause a consultant to become impatient, frustrated, and even angry—all of which can worsen the consulting situation. Len and Zeace Nadler, who have consulted internationally for over thirty-five years, believe that the skill of tolerating and handling high levels of ambiguity is the *key* skill of consultants.

7. *Participating Productively in Other Cultures*. Consultants need to be able to function in the operational mode of the other culture, in their meetings, in their training programs, in their organizational gatherings, etc.

8. *Professional Behavior.* Effective global consultants must manifest professional and mature behavior. They should be thoroughly prepared and accept personal responsibility for the quality of their work and realize that their culture is being evaluated by their behavior, attitudes, and actions.

9. *Developing Independence and Competence.* The tendency in many cultures is to become dependent on the outside, international expert. The global consultant, therefore, should be diligent in not falling into the trap of being the "colonial master" who creates dependence and incompetence.

CONSULTING IN A GOVERNMENT-PLANNED ECONOMY

As the Eastern European countries as well as China and much of Africa move from a government-controlled to a free-market economy, they are seeking the services of consultants from Western, capitalistic economies. Sterniczuk and Lis identified a number of unique cultural aspects of such organizations that impact the work of the consultant:

- Hierarchical relationships are critical, and these relationships dominate the flow of the state economy.
- Shortages of almost all resources exist due to monopolistic structures.
- Suppliers are powerful and customers are weak, thus creating an underground economy.
- There is a poor infrastructure in transportation, energy, market mechanisms, labor flow, and education.
- Local enterprises are strongly affected by government policies. For example, the government can insist on forced hiring, and artificially low prices.
- Money is worth little inside the country and even less outside; therefore compensation for consultants may be in the form of vacations, transportation, or local crafts.
- The growth of an organization may have little to do with profits or demand.
- There is an immutable core of privileges and obligations expected for a select oligarchy.

Sterniczuk and Lis recommend six special rules for consulting in communist cultures:

1. Learn and pay close attention to the political and economic environment, especially the hierarchy of power.
2. Be aware of the economic illogic and incoherence of the state-managed system.
3. Find the delicate balance between the internal organizational logic and the external pressures of an artificial frame of reference.
4. Learn the best balance between change and protection of the status quo.
5. Seek the best means in protecting the organization's well-being in the long-term as well as in the short-term.

6. Identify ways of obtaining participative problem solving in a state-controlled environment.

GUATEMALA: A CASE STUDY

Several years ago one of the authors managed a program in Guatemala that involved consulting in a multicultural community. Two distinctive cultural groups live and work in the Guatemalan highlands: the Latinos and the native Indians. They interact with each other across a gulf formed by contrasting cultures, behavioral patterns, thought processes, and organizational mechanisms.

For example, the leadership styles of the two groups are radically different. Latinos tend to operate well in hierarchical structures and take little initiative without checking with a superior. Thus Latinos will defer decisions to a *jefe* or boss. Consultants need to work at the top, especially with social contacts. Gaining approval at the top will accomplish more throughout the organization.

By contrast, the Indians have a system of community government that is very egalitarian. At meetings, change is a slow process because authoritarian action is unacceptable. An Indian will hold back his opinions, hoping to get a hint that his peers think the same way before committing himself. The consultant, therefore, if he is to be successful, will circulate from house to house suggesting an idea and carefully detailing its rationale to the families in each household. The consultant should not apply pressure to force a decision during his visit. Sufficient time should be provided for Indians to consider the idea.

The consultant must also consider the aspects of friendship and social connections. Since the Spanish conquest, the Latinos have managed their lives by cultivating friendships. Extensive networks of friends and interconnection among kin reach across Guatemala. The consultant must recognize this and cultivate social ties. He should have parties, invite guests, be gracious; these actions constitute a bank of favors that build good will.

The Indians, on the other hand, are more averse to, and suspicious of, outsiders, and their history seems to justify such behavior. Trust is built very slowly.

If an American consultant were to consult based on his own cultural value systems, he would frustrate both the Latinos and the Indians. For example, the American notion that all people should be treated as equals may seem cold to Latinos, for they may feel special treatment is due. On the other hand, American assertiveness would confound the Indian. The Indian wants to be left alone and has no need to be different or unique.

SUMMARY

The past decade has seen enormous growth in the field of international HRD consulting as a result of a number of factors including increased public sector reliance on consultants, downsizing of corporations, increased need for highly specialized skills and knowledge, and the increased demands of global competition.

In serving a client, the global HRD consultant can play any of a number of critical roles ranging from directive to nondirective. These include advocate, informational expert, learning provider, joint problem solver, alternative identifier and linker, fact finder, process counselor, and reflector. A single consultant may play different roles during the five consulting phases: entry, assessment, planning, implementation, and evaluation.

Global HRD consulting is enormously challenging since many of the consultant's most basic beliefs and assumptions must be consciously identified and questioned with regard to their relevance in the target culture. Such fundamental concepts as work ethic, time, management style, and the role of women can vary widely from one culture to another. In addition, in many parts of the world, there are hurdles to be overcome with respect to bureaucracy, limited resources, organizational structure and staffing, and corruption.

Finally, there are a number of self-imposed limitations that must be confronted by global HRD consultants. These include inadequate flexibility with regard to local social, political, and cultural contexts, as well as local learning styles. In addition, the consultant must avoid overreliance on his own culture's models, concepts, and materials and must be willing to make a long-term commitment to providing adequate follow-through and reinforcement. Nine skills that noted global consultants feel are essential to success in international consulting were identified. Strategies for consulting in a socialist setting and in a mixed Latino-Indian environment were discussed.

REFERENCES

BURKE, W. WARNER. *Organization Development.* Reading, Mass.: Addison-Wesley, 1987.

GORMLEY, WILMA. "Consulting across Cultures." In *Corporate Culture:International HRD Perspectives*, edited by Michael Marquardt. Alexandria, Va.: ASTD Press, 1987.

LIPPITT, GORDON, AND RONALD LIPPITT. "The Consulting Function of the HRD Professional." In *The Handbook of Human Resource Development.* New York: John Wiley and Sons, 1984.

RAMCHANDRAN, VENKATRAM. "Training for Work in an Alien Culture" In *Global Strategies for Human Resource Development*. Alexandria, Va.: ASTD Press, 1984.

ROBERTS, LEE. "Management Consulting and Training in Developing Countries." *Training and Development Journal* (October 1983), pp. 48–52.

STERNICZUK, HENRY K., AND KRZYSZTOF LIS. "Rules for Consulting in a Communist Economy." *Organization Development Journal* (Spring 1990), pp. 58–65.

CHAPTER 6

❦ ❦

Administration of Global HRD Programs

INTRODUCTION

A global manager must be cosmopolitan, effective as an intercultural communicator and negotiator who creates cultural synergy and leads cultural change.

Philip Harris and Robert Moran
Managing Cultural Differences

The administration of an HRD program in another culture can be a bewildering challenge. Often the expectations of the other stakeholders are quite different from those that have resulted in success for the administrator in his home country. And since such expectations are taken for granted on both sides, they are usually unspoken until conflict or unexpected behavior bring them to the surface.

A number of years ago, one of the authors went to a South American country to act as principal consultant and temporary administrator of an English language and culture institute until the enterprise was on its feet and a permanent administrator could be identified. Since there was no one else involved with the venture who had relevant administrative or managerial experience, he thought that he had been brought down there to apply his own experience and expertise and that he would have virtually full responsibility for defining and realizing the operation; in short, he expected to be in charge. As it turned out, he was wrong on both counts. Subsequent events made him realize that, for the client, his main appeal was that he was an American native speaker of English with academic credentials. The client expectation was that the author would sit in the corner office in a chair with a higher back than any other in the building, make public appearances, have long lunches with local dignitaries, and let one of the principals, who knew nothing about the business, run it. Until all of this became clear, and even beyond that point, it was a frustrating experience for all parties concerned and one based simply upon conflicting cultural expectations and assumptions about the role of the program administrator.

In this chapter, we will focus on the global HRD program administrator, emphasizing the roles and responsibilities inherent in the job. The administration of global HRD programs will be compared to and contrasted with domestic program administration.

❦ Value

The analysis of the roles and responsibilities of the global HRD administrator will give you a greater understanding of the need for being culturally sensitive and possessing strong management skills for this HRD function. You will also recognize the important role that the global HRD program administrator plays in program success.

❦ Learning Objectives

After studying this chapter, you should be able to:

1. Compare and contrast the roles and responsibilities of domestic and global HRD program administrators
2. Describe the global dimensions of HRD administration
3. Identify the functional responsibilities of the global HRD administrator

ROLES AND DEFINITIONS IN HRD ADMINISTRATION

Before examining the global aspects of HRD administration, we should first review the general responsibilities included in this area of HRD. Generally, three different roles are considered when discussing HRD administrative responsibilities:

1. Management of the HRD Staff
2. Coordination and Management of HRD Programs
3. Marketer and Contractor for HRD Activities

❦ Management of the HRD Staff

The HRD manager is responsible for implementing a number of human resource management (HRM) functions (recruiting, selecting, compensating, evaluating) and HRD functions (training, developing, career counseling) for his HRD staff. Like other managers, he should create an environment that promotes continuous learning and development and encourage staff participation in professional societies.

The HRD administrator will generally be working with two kinds of personnel—those who are full time within the HRD department and those who are contracted on a temporary basis. This latter category is becoming a majority in more and more organizations.

❦ Coordination and Management of HRD Programs

This administrative role involves managing the various elements needed to assure that the HRD program and/or services are actually delivered. Activities include:

1. Assessing organizational HRD needs
2. Ensuring appropriate human resources to design and deliver programs
3. Arranging for facilities
4. Informing the organization of the content, costs, dates, and location of the HRD programs within and outside the organization
5. Managing the financial aspects of organization and individual HRD activities
6. Overseeing the evaluation of internal HRD programs

❦ Marketer and Contractor for HRD Activities

This role involves representing HRD programs, services, and viewpoints both internal and external to the organization.

Internal. A key role for the HRD administrator is to educate others in the organization, especially the top executives, about the strategic contributions of HRD to global success.

Developing HRD policy within the organization is another part of internal representation. This includes identifying internal versus external sources for training, establishing procedures with vendors, and supporting relations between the HRD staff and the organization.

External. The HRD administrator must also identify and gain support of external HRD resources and, in increasing frequency, market the internal HRD capabilities to the outside world.
He needs to identify possible vendors such as universities, consulting and training firms, and individuals who may be selected to provide HRD programs and services to the organization. He may have to coordinate HRD activities with appropriate government organizations and labor unions.

GLOBAL DIMENSIONS OF HRD ADMINISTRATION

The three administrative HRD roles described in the previous section are significantly altered by the following international dynamics.

❧ *Culture*

Every cultural group perceives management, authority, and power differently. Expectations regarding the administrator's style and level of involvement as well as the tasks to be performed vary dramatically from Sweden with its collegiality to Swaziland with its strong, clear authority. Moreover, the dynamics of an American managing Japanese, or Germans, or a multinational HRD team are much more complex than those involved when Americans manage only other Americans.

❧ *Political and Economic Systems*

The responsibilities of the HRD manager as well as the manner in which he carries out those responsibilities depend to a great deal upon the political and economic system within the country. Marketing HRD services, for example, is dramatically different in a country with a small private sector than in a country with a strong capitalist base.

❧ *Geographic Distance*

Even with global telecommunications technology, it is much more difficult to administer, communicate, and interact with people and organizations thousands of miles away.

❦ Resource Limitations

In many developing countries, the HRD administrator will simply be unable to secure the supplies or materials, the facilities, or even the local trainers that he knows are important for a quality HRD program.

❦ Government Regulations

Some governments regulate almost every aspect of an employee's work, detailing the who, what, when, and how of the training. Other governments prescribe very little to the HRD administrator.

ADMINISTRATION AND MANAGEMENT OF HRD STAFF

❦ Administrative Services

In managing an HRD unit or personnel in other countries, there are a large number of additional and complex responsibilities for the HRD manager. He has to oversee and coordinate such areas as:

- Immigration and travel details
- Work permits
- Compensation and allowances for local, third country nationals (TCN) and U.S. staff

- Housing, health care, insurance
- Recreation and schooling
- Family needs of HRD personnel
- Safety and security

❦ Orientation and Relocation

Whether the HRD practitioners are going abroad for two weeks or two years, the HRD manager needs to assure them that they are prepared to go overseas and to return as successfully as possible. Accordingly, appropriate cross-cultural training (the intensity of which will depend on factors such as culture differences, degree of interaction, level within the organization) should be provided. (In Chapter 23, various aspects of predeparture and return training programs are discussed.)

During the person's stay, the HRD manager must provide long-distance, culturally appropriate support. Finally, steps should be taken to assure a smooth transition upon the person's return. Learning should be shared. A position that utilizes and rewards this international experience should be identified before his return.

❦ Recruitment and Selection

When recruiting and hiring HRD staff, it is important to seek the competencies needed in global, cross-cultural assignments. Although international experience and technical competence are important, the key competencies identified by most seasoned global HRD practitioners are attitudinal. Global HRD recruiters agree that interviews should test the applicant's ability to handle situations in which everything is different from what he expected.

❦ Management

The managing and coaching of staff, full time and/or temporary, can be very difficult because of the great distances and the culturally different environment in which the staff is operating. In addition, there is the possibility that the trainer who is perceived as effective at home will not be perceived as effective abroad.

The HRD manager needs to be sure that the overseas staff continually develops HRD and technical competencies, that they are not being cut off from important information and technologies needed for their work. She should create mechanisms for assessing their needs/interests and providing resources and materials. Periodic visits to the field to identify development needs as well as to evaluate performance and effectiveness are necessary.

❦ Evaluations

Evaluation of the manager's HRD staff should take into account input from co-workers and trainees within the culture in which they are working. The evaluation by local people, however, can be problematic since they will be evaluating the expatriate's performance from their own cultural frame of reference and set of expectations. For example, an American trainer who uses participative training methodology in China might be seen as incompetent because he is not enough in control and apparently not enough of an expert.

In addition, the home country HRD manager who is geographically distanced from the expatriate training staff is often not fully aware of what is happening overseas. Local events and cultural differences may make training success much more difficult to achieve and require greater effort with fewer results. If an HRD manager has had limited international experience, it is even more difficult to adequately and fairly evaluate the expatriate's performance.

Mendenhall and Oddou offer the following guidelines on how to appraise an expatriate's performance:

1. Determine the difficulty level of the assignment. For example, it is generally much more difficult for an American to work in Japan or China than in Canada or England. The degree of difficulty is dependent on such variables as language, cultural difference and stability of political and economic forces.
2. Objectify the evaluation by means such as:
   • Utilizing a former expatriate from the same location in the appraisal process
   • Involving on-site and home-site managers
3. Consider all the aspects of the expatriates' experiences and realize that they are not only performing a specific function but also broadening their understanding of the firm's total operations.

❧ Administrative Facilities for Staff

The quality, size, and location of the HRD staff's offices is very important. The status of the trainers, and therefore receptivity from the learner, is based on the office-building status where he is working or on the status of the hotel at which he is staying.

❧ Finance

The handling of financial matters, particularly in developing countries and in the public sector, can be time-consuming and frustrating. HRD programs may be put "on hold" for months; training staff may leave because of payment delays; equipment and materials may be repossessed because the government bureaucracy has delayed payments to your organization; the local organization and/or the local trainers may move elsewhere. Strong planning and political skills as well as patience are obviously critical.

MANAGEMENT OF HRD TRAINING PROGRAMS

❧ Coordination of HRD Team

The global HRD administrator must be sure that an appropriate team of HRD people has been assembled to carry out the training or consulting assignment. The skills and competencies of the team members should complement one another, so they can effectively work with and learn from each other. They should have the administrative support (typing, translation, transportation) necessary so they can focus on their HRD functions.

❧ Materials

Locating and securing materials and supplies can be an adventure. One of the authors had a great deal of difficulty securing electrical equipment for a language laboratory in Japan, not because it wasn't readily available, but because he made a culturally based and mistaken judgment as to who had the authority to release it.

In developing countries, the HRD administrator may need to have the trainer bring such resources with him or have them sent from headquarters. Lassiter recommends these precautions:

- Take basic training supplies (paper, pens, markers) with you.
- Find out where you can purchase or borrow necessary materials.
- Check the audio visual equipment; be sure it is the correct voltage and take along extra bulbs for backup since replacements may be unavailable in the country or village.

Training materials or textbooks are seen as very precious in most developing countries; trainees will be immensely grateful to receive or borrow them and will treat them reverentially.

❧ Training Venue

Selecting the training site and facilities is important. The venue, surroundings, and technology can enhance or diminish the status of and receptivity toward the training.

Some countries have limited facilities available; sometimes the local collaborative organization has no funds available to secure adequate facilities. Or, you may unexpectedly have to find them on your own. In developing countries, do not assume that the facilities have already been identified or that they will be adequate. Check out the training site well in advance.

❧ Trainee Accommodations

In managing the HRD program, the HRD administrator may also need to arrange for living accommodations for the trainees. In societies where power is the basis for a clear and distinct class system, it is important to provide, if possible, different facilities (or floors or rooms) for people of different status levels. Mixing them together can alienate all the trainees, both those of high and low status.

𝕖 *Ceremonies*

A very valuable role that the manager of the HRD program can perform is to arrange for senior-level people from within or outside the organization to be present or speak at the opening or closing ceremonies of the training program. Providing certificates or plaques for program completion is also important throughout the world.

These gestures indicate the importance and prestige of the HRD program to the learners as well as to the instructors. The learners' appreciation will also result in a higher level of learning transference and application.

𝕖 *Food*

There are a large number of considerations in determining the food to be served at training programs. The Hindus do not eat beef, the Muslims do not consume pork or alcohol. Indonesians and most Asians expect rice with their meals. Meridian International Center in Washington, D.C., which trains thousands of leaders annually from all over the world, found chicken to be the most globally accepted food.

MARKETING AND CONTRACTING FOR HRD ACTIVITIES

𝕖 *Internal*

Representing the importance and needs of HRD within the organization from a distance and across cultures can be a trying experience. Headquarters may not appreciate the problems of incorporating the HQ HRD programs into another culture or may not be aware of the obstacles of local labor strikes, government regulations, and religious holidays. The HRD manager must therefore serve as a bridge between the local HRD reality and the needs of top management.

𝕖 *External*

Marketing, Negotiating, and Contracting. Billions of dollars of training and consulting (also known as technical assistance) are marketed and sold each year by HRD managers around the world; it is one of the United States' largest exports. Marketing, and eventually selling, HRD products and services globally requires not only marketing and negotiating skills but exceptional cross-cultural, communication, and political skills.

1. *Marketing.* How one markets and sells HRD is unique to each culture, since what is seen as "benefits to the customer" varies from culture to culture, and even from organization to organization within a culture. Some African cultures, for example, will value the credentials much more than the content because of how those credentials will serve the individual and his family. The Japanese are very concerned about the capability of the organizations providing the HRD programs—their size, clients, history, etc.—and evaluate them before considering the product.

2. *Negotiating and Contracting.* As one attempts to finalize the contract for delivery of HRD services, there are a number of cultural factors which can add a tremendous amount of time and cost in preparing and getting final approval of HRD contracts.

   (a) *Establishing Trust and Rapport.* In the American culture, one may quickly get "down to business" and write up the contract. In most other cultures, the process of developing a trusting relationship between the two parties must occur first, and this may take weeks or even months. Attempts to "bypass" this step will lead to resentment and failure.

   (b) *Power Structure.* In societies in which there is a clear, pyramidlike power structure, lower level officials or managers will never make final decisions without the approval of higher authorities. Only when the top person (who must see hundreds of documents) has reviewed and signed off can one go forward.

   (c) *Context.* In negotiating and signing agreements, low-context and high-context cultures differ significantly. In low-context cultures such as Switzerland and Germany, every detail must be agreed to and put in writing. High-context cultures such as Malaysia may never require a written contract. Good personal relationships and trust mean that a personal handshake may be all that is necessary.

   (d) *Communications.* The cultural context often makes it difficult for the HRD manager to obtain the level of communications necessary. The subordinate, who has the data needed, may be a "shadow" in a meeting that includes his superiors whereas he was very articulate before. A senior official who is open and warm when negotiating alone may become extremely careful and formal when his colleagues are present.

   (e) *Language.* Negotiating and contracting become even more challenging when one is is not using his primary language. The tone, nuance, or even the meaning of a message might be inadvertently lost through mistranslation.

Government Relations. Among the many groups which the HRD administrator must work with in other countries are the various government ministries which must be closely consulted with before and during HRD activities.

In much of Asia, Africa, Europe, and Latin America, the Ministry of Labor closely regulates all aspects of work life. Most European countries have some form of mandatory standardized skills and achievement testing system to qualify workers for occupational status and related pay scales. Usually the Ministry of Labor establishes the standards and administers the test.

The HRD administrator must be cognizant of these regulations when designing training courses and developing job training standards for occupations covered by such regulations. He needs to understand the structure of educational and training systems in the countries in which his corporation is operating. Many countries (e.g.,Switzerland, New Zealand, Germany) have a strong technical/vocational program at the secondary education level.

When working with the public sector or with public funds, one should become acquainted with the funding and administrative arrangements of the government. In Singapore and France, for example, a certain percentage of corporate revenues are taxed for training purposes. A corporation may use/reclaim these taxes for training; what is not used is put in the general fund for government training programs.

Most countries have national manpower plans in which present and future skills needs are identified and reported. National training centers then provide training in these areas.

Labor Unions. Labor unions also play an important, although globally diminished, role for workers around the world. In many countries, the unions strongly oppose training since it is seen as linking management and worker and thereby undermining the role and importance of the union.

The HRD administrator should study labor-management work contracts and national legislation that may stipulate training clauses regarding work hours, wages, program length and scope, and trainee/skilled worker ratios. He should identify ways for employees and labor unions to work together in training.

SUMMARY

The administration of an HRD program in another country is a complex and challenging task. Although the roles of the administrator include those typical of a domestic program (management of the HRD staff, coordination and management of the HRD program, and marketing and contracting for HRD activities), the global setting adds a number of dynamic dimensions. General administrative concerns for global programs include culture, political and economic systems, geographic distance from the home office, local resource limitations, and government regulations.

In terms of the administration and management of HRD staff, the global HRD administrator must deal with such factors as providing financial and administrative services as well as handling orientation and relocation, recruitment and selection, management, and evaluation of staff.

The HRD administrator must also manage all aspects of the training programs ranging from materials selection and preparation through training venue and trainee accommodations to contracting with vendors. Finally, the global HRD administrator must act as a marketing agent, internally with the client and home office and externally with government agencies, vendors, regulatory bodies, and labor organizations.

REFERENCES

COPELAND, LENNIE AND LEWIS GRIGGS. *Going International: How to Make Friends and Deal Effectively in the Global Marketplace*. New York: Random House, 1985.

MENDENHALL, MARK, AND GARY ODDOU. *International Human Resource Management*.Boston: PWS-Kent Publishing Company, 1991.

HRD in Global Organizations

More and more organizations are becoming global organizations, that is, organizations that operate and market as if the entire world were a single entity without walls or borders. They integrate their organizationalwide and functional activities on a worldwide basis. In Section III, we will discuss the HRD programs and activities of global organizations as well as the critical role of HRD in enabling organizations to become, and remain, globally competitive.

Chapter 7, Global Corporations, discusses the elements of corporate globalization and how and why corporations become global. The training and development programs of several of the best global corporations are then described and analyzed, particularly as to how these HRD activities promoted global success.

In Chapter 8, we explore the HRD programs of a number of successful noncorporate organizations including global public agencies, nonprofit organizations, and associations.

In Chapter 9, we will identify the ways in which HRD can assist corporations in becoming global. We will describe how organizations can acquire the competencies necessary to "climb the global learning curve" and how HRD professionals can conduct global needs analysis, develop global leadership, provide world-class training programs, and maintain organizational learning on a global basis.

❦ ❦

HRD in Global Corporations

INTRODUCTION

Globalization is no longer an objective, but an imperative.

Jack Welch
Chairman and CEO
General Electric

When we speak of a global organization, we mean one that operates as if the entire world were a single entity and integrates its activities on a worldwide basis to capture linkages among countries. Such organizations emphasize global operations over national or multinational operations. They select the best people available for management, regardless of nationality, and conduct worldwide searches in recruiting personnel. Their headquarters may be located anywhere in the world. Research and development is conducted wherever the organization can capitalize on costs and technical capabilities. Globalization of an organization has occurred when the organization has developed a global corporate culture, strategy, structure, and communications process.

In this chapter, we will examine and illustrate the role of HRD in global corporations headquartered in countries around the world. The phenomenon of globalization in the corporate environment will be explored in detail, and several examples of HRD programs in global corporations will be provided.

❦ *Value*

This chapter will give you a solid sense of the globalization process as it applies to corporations and enable you to identify how those corporations have become global. You will also learn about a variety of successful HRD programs within global corporations that have different countries of origin.

❦ *Learning Objectives*

After studying this chapter, you should be able to:

1. Define and describe global corporations
2. Discuss the advantages of globalization and list the features that identify a global corporation
3. Cite examples of innovative and effective global HRD programs

THE GLOBAL CORPORATION

What exactly is a global corporation? Adler defines it as an organization that has fully and globally integrated its operations—product design, process design, manufacturing, vendor management—in many parts of the world. For example, Honda, a Japanese auto manufacturer, has a fully integrated operation in the United States for producing the Honda Accord Coupe.

White sees the global corporation as one that has the ability to optimize marketing, purchasing, people, engineering, and manufacturing activities worldwide. Ohmae describes a global organization as one that has become an "insider" in any market or nation where it operates and is thus competitive with domestic firms operating in local markets. However, unlike truly local firms, the global corporation has a global strategic perspective with a capability for local differentiation.

Global corporations search the globe for the best opportunities available, place investments around the world to achieve the highest return at the least risk, purchase materials wherever in the world they are the most economical, produce components or finished products wherever in the world this can be done most effectively, and market the product or service wherever in the world it can be done most profitably.

A global organization does not have a single country bias. The successful global firm, although globally integrated, can respond locally and be sensitive to cultural differences relative to the needs of customers, the political and economic environment, and values of local workers and clients. Learning in a global organization takes place in both a global and local context, encompassing global as well as local knowledge, attitudes, and skills.

Certain industries have globalized earlier than others, including:

- Telecommunications
- Electronics/Computers
- Finance and Insurance
- Pharmaceuticals

- Chemicals
- Transportation
- Automotive
- Construction

Global corporations may be small as well as large, and headquartered anywhere in the world. Among the 500 largest industrial corporations, 157 are American, 150 are Japanese, and 161 are European.

WHY CORPORATIONS GO GLOBAL

There are a number of external forces, according to Moran and Stripp, that are causing organizations to globalize:

- Increased foreign competition in their domestic markets
- Expanded free trade policies such as the European Common Market and North American Free Trade Agreement
- Improved telecommunications and information systems that allow instant decision making and transfer of data
- Better utilization of company personnel
- Lowered transportation costs and time
- Increased global customer bases
- Worldwide financial systems with access to the global money markets that allow for utilization of foreign capital, tax advantages, the opportunity to diversify risks, and the ability to profit from foreign exchange fluctuations
- Opportunities for larger profits due to economies of scale in production, logistics, and marketing
- Ability to earn additional income on existing technology
- Increased product/service life cycle
- Opportunities to gain an edge in reputation and credibility
- Access to foreign technology, skills, knowledge, capital, and human and natural resources

HRD in Global Corporations

Let us now examine HRD programs in five of the top global corporations, looking at the content and process of their HRD activities as well as the HRD levers they use to propel themselves as leaders in the global marketplace.

❦ General Electric

General Electric (GE), a $60-billion-a-year global giant, manufactures aircraft engines, defense electronics, engineering plastics, locomotives, and household appliances in addition to broadcasting programs worldwide and providing financial services. Over 300,000 employees work worldwide; 40 percent of profits come from international activities.

Barham and Devine describe the HRD activities at GE as "global action learning." GE's aim for the nineties "is to become a boundary-less company." Employees are expected to be as comfortable in Seoul and Budapest as in Connecticut and New York.

A key HRD strategy is a participative strategy called "work-out," whereby team meetings bring together large cross sections of people to open up communications, build teams, and work on problems together.

Stewart, in a recent issue of *Fortune*, describes what happens at a typical work-out:

> The three-day sessions begin with a talk by the boss who roughs out an agenda—for example, to eliminate unnecessary meetings, forms, approvals, and other scutwork. Then the boss leaves. Aided by the outside facilitator, the group breaks into five or six teams, each to tackle part of the agenda. For a day-and-a-half they go at it, listing complaints, debating solutions and preparing final preparations for the final day. It is the third day that gives Work-Out its special power. The boss, ignorant of what has been going on, comes back and takes a place at the front of the room. Often senior executives come to watch. By the rules of the game, the boss can make only three responses: he can agree on the spot; he can say no; or he can ask for more information—in which case he must charter a team to get it by an agreed-upon date. [pp. 42-43]

Work-outs have had tremendous results for GE. Millions of dollars have been saved, trust has been built, productivity has improved, creativity and commitment have grown. Now GE suppliers and customers are utilizing the techniques.

GE's Management Development Institute at Crotonville, New York, has been recognized as one of the top corporate training centers in the world. The curriculum has recently changed its focus from developing individual skills to one that seeks to bring about organizational change. GE believes that "thinking globally requires more than just knowledge; People must actually learn how to manage in the more complex and faster-moving global environment." Since, as GE believes, 80 percent of learning and development comes from the job and 20 percent comes from formal training programs, it is important to identify the most appropriate points for training in an individual's career. Based upon these determinations, GE has developed a five-stage training program, each phase of which includes the three interdependent themes of (1) global brains, (2) technical and business best practices, and (3) leadership.

❦ *Unilever*

Unilever, headquartered in London and Rotterdam, is one of the largest consumer businesses in the world and employs more than 300,000 people in seventy-five countries. The headquarters staff includes thirty different nationalities, and most of the top managers have worked in two or more countries. Unilever's philosophy is to expose its managers both to different countries and to the different industries of the company.

Unilever seeks to develop managers who possess language skills, cross-cultural sensitivity, and the unusual combination of being high achievers who also have humility and strong affiliation needs.

Career planning is seen as very critical for Unilever's long-term success. Worldwide guidelines stipulate that future managers and executives be involved in a wide variety of product lines and countries. Careers should also include a variety of experiences within the function. Market managers, for example, should have sales experience, and personnel managers should have factory and industrial relations experience.

Management careers include early opportunities to assume responsibility and demonstrate results. All experiences are supplemented by formal training. Every job is considered both a job to be done *and* an opportunity to develop individual capabilities and expertise.

All managers who are assigned overseas are able to attend, with their spouse, a one-week training program about their new country at the Centre for International Briefing in the U.K. In addition, "contact managers" are available in each country who act as facilitators to the new managers in such areas as taxation, schooling, local customs, etc. Unilever provides strong, continuous support to employees while they are abroad. They also keep them apprised of their next career opportunities so that their transition and reentry is as smooth as possible. Special efforts are made to find employment opportunities for the spouse in the new country.

Unilever is in the forefront of global companies in developing the potential of its women employees. It has introduced such measures as career breaks, weekend schools for those on maternity leave, and arrangements for part-time working and job sharing.

❦ *NEC*

NEC, one of the largest electronics corporations in the world, employs over 115,000 people including 24,000 outside Japan. It manufactures 15,000 different products and is seen as doing *today* what other firms will do tomorrow. Already in 1964, NEC President Kobayashi declared that NEC must "go global." In 1980, NEC created the NEC Institute for International Studies with the sole purpose of internationalizing NEC employees. The Institute seeks:

- To integrate companywide international education
- To develop and support overseas personnel
- To provide management education in Japan for NEC's expatriate managers
- To accumulate and make effective use of international management know-how
- To integrate foreign language training with the management training

NEC has continued to expand its HRD efforts to globalize its thinking and operations. Management education focuses on training managers to be effective in the cross-cultural sphere. Numerous courses in globalization are offered to NEC employees.

NEC realizes that corporatewide English competency is critical for its future global success since the language is important for global sales and marketing, acquisition and assimilation of relevant scientific and technical information, and supervising expatriate employees.

Today NEC strongly supports an active, companywide learning environment. The emphasis is not so much to concentrate on core products as on core competencies, abilities, and skills. NEC's honing of its core competencies is to a very high degree related to the importance it attaches to human resource development (Barham and Devine).

❦ *Rhone-Poulenc Rorer*

Within the past twenty years, Rhone-Poulenc Rorer (RPR) has transformed itself from a struggling French company to a highly successful global corporation with 90,000 employees in 140 countries. A key element for this remarkable transition is its global HRD strategy. The company places strong emphasis on the need to recruit managers on a global scale and to move these managers around the world.

The international assignments provide several learning benefits for the managers as well as economic benefits for RPR:

- Managers become better aware of the geographic and industrial aspects of the company.
- There is a greater integration of the businesses as well as building of an *esprit de corp.*
- The flow of information about technical and marketing areas increases.

An important HRD element at RPR is the mentoring of the new expatriate manager. This mentor or "godfather" is generally a senior manager at headquarters who is technically higher skilled and is a good communicator/adviser. The new expatriate manager stays in regular contact with the mentor and consults with him on next career moves. The mentor then works with the appropriate executive to negotiate some sort of arrangement for the up-and-coming global manager.

RPR has rapidly increased its number of non-French employees and managers and is well on its way to achieving its ultimate aim of developing "citizens of the world" (*citoyens du monde*), people who think of "world" as the corporate center.

✌ *Johnson and Johnson*

Johnson and Johnson (J & J) is one of the world's largest manufacturers of pharmaceutical and health care products and equipment. It has 82,000 employees, half of whom are located in some sixty countries around the world. Annual sales are over $12 billion.

Management training and development as well as succession planning are considered the most globally leveraged of all the human resource functions. In developing managers for the global business, J & J has instituted a number of management programs at its training center in New Brunswick, New Jersey. An Advanced Management Program is run at different centers around the world; it is currently offered at IMD (International Center for Management Development) in Lausanne and the University of Singapore, with plans to expand to Tokyo and South America.

In addition, Johnson and Johnson conducts a one-week "World Class Manufacturing Program," which is a diagnostic program devoted to developing a strategic plan for each operating unit. Topics include computer-integrated manufacturing, just-in-time inventory control, statistical process control, and total employee involvement.

J & J is committed to the principle that its overseas companies should be managed by local managers. Under its International Development Program, the company takes mid-level managers out of their existing overseas jobs and transfers them into one- to two-year assignments in the United States to give them headquarters experience and to learn about company systems, principles, and ways of thinking. J & J provides language training, housing, and cross-cultural briefings to make the learning experience in the United States as smooth as possible.

SUMMARY

Corporations around the world are becoming global in both their strategic vision and day-to-day operations. When we speak of a global organization, we mean one that operates as if the entire world were a single entity and integrates its activities on a worldwide basis to capture linkages among countries. Such organizations emphasize global operations over national or multinational operations. They select the best people available for management, regardless of nationality, and conduct worldwide searches in recruiting personnel.

Their headquarters may be located anywhere in the world. Research and development is conducted wherever the organization can capitalize on costs and technical capabilities. Globalization of an organization has occurred when the organization has developed a global corporate culture, strategy, structure, and communication process.

In the global corporation, HRD plays a critical role in the strategic planning activities and in the establishment of a learning organization that supports the constant changing dimensions of global corporations. Learning in a global organization takes place in both a global and a local context, encompassing global as well as local knowledge, attitudes, and skills. HRD practices in a number of corporations already reflect corporate movement toward globalization; in this chapter, we consider such programs at General Electric, Unilever, NEC, Rhone-Poulenc Rorer, and Johnson and Johnson.

REFERENCES

ADLER, NANCY. *International Dimensions of Organizational Behavior*. Belmont, Calif.: Kent Press, 1986.

BARHAM, KEVIN, AND MARION DEVINE. *The Quest for the International Manager: A Survey of Global Human Resource Strategies*. London: Business International Press, 1991.

MORAN, ROBERT, AND WILLIAM G. STRIPP. *International Negotiation*. Houston: Gulf Publishing, 1991.

OHMAE, KENICHI. *The Borderless World*. New York: Harper Business, 1990.

STEWART, THOMAS A. "GE Keeps Those Ideas Coming." *Fortune* (August 12, 1991), pp. 41–49.

WHITE, BREN. *World Class Training*. Dallas: Odenwald Press, 1992.

CHAPTER **8**

❦ ❦

Public and Nonprofit Global Organizations

INTRODUCTION

Today, in an age of dazzling technology, over one billion people live in absolute poverty...The challenge is to empower the people to shape their own future.

William Draper
United Nations Development Program

As the nations and the peoples of the world come closer in fact and realization to becoming a single community, HRD professionals are going to play an even more critical role in nonprofit and public development global organizations. The challenges we face on the eve of the twenty-first century will test the limits of HRD skills and expertise in a way that has never been seen before and provide opportunities for HRD professionals to make valuable contributions to world development. In this chapter, we will explore highly acclaimed HRD programs in the global public and nonprofit sectors as well as in global HRD associations.

❦ *Value*

Learning about the HRD activities of global public and nonprofit development organizations will increase your understanding of the important contributions of these organizations to the economic and social growth of developing nations. An understanding of the resources of global associations will enable you to identify which ones might most benefit you in your professional development.

❧ Learning Objectives

After studying this chapter, you should be able to:

1. Recognize the critical role that HRD is playing in global public and nonprofit development organizations
2. Identify key public organizations and describe some of their HRD programs
3. Recognize the missions and goals of a number of nonprofit development organizations as they operate around the world
4. Understand the purposes and activities of the major global HRD associations

GOALS OF PUBLIC AND NONPROFIT ORGANIZATIONS

The first truly global organizations were the public ones which began to emerge after the ravages of World Wars I and II. The focus of these organizations was to accomplish one or more of the following goals:

- Build a world of peace
- Share human and financial resources to provide relief and development
- Exchange information to better implement the programs of national or local organizations

These public organizations, both governmental and nongovernmental, have continued their focus on the development of people and nations around the world, especially the developing countries of Asia, Africa, and Latin America.

In this chapter, we will examine three categories of public organizations: (1) global, public, government-to-government organizations, (2) global, private, people-to-people voluntary organizations, and (3) global HRD associations.

PUBLIC GLOBAL ORGANIZATIONS

❧ United Nations Development Program

The United Nations Development Program (UNDP) delivers more training and technical assistance programs than any other development agency.

UNDP has field offices in 112 countries with over 7,000 employees and 20,000 consultants from 179 countries—a truly global organization.

The present mandate endorsed by UNDP's Governing Council is for UNDP to concentrate on building developing nations' capabilities in six specific areas:

- Poverty Eradication
- Environmental Protection
- Management Development
- Technical Cooperation among Developing Countries
- Technology Transfer
- Promotion of Women in Development

Currently over 6,000 technical assistance and training projects are occurring in the following sectors:

Sector	Number of Projects
Management planning and policy	1391
Agriculture, forestry, and fisheries	1024
Industry	805
Natural Resources	531
Health and Education	529
Transport and Communications	480
Science and Technology	368
Employment	295
Miscellaneous	717

Examples of global and regional technical assistance programs include:

- Training for small-scale business development for the disabled in Africa and Latin America
- Development of training materials for government personnel in Africa and Asia to increase knowledge and treatment of HIV/AIDS pandemic
- Global conference on ways to assist the one billion people lacking basic water and sanitation services
- Urban development and management projects to assist the urban dwellers in developing countries, the number of whom has grown to 1.4 billion
- Soil and water conservation training in Tunisia, where two-thirds of the available arable land is threatened by desertification
- A twenty-five-year, multibillion dollar technical assistance program for forestry development in the Philippines

- National literacy and agricultural education program for 50,000 illiterate men and women in Bangladesh
- Grass-roots education programs in agroforestry and health for remote sections of Nepal
- Training small business entrepreneurs in Kenya, Ivory Coast, Nigeria, Botswana, and Zimbabwe
- Rural development training for 2,800 farmers in Antigua, Anguilla, Dominica, Grenada, Montserrat, St. Kitts and Nevis, St. Lucia and St. Vincent

❦ *International Labor Office*

Created in 1919 and headquartered in Geneva, Switzerland, the International Labor Office (ILO) has over 150 member nations. While improved working conditions and the promotion of full employment remain central aims of the ILO, it also deals with occupational safety and health, labor-management relations, women and migrant workers, as well as training. The ILO currently devotes more than half of its resources to vocational and management training and labor research.

Turin Center. The depth and breadth of HRD activities of the ILO are astounding. At the Turin, Italy, training center alone, over 35,000 participants from 170 countries have been trained since its establishment in 1964. In addition, the International Centre for Advanced Technical and Vocational Training has produced over 400 training publications. The staff consists of 500 trainers from every part of the world who are capable of speaking scores of languages.

Each year, over forty advanced training courses are conducted in several different languages including Arabic, Russian, Chinese, Farsi, and Greek. These specially designed courses aim at fulfilling training needs identified within the framework of the development plans of the nations with whom the ILO works. The focus of the training courses is to promote local self-reliance in technical and managerial skills and to improve the capability of national staff in key industries and vocational training programs.

Current courses include entrepreneurship, marketing, consultancy, productivity improvement, human resource management, training policies and methodologies, cooperative management, occupational health and safety, project management, and procurement policies.

The ILO has been especially committed to the training of women because of the low socioeconomic status of women in most developing nations. Four courses are presently taught throughout the world: (1) Management Training for Women Entrepreneurs, (2) How to Integrate

Women in Development Projects, (3) How to Plan and Organize Income—
Generating Activities for Rural Women, and (4) How to Promote Women
into Technical Trades.

The Turin Center is also responsible for the organization and monitoring
of all individual international fellowships awarded for overseas training.
Nearly 500 such individual fellowship programs are organized each year and
enable the participants to view technical programs in the United States,
Canada, Japan, and Western Europe.

Management Development. The effective management of scarce
resources, whether material, financial, or human, is critical to economic and
social development. For this reason, the ILO places a high priority on
improving the quality of management performance in the areas of manufacturing, transportation, distribution, construction, rural development, energy,
and water supply. Since 1960, the ILO has trained over 500,000 managers
and established and strengthened management development institutions in
more than eighty countries.

ILO efforts have resulted in concrete and innovative projects throughout
the developing world. In Sri Lanka, for example, the ILO assisted the
National Institute of Business Management in applying minicomputers to the
problems of public enterprise management. An ILO project in Pakistan
improved the distribution of basic commodities to the poorest strata within
the local villages. Training in the development of small businesses has been
provided to several countries including the Congo, Zimbabwe, and many of
the smaller island nations of the South Pacific. ILO's "Improve Your
Business" training package has been used extensively in Kenya, India, and
Zambia.

Vocational Training. Aware that a skilled work force is an essential
ingredient of national economic development, the ILO has trained hundreds
of thousands of technicians in various occupational skills over the past seventy years. Skills training is provided in most construction and manufacturing areas and includes special segments of the population such as women,
youth, migrants, and other disadvantaged groups.

ILO makes a special effort to train trainers and instructors. For instance,
in Senegal, 2,000 instructors were taught to train thousands of rural artisans
and farmers. In Zaire, a project was recently launched for training in water
distribution and treatment. The ILO is also training Malaysians in electric
supply and distribution, while in Peru there is a training project to improve
efficiency and safety in the copper mines.

The ILO also helps governments develop national HRD policies by assisting them in researching macroeconomic trends, employment perspectives, and present government policies affecting training supply and demand and then recommending policy alternatives to improve HRD activities in the particular country. The ILO even works with relevant government ministries in designing policy-change strategies and in drafting HRD legislation.

☜ World Bank

The World Bank conducts a wide range of training programs not only for its 6,000 global employees though the Training Division but also for senior officials worldwide through its Economic Development Institute. Let's briefly explore each of their HRD activities.

Economic Development Institute. Since 1955, the Economic Development Institute (EDI) has trained over 40,000 government and nongovernment leaders of the 150 member countries so that these countries can better plan and manage their economic and social development programs. While most of the training is conducted in English, EDI also trains in Arabic, Chinese, French, Portuguese, and Spanish. EDI collaborates with over 100 training institutions around the globe.

EDI's mission is "to mobilize knowledge and experience" and transfer them to its member countries. It fulfills this mission through three HRD activities: training seminars, organization building and development, and developing training materials.

Training seminars. Training seminars are conducted at the global, regional, and national levels. Examples of current seminars and locations include:

- Executive Development for Finance Institutions—Bangkok
- Techno-Economic Feasibility of Road Design and Construction—Belgrade
- Industrialization Management—Tokyo
- African Women Management Training—Douala, Cameroon
- Water Supply Sector Development—Manila, Philippines
- Developing Training Designs in China—Beijing
- Macroeconomic Management and Inflation—Hanoi
- Delivery of Vocational and Technical Education—San Jose, Costa Rica

Organization Building and Development. EDI assists each country or regional group of countries to establish its own training institutions and to conduct training programs. It assists these institutions in the following ways

- Jointly designing, delivering, and/or evaluating seminars
- Training trainers and granting fellowships for advanced HRD study
- Improving training materials
- Reviewing and formulating basic institutional strategy
- Analyzing external environment, marketing, and needs assessments
- Establishing financial and program accountability
- Interacting and "twinning" with training institutes in other countries

Developing Training Materials. Over the past thirty-five years, EDI has produced an extensive and unique collection of training materials covering all aspects of economic development, agriculture, education, finance, training and development, and health. These materials are culturally specific and are designed to enable trainers and trainees to develop specific technical skills. The 1992 *Catalogue of Training Materials* lists over 1,500 training packages including case studies, simulations, structured exercises, and learning instruments.

Training Division. The World Bank has extensive training and career development programs for its employees. Over 300 in-house courses are available in the categories of (1) technical skills, (2) economics, (3) finance, (4) bank skills, (5) management training, (6) information management and technology, (7) communications, and (8) languages.

☝ Food and Agriculture Organization

The Food and Agriculture Organization (FAO), headquartered in Rome with a membership of 160 countries, provides technical assistance to improve the production and distribution of food and agricultural products and to raise the levels of nutrition and standards of living of people in developing nations. Founded in 1945, FAO is the largest of the UN specialized agencies. Over $35 billion of foreign and domestic assistance has been provided to over 100 countries.

FAO currently has nearly 3,000 field projects that strengthen local institutions, support research and training, and enable the development and demonstration of new techniques. They vary in length from a ten-year project staffed by a large team of international experts and local technicians building in-country capability to control watershed erosion to a two-week training program in marketing local agricultural produce.

Typical FAO field projects include:

* Providing aquaculture technical assistance for fishermen in fifteen Pacific island countries for raising fish, mollusks, and edible seaweeds
* Developing and conducting training programs for rural Zambians in metalwork and blacksmithing
* Training in tractor maintenance in Indonesia
* Assisting farmers in Niger in the planting of more than one million trees with the fodder legume "prosopis," which thrives on desert soils and helps improve their fertility

FAO also serves as an information and development center on the topics of agriculture, fisheries, and forestry. Educational and training manuals, guides, and kits are prepared for use by government officials, schools, and rural leaders. In Peru, an FAO project has produced more than 800 video programs for training illiterate peasants in new farming and household methods.

FAO provides data to governments, businesses, and research workers on the production, use, and trade of 648 commodities. For example, the International Information System for the Agricultural Sciences and Technology (AGRIS) contains nearly two million references reported by national agricultural centers in 130 countries. The Global Information System on Food and Agriculture issues monthly reports on the world food situation, information which is critical for technical advisers in the affected countries.

FAO also helps national governments by encouraging information and technical assistance among regional groupings such as the Economic Community of West African States, the Center for Integrated Rural Development in Asia and the Pacific, and the Organization of Andean Pact Countries.

❦ *United Nations Industrial Development Organization*

The United Nations Industrial Development Organization (UNIDO), headquartered in Vienna, provides technical assistance in global, regional, national, and sectoral levels to promote and accelerate industrial development around the world. UNIDO projects include three main components:

1. Technical expertise for consulting and training
2. Educational opportunities in the form of fellowships to individuals and organizational groups to develop local expertise
3. Research by industry sector as well as by country

The global operations of UNIDO cover virtually every branch of industrial enterprise. UNIDO staff constantly monitor the latest technical advances and transfer this technology to the least developed countries. UNIDO assists developing countries to identify and quantify their training skill requirements and to develop appropriate HRD policies and training programs for meeting these needs. UNIDO also conducts training workshops for engineers, managers, and other senior technical personnel in areas such as petrochemicals, pharmaceuticals, wood products, leather products, food processing, agricultural machinery, and construction. Special consultations are provided to industry and government to increase the industrialization process.

For the nineties, UNIDO is placing special emphasis on industrial development in Africa, on training women to participate in industrial activities, and on the manufacturing sector of the least developed countries in the world.

NONPROFIT DEVELOPMENT GLOBAL ORGANIZATIONS

☜ *Organization for Educational Resources and Technological Training*

The Organization for Educational Resources and Technological Training (ORT) is one of the largest nonprofit, nongovernmental training institutions in the world. With world headquarters in London and regional offices in Geneva, Paris, New York, and Washington, D.C., this global organization began in 1960 with a grant to survey the vocational training needs of eight newly independent African countries. Since that time ORT has implemented more than 250 training and technical assistance programs in more than sixty developing countries in Latin America, the Middle East, Eastern Europe, Africa, Asia, and the Caribbean. Presently, more than 200,000 people are enrolled in ORT's worldwide network of secondary and industrial schools, apprenticeship programs, technical institutes, junior colleges, and teachers' training institutes. Most ORT projects are financed by multilateral and bilateral agencies such as the World Bank, the European Economic Community, the Canadian International Development Agency, and the U.S. Agency for International Development.

The motivational force behind every ORT project is (a) to provide training that will lead toward employment, and/or (b) to provide technical assistance leading toward sustainable growth for vocational education institutions.

ORT offers training for personnel in government ministries, public utilities, and industrial enterprises in areas ranging from robotics, electronics, computer technology, management, to child care and agrotechnology, as well as in a variety of industrial and agricultural skills. The programs include needs assessment and analysis, program design, and program implementation.

To assure a self-sustaining, institutional capacity within the country, ORT works closely with local managers and technicians in developing the vocational training programs. ORT designs and equips training centers as well as trains instructors in the preparation of courses and the production of teaching materials. ORT is one of the world's leaders in vocational technology and has developed packages such as "Robotics and Automation Literacy" hardware, software, and courseware. It has also created an integrated factory environment package which enables trainees to undertake the complete production cycle from design to manufacturing to testing.

Current HRD projects of ORT include:

- Establishing advanced training centers in Russia, Bulgaria, Poland, Hungary, and Czechoslovakia
- Developing distance education courses in office administration and electrical maintenance in Brazil
- Implementing a network of artisan training centers for low-income women in Uruguay
- Designing a job-oriented training program in Albania for former political prisoners and their families
- Training unemployed youth in Great Britain in carpentry, typing, hairdressing, child care, and catering
- Supporting a joint project with Peugeot Automobile of Nigeria to retrain and upgrade automotive employees

❦ *International Red Cross*

The International Red Cross encompasses both the International Committee of the Red Cross and the World Federation of 149 national Red Cross and Red Crescent (in Islamic countries) societies. Inspired by Henry Dunant, a Swiss businessman, the Red Cross was organized in 1893 in Geneva. Known primarily as a relief organization assisting victims of war and of natural disasters such as famines, earthquakes, and floods, the Red Cross also provides training to literally millions of volunteers all over the world who carry out the rehabilitative as well as the emergency work of the Red Cross. Millions of training materials and numerous training films are produced in all the major languages. A worldwide staff of 6,000 also are trained to provide technical assistance for victims around the globe.

❦ *World Rehabilitation Fund*

The World Rehabilitation Fund (WRF) has trained thousands of disabled people from 153 countries over the past two decades. For the past fifteen years, the World Rehabilitation Fund has coordinated an International Exchange of Experts and Information in Rehabilitation (IEEIR) program that enables American disability experts to share experiences and ideas with other specialists around the world. Examples of regional and national HRD programs for the handicapped include the following:

Nicaragua. Over 100,000 refugees were maimed by the civil strife in Nicaragua. In a remarkably symbolic program called "Arms for Arms," the WRF Central American Center in Honduras received over fourteen tons of scrapped military material such as rifles, land mines, mortars, grenades, and missiles formerly belonging to Nicaraguan soldiers and recycled these weapons to make parts of arms and leg braces. The enormity of disabled in this region—over 10 percent of the population!—and the shortage of qualified professionals has made training in physical and occupational therapy a high priority for WRF.

India. Two centers in India offer vocational training to mentally retarded youth and long-term home education for handicapped children.

Lebanon. Training in emergency medical care is provided in local health centers with special emphasis for those who have been severely burned from exploding shells and uncontrolled fires. Families are taught rehabilitation and basic medical care for treatment in the home.

China. Over five million Chinese are served by the WRF's community based rehabilitation services and training programs. The hope is that all of China will be reached by the year 2000.

❦ *World Education*

For over four decades, World Education has worked throughout Asia, Africa, and Latin America in training low-income adults and youth for skills which will increase their incomes and improve their communities.

World Education began in 1951 training teachers in India and preparing reading materials for illiterate adults. World Education works closely with local organizations and government agencies so that the projects can become part of a broader process for learning and long-term development. The experience gained overseas is shared with service agencies and schools in the United States to promote global awareness. World Education produces numerous training publications for worldwide use, and its training evaluations are used by policy makers around the globe. Recent World Education HRD projects include:

- Training Indochinese refugees in camps in Thailand to become productive citizens of the countries to which they will be migrating
- Training farmers in Nepal to learn how to read and write with materials that focus on health and family planning
- Conducting training workshops for men and women entrepreneurs in Kenya in the areas of marketing, bookkeeping and accounting, and credit administration

GLOBAL HRD ASSOCIATIONS

❦ *International Federation of Training and Development Organizations*

The International Federation of Training and Development Organizations (IFTDO) was formed in 1972 and includes more than eighty national training associations and educational organizations from thirty-five countries. The general purpose of the global association is to improve the field of HRD throughout the world by:

- Holding annual world training and development congresses. Congresses have taken place in venues such as Geneva, Dublin, Rio de Janeiro, Manila, Mexico City, Sidney, Amsterdam, Stockholm, Buenos Aires, and Madrid.
- Assisting in the formation of new national HRD organizations. Among the IFTDO publications is a manual entitled "How to Form a National Training and Development Organization."
- Encouraging worldwide cooperation and assistance among global HRD practitioners. A *Who's Who in International HRD* is published periodically.

❦ *Interman*

Interman is an association of over 400 management development institutions in nearly ninety countries. Member organizations include the American Assembly of Collegiate Schools of Business, Ashridge Management College (U.K.), Algerian National School of Administration, China Enterprise Management Training Center, Asian Productivity Organization, and the Argentina Center for Training.

Interman's objectives are:

- To facilitate and strengthen the networking of member organizations
- To strengthen member institutions through technical assistance and support
- To identify joint venture training projects

Interman conducts research on global management issues and identifies innovative management development activities around the world. It also publishes technical guides and policy papers and holds regional conferences.

❦ *International Society for Intercultural Education, Training, and Research*

Founded in 1974, the International Society for Intercultural Education, Training, and Research (SIETAR International) is a global professional and service organization with more than 2,000 members from nearly seventy countries worldwide. Its purpose is "the development and application of knowledge, values and skills which enable effective intercultural, interracial and inter-ethnic actions of the individual, group, organization and community levels."

Each year, SIETAR International holds a global congress which features workshops, seminars, formal presentations, and symposia on a variety of HRD topics. Recent congresses have been held in Jamaica, Canada, Netherlands, Italy, Mexico, and the United States. In addition, a "training of intercultural trainers" institute is held each summer at Georgetown University in Washington, D.C.

SIETAR International's membership is composed of trainers, educators, consultants, and researchers involved in improving the organizational operations and the effective training of personnel working in both multicultural and international environments. SIETAR International produces a bimonthly newsletter, *Communique*, and a quarterly journal, *International Journal of Intercultural Relations.*

❦ *Society for International Development*

The Society for International Development (SID) is a worldwide professional association for professionals with an interest in international economic, political, and social development. SID was founded in 1957 and has members in 120 countries and a network of over ninety-five national and local chapters. The Washington, D.C. chapter alone has over 1,400 individual and forty-nine institutional members.

There are numerous technical work groups in areas such as human resource development, trade, agriculture and rural development, careers in international development, health and nutrition, education and marketing in development. Other activities and programs include annual conferences, monthly luncheons, and international development forums. An international conference is held every three years as is the North-South Roundtable. Publications include a quarterly journal, *Development*, and a quarterly newsletter, *Compass*.

SUMMARY

In the past fifty years, global public and nonprofit organizations have played an increasingly critical role in supporting the development of people around the world and especially in developing regions of Africa and Asia. There are three categories of public and nonprofit organizations that have had an impact on HRD around the world: (1) global, public, government-to-government organizations, (2) global, private, people-to-people voluntary organizations, and global HRD associations.

The major public global organizations include the United Nations Development Program (UNDP), the International Labor Office (ILO), the World Bank, the Food and Agriculture Organization (FAO), and the United Nations Industrial Development Organization (UNIDO). These institutions and others like them have provided direct government-to-government support of efforts to strengthen the governmental structures of developing nations, establish labor and other standards, and transfer knowledge and technology that is applicable in the development process.

From the many nonprofit organizations that have been working globally, we selected and profiled the following as representative of HRD programs that are succeeding: the Organization for Educational Resources and Technological Training (ORT), the International Red Cross, World Rehabilitation Fund (WRF), and World Education.

Global HRD organizations provide a means for HRD professionals around the world to communicate new information and technologies and respond as a group to new HRD challenges. Organizations profiled in this chapter include the International Federation of Training and Development Organizations (IFTDO), Interman, the International Society for Intercultural Education, Training, and Research (SIETAR International), and the Society for International Development (SID).

REFERENCES

ALISBAH, BILSEL. *The World Bank Training Handbook.* Washington, D.C.: World Bank Press, 1991.

DRAPER, WILLIAM H. *Putting People First: UNDP Annual Report.* New York:UNDP, 1991.

ECONOMIC DEVELOPMENT INSTITUTE. Washington, D.C.: World Bank Press, 1990.

Food and Agriculture Organization: What It Is, What It Does. Rome: FAO, 1988.

ILO Turin Center—Training for Development. Turin, Italy: ILO Press, 1989.

INTERMAN Directory. Geneva: ILO, 1990.

ORT International Cooperation Activities Since 1960. Washington, D.C.: ORT, 1991.

SIETAR International Brochure. Washington, D.C.: SIETAR, 1991.

❦ ❦

CHAPTER 9

HRD and Globalizing the Organization

INTRODUCTION

> When globalizatiobn efforts fail, chances are it's because of a mistaken vision of the organization and the values needed for success. Too often we do not properly plant for the global harvest.
>
> *Kenichi Ohmae*

According to White, Porter, Carnevale, and other experts in the field, HRD should be the center, the strategic lever in enabling an organization to successfully transform itself and enter the global arena. Without HRD, companies attempting to globalize will move too slowly and too ineffectively to retain their competitive advantages at the global level. HRD is also critical in enabling companies that are already globalized to remain competitive in the global marketplace.

In this chapter we will discuss the ways in which HRD can guide the globalization process and assist corporations in evolving into global learning organizations capable of successfully entering the twenty-first century's competitive global environment. As Bartlett and Ghoshal have noted, even if companies have identified what must be done to enhance their global competitiveness, the challenge is to learn how to develop the organizational capability to do it.

❦ Value

An understanding of the critical role that HRD plays in the globalization of organizations will enable the HRD professional to work alongside strategic planners as they move a company up the global learning curve. HRD can create a global *learning* organization by providing organization assessment, leadership development, global education, and world-class training.

❦ Learning Objectives

After studying this chapter, you should be able to:

1. Outline the steps in the evolution from a domestic to a global organization
2. Identify the functions of HRD in transforming a nonglobal organization into one that is global in outlook and operations
3. Recognize the leadership and executive development needs of a globalizing organization
4. Understand the role and dimensions of training in the globalization process
5. Recognize the need to and advantage of creating global *learning* organizations

STEPS IN GLOBALIZATION

❦ Domestic to Global Corporate Evolution

According to Adler, corporations typically go through four conceptually distinct, progressively more complex phases or stages as they evolve from a domestic to a global status (see Table 9.1).

In Phase I, the domestic phase, companies operate on domestic terms and focus solely on domestic markets. They focus on either product or service, and technology is highly proprietary and protected. These companies have relatively few competitors and are structurally centralized. The perspective is generally ethnocentric and cultural sensitivity is relatively unimportant.

International or Phase II companies are those that begin to export their products or services abroad. Usually, in such companies, international human resource development activities focus only on the small group of expatriate managers involved directly in foreign operations. Structurally, the company is decentralized and often forms a single international division for its foreign operations. The corporate strategy is multidomestic. Cultural sensitivity begins to be important.

TABLE 9.1
Domestic to Global Corporate Evolution

Corporate Activities	Phase I Domestic	Phase II International	Phase III Multinational	Phase IV Global
Competitive Strategy	Domestic	Multidomestic	Multinational	Global
Importance of World Business	Marginal	Important	Extremely Important	Dominant
Primary Orientation	Product or Service	Market	Price	Strategy
Product/ Service	New, Unique	More Standardization	Completely Standardized (Commodity)	Mass-Customized
	Product Engineering Emphasized	Process Engineering Emphasized	Engineering Not Emphasized	Product & Process Engineering
Technology	Proprietary	Shared	Widely Shared	Instantly & Extensively Shared
R&D/Sales	High	Decreasing	Very Low	High
Profit Margin	High	Decreasing	Very Low	High
Competitors	None	Few	Many	Significant (Few or Many)
Market	Small, Domestic	Large, Multidomestic	Larger, Multinational	Largest, Global
Production Location	Domestic	Domestic & Primary Markets	Multinational, Least Cost	Global, Least Cost
Exports	None	Growing, High Potential	Large & Saturated	Imports & Exports
Structure	Functional Divisions	Functional with International Division	Multinational Lines of Business	Global Alliance Heteroarchy
	Centralized	Decentralized	Centralized	Centralized & Decentralized
Cultural Sensitivity	Unimportant	Very Important	Somewhat Important	Critically Important
With/Whom	No one	Clients	Employees	Employees & Clients
Level	No one	Workers & Clients	Managers	Executives

Phase III is the multinational phase. Companies focus on least-cost production with sourcing, manufacturing, and marketing worldwide. The parent company operates with a centralized view of strategy, technology, and resource allocation, but decision making and customer service shift to the national level for marketing, selling, manufacturing, and competitive tactics. There are many competitors, and profit margins are low. Products and services are standardized, and the primary orientation is price.

In Phase IV, the global phase, the corporation operates globally. Global thinking and global competencies become critical for survival. The company is constantly scanning, organizing, and reorganizing its resources and capabilities so that national or regional boundaries are not barriers to potential products, business opportunities, and manufacturing locations. Companies send their best, fast-track managers as well as senior executives for global assignments. Cultural sensitivity becomes critically important as do language skills. Products are mass-customized. Imports as well as exports are part of the company's operations in manufacturing and sales. There are globally coordinated strategies, global structures, and a global corporate culture.

☜ The Global Learning Curve

To assist organizations in identifying their location on the road to corporate globalization, White has developed the Global Learning Curve (Figure 9.1), which combines Adler's four phases with key corporate events, activities, and strategies. As the figure demonstrates, firms often begin their ascent toward global status by international travel and then begin to export and get involved in international law, tax, and finance issues. The multinational phase includes new marketing, quality, service, and telecommunications systems. In the global stage, a corporation transforms its structure, policies, organizational dynamics, HRD activities, and, most importantly and with greatest difficulty, its corporate culture.

Of course, not all companies systematically and clearly traverse each of the phases. In addition, companies may be in Phase I (Domestic) for some corporate activities (e.g., primary orientation and structure) and in Phase IV (Global) for other corporate activities such as technology. To the degree this mixed-corporate evolution exists so also exists dysfunction and inefficient results and ultimately economic failure. Hence, the critical need for HRD to assist and lead corporations in the journey toward globalization, which will be the focus of the remainder of the chapter.

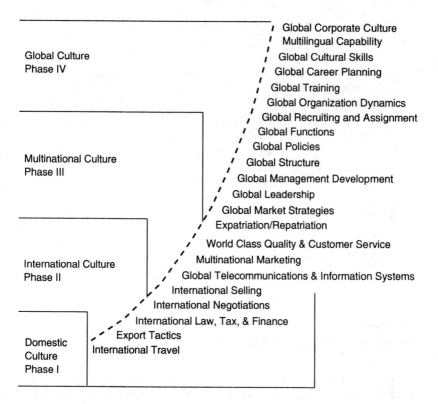

FIGURE 9.1
Global Learning Curve

HRD GLOBALIZATION MODEL

Transforming a nonglobal organization into a global one is a challenging, formidable task that should not take place in a haphazard or "trickle-up" fashion. Globalization requires a top-down, organizationwide commitment. The top leadership must understand its importance, its complexity and the need for comprehensive, continuous, enthusiastic support. HRD programs then can assist in the creation of a successful global enterprise.

Globalization through HRD is systematic and multidimensional, involving four distinct inputs—global organizational assessment and development, global leadership development, global training, and global education (Figure 9.2). There is not necessarily a best input to begin or end with, although

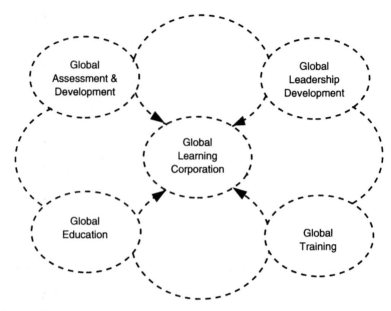

FIGURE 9.2
Globalization through HRD Model

organizational assessment and development are often logical starting points. However, for some organizations, gaining leadership's complete support and commitment requires beginning with these activities. Other organizations want to "put their toe in" by receiving a training course or a global briefing. Most organizations probably are best served by eventually having all inputs occurring simultaneously and continuously. As indicated in the figure, the desired goal is not just a global organization, but a global learning organization for, as we will see later in this chapter, only an organization that is continually learning is able to remain competitive in a rapidly changing global environment.

The following discussion shows how each of these HRD inputs can build the global learning corporation in different ways.

ORGANIZATION ASSESSMENT AND DEVELOPMENT

❦ *Global Assessment*

There are a number of both organizationwide and functional systems that can be assessed to determine the phase (domestic, international, multina-

1. Organizationwide	2. Functions
a. Corporate Culture	a. Human Resource Management
b. Leadership	b. Marketing
c. Work Force	c. Technology Development (R&D)
d. Structure	d. Finance and Purchasing
e. Strategy	e. Telecommunications and Information Systems
f. Policy and Procedures	f. Manufacturing
g. Management Controls	g. Sales and Service
h. Organizational Dynamics	h. Training and Development

FIGURE 9.3
Global Assessment Systems

tional, or global) to which an organization has evolved and how it "stacks up" against other global competitors of that particular industry (Figure 9.3).

In a global audit, each of these organizational and functional elements are measured against global standards, especially with those firms that are considered the top global companies in the industry. The gaps identified serve as a foundation in determining key organizational competency needs and structural changes.

❦ *Global Organization Development*

As an organization becomes more aware of its strengths and limitations, the change process can continue. The corporation attempts to resolve the incongruity or "disconnect" between its global goals and its organization structure and capability. The global HRD consultant can utilize a number of organization development strategies—e.g., organizational and process mapping, team building, process reengineering and regrouping—to promote the development of a focused global corporate structure and build a global learning organization. Chakravarthy and Perlmutter, among others, have developed strategic models to guide corporations to the global stage.

A number of corporations—Oryx Energy, NEC, Millipore, and Xerox—have undergone planned, extensive global assessments and organization change to become more functionally and systematically global.

GLOBAL LEADERSHIP DEVELOPMENT

Developing global awareness and global competencies for corporate executives is critical for the global organization. A number of global HRD activities can be employed in training and developing top corporate leaders:

- Individual profiling and consultations
- Global executive seminars
- Structured learning exchanges with other global executives
- Global briefings and conferences
- Executive retreats
- Leadership development programs

ASTD recently developed a skill model for the Global Executive which included the following four skill areas:

1. Skills for understanding global business opportunities
2. Skills for setting an organization's direction, for creating vision, mission and purpose
3. Skills for implementing the vision, mission, and purpose
4. Skills for personal understanding and effectiveness with multicultural teams and alliances in a global context

ASTD recommends that a variety of HRD strategies might be considered to enable executives to broaden their horizons from domestic thinking to global thinking:

- Rotating the high potential in global assignments
- Sending executives to visit key competitors in other countries
- Teaching foreign languages on a just-in-time basis
- Offering reentry programs for executives returning from foreign assignments
- Establishing worldwide electronic study groups

A number of corporations have begun excellent leadership development programs. Emhart, a manufacturer and marketer of hardware and machinery, has initiated an executive development program on global competitiveness which includes topics such as, "The World in the Year 2000," "The Dynamics of World Trade," "Operations in Global Business," and "Building a Global Business Perspective." Colgate-Palmolive and Cray Research give executives expatriate assignments to boost their global awareness. Aetna Insurance has established a deliberate system of promotions and rotations between domestic and international assignments. Bethlehem Steel includes global competitiveness in its executive development programs.

GLOBAL TRAINING

Michael Porter, in *The Competitive Advantage of Nations*, writes, "Sustaining and improving competitive position ultimately requires that a firm develop its internal capabilities in areas important to competitive advantage" (p. 55). World-class training should be at the center of such strategic thinking.

World-class training incorporates many different disciplines into the development of the organization. White identifies nine areas for "global training for the global corporation," or what he calls World-Class Training (see Figure 9.4).

Rhinesmith suggests the following training programs to develop the kinds of skills and attitudes that are necessary for the staff of global corporations:

1. *Orientation programs* for global cohorts across functions, regions, and product groups to instill common global visions and global corporate strategies and values.

2. *Global scanning seminars* to ensure familiarity with global social, economic, and political trends and to teach managers how to balance global integration

FIGURE 9.4
World Class Training
Global Training for the Global Corporation

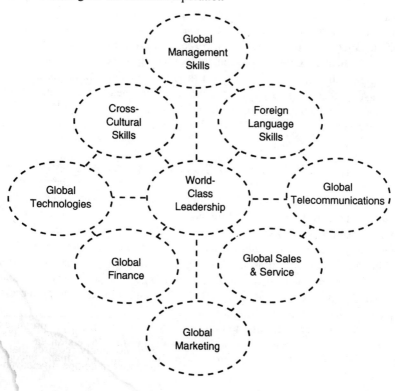

needs for efficiency, global coordination for learning, and effectiveness and local responsiveness by business, function, and tasks.

3. *Cross-cultural and multicultural skill training* emphasizing problem solving, decision making, communicating, selling, negotiating, coaching, appraising, and leading in multicultural contexts.

4. *Right-brain/left-brain training* for reframing and managing contradictions and complexities, ambiguity, and chaos and change.

The training curriculum courses within the organization should be fully globalized. Each course should be integrated, reinforcing and, above all, supporting the successful implementation of global business strategies. A number of companies, including AT&T, GTE, AMP, Royal Bank of Canada, and COMSAT, have already globalized their training programs.

GLOBAL EDUCATION

The acceleration of global change and global competition requires a regular, continual flow of relevant, strategic information entering the organization. Key professional journals and international newspapers should be made available, and appropriate global and technical computer networks should be identified. Briefings and roundtables on corporately critical topics should be held on topics such as "Global Management Issues in the Nineties," "Competing in the New Europe," "Impact of a North American Free Trade Zone," and "Global Leadership in a High Tech World." Only then can the organization gain a strategic window of the world and be in tune with constantly changing global realities.

BECOMING A GLOBAL LEARNING ORGANIZATION

The cherished goal for today's global organization is to become a global *learning* organization. The need for global integration and local differentiation, as well as for worldwide innovation and networking, requires the creation of an adaptive and flexible learning organization to meet these challenges. Global organizations must have *collective* learning competence and a corporate environment with world-class training that equip everyone, from the CEO to the receptionist, with global values and skills crucial for success in the rapidly changing global marketplace.

It is necessary, therefore, to build a learning environment that promotes a sharing of experience on a worldwide scale and that fosters an easy dialogue between the different countries and cultures that a company encompasses. Barham and Devine note that "the future is not just about international competition or collaboration; it is also about international learning. Managing across borders means learning across borders" (p. 37).

The process of becoming a learning organization appears to fit more easily into the Japanese business environment than other business cultures. The Japanese believe that business success is a ceaseless process of learning. Self-betterment leads to national development. In Japan, company education has psychosocial underpinnings that fall outside Western experience. Company education is seen as a major instrument for long-term organization development and for shaping corporate culture.

Several U.S. companies have now begun the process of becoming global learning organizations. Colgate-Palmolive's present human resource strategy includes development of an organizational capability for continuous learning, a "process through which Colgate-Palmolive people continuously expand their capacity to perform, where expansive new thinking is nurtured, and where people are continuously learning to learn together." Other global learning corporations include Analog Devices, Rover, Honda, Shell, and Motorola.

SUMMARY

As corporations transform themselves from domestic or multinational organizations, HRD should be the center, the strategic lever in enabling them to successfully enter the global arena. Without HRD, companies attempting to globalize will move too slowly and too ineffectively to retain their competitive advantages at the global level. HRD is also critical in enabling companies that are already globalized to remain competitive in the global marketplace.

Adler has defined four stages that corporations go through in the process of globalization: domestic, international, multinational, and global. Each of these stages can be characterized in terms of competitive strategy, primary orientation, nature of product or service, markets, the degree of need for cultural sensitivity, and other factors. To assist organizations in identifying their location in the globalization process, White has developed a global learning model that combines Adler's four phases with key corporate events, activities, and strategies.

HRD plays an important role in the organization assessment and development process that is fundamental to a corporation's successful globalization. In areas such as global assessment, global organization, leadership, executive development, and global training, the HRD professional brings critical skills and knowledge. Vital training areas include regional orientation, global scanning seminars, cross-cultural training, foreign language skills training, and global leadership development.

In order to succeed, a global organization must become a global *learning* organization in which the corporate environment and world-class training equip everyone with global values and skills crucial for success in the rapidly changing global marketplace.

REFERENCES

ADLER, NANCY AND FARIBORZ GHADAR. "Strategic Human Resource Management: A Global Perspective" in *Human Resource Management in International Comparison*. Berlin: de Guyter, 1990.

BARHAM, KEVIN, AND MARION DEVINE. *The Quest for the International Manager:A Survey of Global Human Resource Strategies*. London: Business International Press, 1991.

BARTLETT, CHRISTOPHER, AND SUMANTRA GHOSHAL. *Managing across Borders:The Transnational Solution*. Cambridge: Harvard Business School Press, 1989.

CARNEVALE, ANTHONY. "Learning: The Critical Technology." *Training and Development* 1992.

CHAKRAVARTHY, BALAJI AND HOWARD PERLMUTTER. "Strategic Planning for Global Business." *Columbia Journal for World Business* (Summer 1985), pp. 3–10.

GALAGAN, PATRICIA A. "Executive Development in a Changing World." *Training and Development Journal*. Alexandria, Va.: ASTD Press, 1990.

OHMAE, KENICHI: *The Borderless World*. New York: Harper Business, 1990.

PORTER, MICHAEL. *The Competitive Advantage of Nations*. New York: Free Press, 1990.

RHINESMITH, STEPHEN. "An Agenda for Globalization." *Training and Development Journal* (February 1991), pp. 22–29.

RHINESMITH, STEPHEN. "Going Global from the Inside Out." *Training and Development Journal* (November 1991), pp. 42–47.

WHITE, BREN. *World Class Training*. Dallas: Odenwald Press, 1992.

❦ ❦

HRD Practices and Programs around the World

The field of human resource development has blossomed worldwide. Every country has developed powerful, culturally appropriate HRD programs that have enabled organizations and countries to become ever more successful. No single country or region has a monopoly on HRD excellence since there are a rich array and variety of HRD programs in every corner of the globe that offer creative and exciting solutions to the human resource needs in that region of the world.

In Section IV, the HRD programs and practices of eleven regions are surveyed:

- Western Europe (Chapter 10)
- Eastern Europe (Chapter 11)
- Middle East and North Africa (Chapter 12)
- Africa (Chapter 13)
- South Central Asia (Chapter 14)
- East Asia (Chapter 15)
- Japan (Chapter 16)
- South Pacific Region (Chapter 17)
- Canada (Chapter 18)
- Latin America and the Caribbean (Chapter 19)
- United States (Chapter 20)

In each chapter, we first examine the cultural factors and economic environment that impact HRD in that region. Following an exploration of general HRD practices, the best HRD programs of organizations in the region will be described. The organizations selected include a wide spectrum—large and small, corporate and public, national and global. Each of the more than 40 organizations cited have received national as well as global acclaim and recognition for their HRD programs.

CHAPTER 10

❦ ❦

Western Europe

INTRODUCTION

If Europe is to attract foreign investment and compete effectively with the U.S. and Asia, the continent's nations must begin to work more effectively—and training is a fundamental part of that effort.

Robert O'Connor
New Training Approaches for Europe '93

As Europe faces the challenge of becoming a single entity, powerful political, social and cultural factors continue to push the continent's countries apart. The European single market will not exist until the historical barriers of national pride and prejudice are torn down. Human resource development is seen as the key to ecomonic unity and growth in Western Europe.

In this chapter, we will examine the HRD environment in Western Europe and outline some successful HRD responses in both the private and public sectors of a number of countries.

❦ *Learning Objectives*

After studying this chapter, you should be able to:

1. Understand how the history, demographics, geography, key cultural beliefs, languages, and religions of Western Europe affect HRD activities

122

2. Recognize the key economic and political factors in the region that have an impact on the practice of HRD
3. Outline the evolving role of HRD in light of European unification, especially with regard to integrating women into the work-force and providing vocational training
4. Give examples of successful HRD programs in both corporate and public sectors

CULTURAL FACTORS IMPACTING HRD

❦ *Geography, Demographics, and Language*

Western Europe is increasingly coming together as a single political, economic, and social entity as a result of the cooperative efforts of the European Community. In this chapter, we include the twelve EC members (Belgium, Denmark, France, Germany, Greece, Ireland, Italy, Luxembourg, the Netherlands, Portugal, Spain, and the United Kingdom), as well as the seven European Free Trade Association (EFTA) members (Austria, Finland, Iceland, Liechtenstein, Norway, Sweden, and Switzerland).

The 380 million people of Western Europe live in one of the most densely populated and urbanized regions of the world. More than 60 percent of the population of most European countries lives in cities, with the highest proportion (95 percent) of urban dwellers in Belgium. In most countries, a single city dominates in terms of population, economy, politics, and culture, with Berlin, London, Madrid, Paris, and Rome being among the largest. As a result of increasing affluence, an emphasis on birth control policies, and individual desire to limit family size, annual growth rates in Western Europe are among the lowest in the world. A long tradition of emphasis on education has contributed to extremely high literacy rates throughout the region.

The diversity of ethnic and cultural groups in Western Europe is seen in the large number of relatively small political units. Attempts in the last two centuries to redraw national boundaries along ethnic, cultural, or linguistic lines have resulted in there being far more separate countries today than there were 100 years ago. Even so, nearly all of the native people are classified as Caucasian, although there are wide differences in coloring, with fair pigmentation dominant in the northwest and darker pigmentation more common in the south. Although most of the region's languages fall into the Germanic or Romance families, there are other indigenous languages, including Basque, spoken along the French-Spanish border, Celtic, found in Brittany and the western parts of Wales, Ireland, and Scotland, and a group of Finno-Ugric languages spoken in Scandinavia.

❦ Religion

Christianity is by far the religion of most Western Europeans, with Protestants in the majority in Germany, the United Kingdom, and the Scandinavian countries. Roman Catholicism is the predominant religion in Austria, Belgium, France, Ireland, Italy, Luxembourg, the Netherlands, Portugal, Spain, and Switzerland. Ninety-eight percent of the people of Greece belong to the Eastern (Greek) Orthodox Church. Judaism is common in urban areas, and recent immigrants throughout the region constitute sizable communities of believers in Islam, Hinduism, Buddhism, and other world religions.

❦ History

Europe, and especially Western Europe, has held an importance in the world that far exceeded its relative size and population. The region has long been a center of education and a source of new ideas. Three universities in Italy and one each in France and England were established prior to 1200, with Spain and Germany also developing major centers of learning prior to 1500.

Colonial empires established from the seventeenth through the nineteenth centuries lured many people to the colonized areas. During the nineteenth and early twentieth centuries, millions more migrated west, particularly to the United States and Canada. Others moved in large numbers to Australia, New Zealand, South America, and South Africa. Of course, in each of these migrations, the people of Western Europe carried their languages, cultures, and ethnic belief systems with them to their new lands. As a result of these two features—an emphasis on education and large-scale emigration—many of today's world social movements, political and economic systems, philosophies, and belief systems have their origins in Europe.

Western Europe was devastated by the two World Wars of the twentieth century and then by its separation from its eastern neighbors that became part of the Soviet bloc during the cold war era. Postwar recovery, aided massively by the United States with whom the area was militarily aligned, led to a vigorous, if considerably smaller, role in world events. In response to a need for more unified political and economic power in the region, the European Economic Community (EEC) was founded in 1958, and was followed in 1967 by the establishment of the European Community. The end of 1992 has seen the elimination of all remaining legal, fiscal, and technical barriers to the completion of communitywide unification and eventual common rules in areas such as energy, environmental protection, education and training, research and development, technology, and currency. With the collapse of the former Soviet Union and the resulting reunification of Germany, the former German Democratic Republic was automatically included in the European Community, and a number of countries in Eastern Europe have shown interest in joining.

❦ *Values and Customs*

The principal cultural influences in Western Europe have historically been those associated with Christianity: hard work, faith in God, responsibility to family, church and community, modesty, charity, and tolerance. These last three especially have been tempered to some degree by social, economic, political, and religious developments but are still held as important by most people. Europeans are proud of their long and distinguished history and place special emphasis on culture and the arts. There is general respect for education, and evidence of learning and culture is appreciated.

An easygoing, friendly, hospitable approach to life is seen in the southern countries, with family and community playing an important role in everyday life. The northern population tends to be more business focused, with an emphasis on industry, punctuality, orderliness, and thrift. In all countries, there is more of an emphasis on family reputation, educational background, and financial standing than is found in countries such as the United States. One's social position is important, and, for the most part, family matters are thought to be private and not open for general discussion. Even in the more outgoing areas, people are reserved with strangers and take time to establish friendships.

❦ *Family*

In Western Europe, as in most of the industrialized world, attitudes toward the family are undergoing enormous changes. Especially in the northern countries, extended families are spread among many households, and the typical nuclear family is small. Women commonly work outside the home, so there's been considerable breakdown of traditional gender roles. Extended families more commonly live together in the south, and in countries like Spain, Portugal, Italy, and Greece, the family unit continues to be very important, with more traditional roles taken by men and women. In these countries, there is also more concern about whether an individual might bring shame or dishonor to the family name. Although there's been an increase in divorce rates, even in countries where there is a Catholic majority, they still tend to be relatively low.

ECONOMIC ENVIRONMENT FOR HRD

In 1992, Western Europe became the world's largest single market with nineteen countries (twelve EC countries and seven EFTA countries) with more than 380 million people and a GNP of over $10 trillion, 43 percent of the world's total. In addition to economic unity, a single currency—the ECU— is gradually being introduced. The free movement of labor, goods, services, and capital has begun in earnest. Workers, employers, the self-employed, mechanics and accountants, teachers and researchers, physicians and architects are now able to work in the member country of their choice, on equal terms as the citizens of that country.

By the year 2000, this membership may extend to more than thirty countries as old and new Eastern European countries (e.g., Poland, Hungary, Ukraine, Croatia, Slovenia, Moldavia, Latvia, Estonia, Lithuania) consider joining and thereby creating a free trade zone of over 500 million people. These Eastern European countries will be expecting Western Europe to provide much needed investment capital, advanced technology, and expert guidance for their desperate economic and environmental problems.

The new economic realities will have a significant impact on the European corporate world. The single market will add urgency to cross-border courtships since the European firms face intensified competition from U.S. and Japanese firms that have already reaped economies of scale in manufacturing, marketing, and research and development because of their giant domestic markets.

European firms have begun to pool their activities in industries such as telecommunications, railroad equipment, artificial intelligence, robotics, and metallurgy to boost their competitiveness in world markets. These alliances have spread to many other sectors ranging from high technology to construction materials. The surge in mergers and acquisitions totaled over $66 billion in 1991 and is the clearest evidence yet of an emerging pan-European business climate.

Friberg notes that Western European countries are responding in different ways to the new Europe. Italian firms are focusing on lowering distribution costs and improving worldwide logistics. Germany is concerned about high wages and the strong social guarantees built into their labor-management systems. Spain recognizes the need to close the productivity gaps with its European rivals. Great Britain is attempting to increase efficiency by increasing volume of production. Belgium will continue to emphasize exports.

There are a number of economic challenges Western European firms are now facing which will require significant HRD help:

1. *Economic Output per Worker*. Western Europe's economic output per worker is much less than that of either the United States or Japan. For example, in the automotive industry, it takes Europeans thirty-six hours to build a car versus twenty-five hours for Americans and less than seventeen hours for Japanese.
2. *Economy of scale*. Many Western European companies in the same industry suffer from fragmented structures and over competition. Alliances and downsizing will continue and dramatically affect the European work-force.
3. *Quality and R&D*. European firms have generally spent less on R&D than Japan or the United States, and the quality of their products has begun falling behind.
4. *Immigration*. Large numbers of Eastern Europeans have entered Western Europe, bringing with them few vocational skills, as well as different cultures and customs for working and learning.
5. *Collaboration between Universities and Industry*. Business leaders feel that European universities are not assisting and collaborating as much as they should to help Europe become more competitive on a global scale.

TRAINING NEEDS AND HRD IN WESTERN EUROPE

In an extensive Western Europe survey, Price Waterhouse and Cransfield School of Management found that employers throughout Western Europe perceive a common handicap—a continued and deteriorating shortage of skilled labor that is threatening their competitiveness at a time when the new European single market will impose unprecedented trading pressure. The survey also noted that a number of states throughout Europe are facing severe skill shortages because employers failed to invest enough resources in education and training in the crucial decade of the eighties, when the world economy underwent major structural changes.

The survey, based on interviews with 6,000 employers in France, Germany, Spain, Sweden, and the United Kingdom, found that employers in all five countries are realizing that "long-term training and career management is a more productive solution to overcoming shortages than throwing more money at the existing group of suitably qualified workers" (Friberg, p. 30). This increased commitment to training, however, has not always been backed up by a proper assessment of employers' future needs and a systematic evaluation of training program effectiveness.

Training in most countries is seen not only as a means of increasing the company's stock of skilled workers but also as a far more effective incentive to potential recruits and existing workers. Michael Eydoux of the French *banque d'affaires*, Paribas, saw that the quality of an organization's training would give it a competitive edge in attracting both new graduates and more experienced professional and technical staff. Attitudes in Germany were similar. For example, two-thirds of German distribution companies and nearly three-quarters of German banks saw better career planning as a critical measure for improving and retaining staff (Freburg, pp. 31-32).

The growing importance of training is also demonstrated by the increase in financial resources now being allocated to support the effective development of staff. The survey found that employers in all countries have spent more on training in the last three years. More than 60 percent of organizations, for example, have increased the amount they spend on training managers and professional staff.

What skills do companies anticipate they will need in the nineties? Those listed as top priority were people-management skills—such as motivation, working in teams, etc. Computers and technology came second. Other frequently cited skills included business strategy and administration, change management, and customer service.

The survey found that, while the majority of companies adopt some formal way of assessing their future training needs, fewer firms link their training strategies to any analysis of the company's business plan. Swedish organizations are the most likely to involve their HRD specialist in the process of determining corporate strategy from the onset. By contrast, only two-fifths of German HRD specialists are directly involved in mainstream decision making. Most aspects of personnel management in Germany are strictly regulated by law.

In France, the direct involvement of HRD specialists in determining strategy is second only to that of Sweden. France also has the highest proportion of HRD directors with board room status. The level of personnel involvement in board room issues is important because almost all strategies adopted by organizations are highly dependent on having the right workforce to carry them out.

Overall, the survey concluded that the potential role for personnel and HRD professionals is far more broad reaching and influential in Western Europe than it has been in the past.

ROLE OF HRD IN INTEGRATING WOMEN INTO THE WORK FORCE

With its limited population growth, or actual decline in some countries, the integration of women into the work-force has become a critical goal for Western European countries. Recent policies have been developed to include women in training programs, especially those related to occupations of the future, and to develop specific measures for training in those occupations in which they are underrepresented. The European Commission recommended the following steps:

- Put qualified people who can respond to the specific problems of women in the vocational guidance, training, and placement services
- Improve school, university, and vocational guidance services in such a way that they cater to these groups
- Present women and those around them with the image of women undertaking nontraditional activities, in particular those linked to the occupations of the future
- Encourage the participation of girls in higher education and, in particular, in technical and technological fields
- Encourage more participation of women in the field of initial vocational training outside the formal educational system
- Encourage young girls and women to create their own activity, set up their own business or cooperative
- Provide training reserved for certain categories of women, especially the under-privileged groups, or those returning to work after a break
- Enable the spouses of self-employed persons who participate in the activity of their partners to benefit from training schemes under the same conditions as their partners
- Create flexible provisions for child care and set up the appropriate social infra-structures which will enable mothers to acquire vocational training
- Recognize skills acquired within the context of the household and the family (Frank)

VOCATIONAL TRAINING IN GERMANY

The vocational training system in Germany is considered among the very best in the world. German companies spend over $15 billion per year in the training of 1.8 million youth. Nearly every large firm offers vocational training in several occupations, and every young person involved receives a monthly wage of about $500. The government, companies, associations, unions, teachers, students, and parents all strongly support vocational training.

Although training costs are high, neither the German government nor the companies step back from their responsibility for youth training. It is considered "indispensable" that trade and industry provide training positions for every applicant. With the growing demand for workers and the decrease in population growth, the number of training positions offered actually exceeds the demand.

There are many reasons why companies are willing to finance vocational training. According to Schenkel, a senior staff person with the Federal Vocational Institute, "a master craftsman is proud of his apprentice, and the success of the firm's training program director is measured partly by the number of trainees who pass the final exam. The firms are convinced that they, themselves, know best what should be taught and how it should be taught. They possess modern equipment, are more likely to be confronted with technical innovation, can train the youth through practical work, and can provide a glimpse at practical working life" (p. 47).

The company is also given the opportunity to have three years in which to observe the apprentices and decide if they want to hire them as permanent employees.

The high quality of training occurs both (1) during in-company training which takes place three to four days a week during the normal working hours of the firm, and (2) at the public vocational school which the trainee attends one or two days a week.

The Federal Institute of Vocational Training is responsible for coordinating the vocational training programs throughout Germany. The employers and trade unions, as well as federal and state governments, are represented on the board of the institute. The institute also develops social training projects and conducts research in the field of vocational structures, planning, financing of training, development of regulations and curricula, and use of media.

HRD PROGRAMS OF WESTERN EUROPE

❦ *AIB Group (Ireland)*

AIB Group was formed in 1966 as the Allied Irish Bank. It has now grown to over 10,000 employees with operations in the U.K., Belgium, Singapore, the United States, and Australia. Its HRD philosophy and activities have launched AIB into a worldwide success story. G.B. Scanlon, AIB's CEO, has publicly challenged all staff to "change the way they think about learning and development so they can make the company the premier Irish financial services organization—capable of competing worldwide."

AIB has developed a "Charter for Employee Development" that contains the following four principles:

1. Professional development is a top priority of each employee
2. Training and development should complement and are driven by business plans
3. Self-development is the primary responsibility of employees
4. All employees have a responsibility for the individual and collective development of colleagues

AIB realizes that most learning can and should occur through the day-to-day work activities and involve elements such as:

- Accepting delegation, seeking and giving responsibility
- Learning from others and from one's own successes and mistakes
- Working as part of a team or as part of a task force on a specific assignment
- Obtaining and providing coaching and feedback on performance

At the annual review, all staff are to ask themselves these questions:

1. What have I done over the past twelve months to improve my professionalism and that of my colleagues?
2. What positive action will I take in the next twelve months relative to my self-development and that of my colleagues?

❦ *Aerospatiale (France)*

The Paris-headquartered company with annual sales of over $7 billion and more than 33,000 employees is a world leader in aircraft, helicopters, and space systems. Over 5 percent of total wages and salaries are "invested" in staff training, a doubling of expenditures in the past five years.

The aerospace industry is marked by globalization forces and the rapid evolution of technologies. Aerospatiale is cognizant of the fact that it must employ comprehensive HRD measures now to guarantee a global work-force to design, manufacture, and market its products. "Indeed, the high level of professionalism and sense of initiative of Aerospatiale's employees are the source of our company's global competitiveness," states Henri Martre, chairman of the board, in a recent annual report of Aerospatiale.

Aerospatiale has developed a career and skills management planning program designed to ensure a match between its human resources and personnel needs. A global analysis of the professions and skills utilized within the company has resulted in a list of measures required to avoid discrepancies between current and future needs. The annual interview for management and nonmanagement is seen as the fundamental tool for spurring career advancement as well as providing a framework for designation of high-potential employees.

In addition to management development programs for senior managers, Aerospatiale has established a groupwide training scheme for program managers and their teams. Aerospatiale is also one of the co-founders of NAME, the Network for Aeronautical Managers in Europe. This network organizes training for senior managers in leadership of multicultural teams.

Since 1985, Aerospatiale has sponsored students from prestigious engineering and business schools in Europe ("grande écoles") and has exchanges of teaching staff, twinning agreements, and research accords with these schools.

Internal career advancement and job mobility is receiving greater emphasis. The *Espace Carrière* career magazine, career orientation centers, and other career development activities have resulted in an increase of 40 percent in geographic mobility.

Aerospatiale has also placed the maintenance of a positive labor relations climate as essential for employee motivation and company success. Office and shop committees have been transformed into forums for exchange and learning. Quality Circles have also been seen as an opportunity for problem-solving, creativity, and learning for all participants.

❧ *Rover Group (Great Britain)*

The Rover Group has committed itself to becoming the top automotive company in Europe. To get to the top and stay there, Rover management realized that it had to develop a corporate culture of continuous learning and launched the Rover Learning Business in 1990. This new learning company has an annual budget of over $50 million to train the 40,000 employees of the Rover Group.

The Rover Learning Business has identified the following objectives:

* To distinguish Rover Group as the best in Europe for attracting, retaining, and developing people
* To emphasize the view that people are its greatest asset
* To gain recognition by its own employees that the company's commitment to every individual has increased
* To unlock and recognize employee talents and to make better use of these talents
* To gain recognition for employees through external accrediting bodies such as Warwick University
* To improve the competitive edge of the company

Rover Group has been a pioneer since the eighties in open learning and has set up open learning centers, now called Employee Development Centers, at each of its manufacturing sites. The centers provide not only numerous training programs but also career counseling and opportunities for face-to-face interaction.

Rover pays for all training that is relevant to the job, and in addition, the company has introduced a program called REAL (Rover Employees Assisted Learning), which offers up to $175 per annum to each employee for a learning experience that may not be directly related to his or her job.

For example, an employee in production can learn French or computing, since the company feels that he or she will be a better person for having taken such a course.

The process for matching the employee's needs with appropriate training providers may result in any of the following options:

- Using existing facilities at Rover Group, which include language laboratories
- Discussing options with outside learning experience providers such as the local technical college
- Custom designing a course for in-house presentation. If a course proves applicable to employees across a variety of work areas, a training program is developed for them all to work through together

As the nature of the work changes at Rover and as demand for direct OJT (On the Job Training) falls, the demand for design and facilitation skills will rise. HRD personnel at Rover prefer the word *learning* to *training,* since *learning* implies that people do it for themselves rather than have it done by others.

❦ Electrolux (Sweden)

Electrolux, the world's largest manufacturer of household appliances, employs more than 150,000 people in forty-six countries. The company has globalized many of its product lines and has developed a multicentered approach in management and decision making.

Electrolux is anxious to globalize its work-force and to create global-thinking managers throughout the organization. Two highly successful HRD programs have been implemented.

Electrolux International Executive Program. This annual training program is conducted for high-potential managers from forty to fifty countries who already hold senior positions involving international responsibilities. The program consists of three modules of four to five weeks total held at intervals in three different countries. Module one examines the Electrolux context for management, cultural integration, environmental analysis, and strategic management. Module two explores functional strategies, business alliances, and international management. Module three deals with media management and leadership.

Electrolux sees the program as generating synergy and energy for global corporate development. The instructors are drawn from top management and leading business schools. The program helps create a common corporate industry and culture, as well as build global perspectives and networks. The creation of networks lasts long after the conclusion of the program as participants contact one another for advice and assistance.

Electrolux International Business Leadership Program. This program is conducted in conjunction with Ashridge Management College in the U.K. and is for younger managers who have responsibility for resourcing or marketing. The program intent is to speed up the participant's transition from a functional-only to a "general management focus within a multinational setting, stimulating entrepreneurial flair across national boundaries, understanding the globalization issues...and working in English as the company language. Topics include globalization, international leadership, teamwork, strategic analysis, marketing and service, flexible manufacturing, international financial management and strategic implementation. The learning is applied through the undertaking of a major project that has been sponsored by their own organization within Electrolux" (Barham and Devine, p. 61).

❦ *Fiat (Italy)*

Fiat, the world's fifth largest car manufacturer, has more than 300,000 employees in fifty-eight countries. Unlike other European car manufacturers, however, the company is relatively dependent on its home market, and, with trade barriers having fallen in Europe in 1992, Fiat has set as its most important target the transformation of Europe to a "domestic market."

The top 350 managers in Fiat travel abroad for seminars in the United States, Japan or a European country, visiting leading world-class companies to learn their approaches to customer service, quality, and strategic alliances.

Fiat has also established intercultural sensitivity programs. A "Fiat Italian Briefing" program is conducted for non-Italian managers and includes Italian language training. Specific country briefings are held for managers to enable them to understand the most important features of that culture and to help change the stereotypes that employees may have.

Realizing that English is the international language of business and an "indispensable work tool," Fiat runs an intensive English language program for its new employees. Since key documentation is translated into English, French, German, Portuguese, and Spanish, language training is provided for senior secretaries (Barham and Devine, p.70).

SUMMARY

This chapter examined the HRD environment in Western Europe in terms of its geography, demographics, languages, religions, history, values, customs, and families. The economic environment for HRD and the evolving role of HRD as Europe moves toward unification were also considered in detail. The highly acclaimed Germany vocational training system was explored. Case studies of successful HRD programs were presented, including AIB Group (Ireland), Aerospatiale (France), Rover Group (Great Britain), Electrolux (Sweden), and Fiat (Italy).

REFERENCES

BARHAM, KEVIN, AND MARION DEVINE. *The Quest for the International Manager: A Survey of Global Human Resource Strategies.* London: Business International Press, 1991.

FRANK, ERIC. "Recent Development in Some EEC Member States." *Journal of European Industrial Training* (May 1988), pp. 24–29.

FRIBERG, ERIC. "Training: Who Does it Well." *Eurobusiness* (July-August 1990), pp. 30–33.

MARTRE, HENRI. *Aerospatiale Annual Report*, Paris, 1992.

NADLER, NEAL, AND KEVIN P. O'KELLY. "HRD in Europe." In *The Handbook for Human Resource Development*, 2nd ed., edited by Leonard Nadler. New York: John Wiley and Sons, 1990.

O'CONNOR, ROBERT. "New Training Approaches in Europe '93." *Personnel Journal* (May 1992), pp. 96–103.

SCHENKEL, PETER. "West Germany's Dual Training System." *Vocational Education Journal* (April 1988), pp. 29–47.

CHAPTER 11

Eastern Europe

INTRODUCTION

We have been living in a time warp. We have regressed to the status of a developing nation. Our industries are efficient only in polluting our environment. We desperately need training and technology so we can rejoin the world.

Polish engineer at recent World Labor Conference

Eastern Europe and the new republics of the former Soviet Union represent a region rich in cultural traditions but now alarmingly poor in economic and human resource development. Leaders such as Havel, Yeltsin and Walesa recognize the critical importance of rapidly acquiring entrepreneurial and management skills to assist in their transformation from communism to capitalism. Hundreds of HRD professionals have been called in to begin assisting these "new" nations to become economically viable.

In this chapter, we will explore the HRD environment as well as look at five highly acclaimed HRD programs that are propelling human resource development in Eastern Europe and the new countries of the former Soviet Union.

🐾 *Learning Objectives*

After studying this chapter, you should be able to:

1. Understand how the geography, demographics, languages, religions, history, and principal cultural beliefs of Eastern Europe and the former countries of the Soviet Union.
2. Recognize the key economic and political factors in the region that have an impact on the practice of HRD
3. Outline the evolving role of HRD in light of the region's sweeping redefinition and restructuring of business practices and systems
4. Give examples of successful HRD programs in the private sector as well as in government and education projects

Cultural Factors Impacting HRD

🐾 *Geography and Demographics*

Eastern Europe encompasses the region of Europe extending from the western borders of Poland, Hungary, the Czech and Slovak Federative Republics, Solvenia, Croatia, Yugoslavia, and Albania eastward through Romania and Bulgaria and across the former USSR, now the new countries of Armenia, Azerbaijan, Belarus (formerly Byelorussia), Kazakhstan, Kyrgyzstan, Moldavia, Russia, Tajikistan, Turkmenistan, Ukraine, and Uzbekistan.

It is estimated that the 400 million people who live in the region belong to more than 100 ethnic and nationality groups, with the majority being Russian. Other substantial populations in the former USSR are Armenian, Azerbaijani, Byelorussian, Georgian, Kazak, and Ukranian with smaller numbers of Bashkirs, Germans, Jews, and Tartars. Major ethnic groups in the other countries of the region include Albanians, Bulgarians, Croats, Czechs, Macedonians, Magyars (Hungarians), Romanians, Poles, Serbs, Slovaks, and Slovenes.

🐾 *Language*

With the exception of Hungarian, a Finno-Ugrian language related to Estonian and Finnish, Romanian, a Latin-based Romance Language written with the Latin alphabet, and the Iranian language of the Tajiks as Ossetes, the major languages of the region are Slavic in origin. Armenian and Georgian each have their own unique alphabet. Except for Polish, which is written with a modified Latin alphabet, the Slavic languages are written in the Cyrillic script. Russian, English, and German are the most common second languages in the area, with Russian serving as the lingua franca of the former states of the USSR.

❦ Religion

During the seven decades of strict communist rule, religious worship was officially discouraged and carefully monitored. Nonetheless, significant portions of the population of both the separate countries of Eastern Europe and the new countries of the former USSR have a religious faith. Christianity is represented by the Roman Catholic and various national Eastern Orthodox churches as well as a number of Protestant denominations, notably Lutheran and Calvinist. Islam is the religion of a considerable minority population in the region, and there are also Jewish communities.

❦ History

The collapse of the Soviet Union has thrown Eastern Europe into a turmoil that more resembles its early history than it does conditions of the past seven decades. Records of native people in the region go back at least as far as the Paleolithic period, with evidence of seventh century B.C. populations along the northern shore of the Black Sea and the Crimea. In the 4th Century B.C., the Dacians left records of their life in what is now Romania. Over the centuries, the vast territory was conquered and ruled by a series of foreign and local empires including the Scythian, Samartian, Roman, Byzantine, Goth, Hun, Avar, Khazar, Moravian, Magyar, Hungarian, Bohemian, Ottoman Turk, Prussian, Serbian, Austrian, and Russian, to name a few.

Although the twentieth century history of the region is marked by numerous political realignments and changes in national boundaries, certainly the most important regional development was the establishment of the Soviet Union and its subsequent occupation of the countries of Eastern Europe. Consisting of only four member republics when it was officially formed in 1922, the Union of Soviet Socialist Republics grew to include fifteen union republics, twenty autonomous republics, eight autonomous regions, ten autonomous districts, six territories, and 123 regions. At the time of its collapse, it encompassed one-sixth of the Earth's land surface, including the eastern half of Europe and the northern third of Asia.

In 1991, after several years of turmoil and uncertainty, the already weakened Soviet Communist party was removed from power, and most of the republics declared their independence. Within months, the Eastern European countries that had been annexed after World War II, including Bulgaria, Czechoslovakia, Hungary, Poland, and Romania, regained their status as independent countries, and the two postwar German states reunited. In December 1991, eleven of the fourteen former Soviet republics joined together to form the Commonwealth of Independent States. By 1992, all fourteen had become independent countries.

❦ New Freedoms

The peoples of Eastern Europe are emerging from decades of tight central government control enforced by the military and secret police. They are eager to embrace freedom of speech, assembly, religion, and the press but have little experience with the institutions that foster and support these new freedoms. But in many cases, they are totally unprepared for the economic and political changes that have swirled around them these past two years.

Reaction to the upheaval has, of course, varied by region and ethnic group, as well as by social and economic class. In Yugoslavia and the former republics of Armenia and Azarbaijan, bitter divisions among the ethnic groups have led to cruel and seemingly unavoidable civil wars. In Poland and Romania, the hopes of the people following their liberation have been tempered by disillusionment with the leaders who have followed and a recognition of the painful economic realities that have to be faced. Even in Albania and Bulgaria, long isolated from the modern world, the people are struggling to shift from centrally controlled economic and political systems.

Throughout the region, however, we can say that there is a heightened sense of nationalism and pride in ethnic and regional history. Traditions and beliefs that were long moribund under the communist system have reappeared with surprising vigor. And it seems that this revival of the old ways is providing the necessary will and energy to create the new world that many seek. Proud of their ability to withstand the hardships of war, loss of territory, and foreign domination and proud also of their rich cultural and artistic heritages, the people of the region seem firm in their commitment to freedom and independence.

❦ Family

Families tend to be small, with only one or two children even in rural areas. The shortage of housing for the majority of the population who live in urban areas has contributed to unusually low birthrates and, in some countries, high rates of abortion. City dwellers usually live in small apartments, many of which have inadequate heat and utilities. Usually both parents work outside the home, and children are expected to be independent and to provide care for the elderly. Family responsibilities are equally divided between the parents, although the father is usually accorded the traditional respect and authority in rural areas.

ECONOMIC ENVIRONMENT FOR HRD

No region in the world is undergoing such rapid political and economic change as Eastern Europe and the independent republics of the former USSR. The number of countries has increased from eight to over thirty. Communism and centralized planning has turned to free markets with chaotic, if any, economic planning on the part of the governments.

Although the general level of education and technical training of the regional work-force surpasses that of most non-Western industrialized countries, this region represents a market of more than 400 million people starved for technology and training.

Although the economies are shrinking, the private sector is surprisingly strong, and more than one million new companies were established in Eastern Europe in 1990 and 1991 alone. Billions of dollars in joint ventures between Western companies and East Europeans have begun (Schares).

The most important concept to remember in examining the focus of East European HRD programs is the difference in economic approach as compared to that in the West. In Eastern Europe and the former Soviet Union, where full-scale planning and administrative methods were adopted to guide economic activity in line with development goals, there was no real role for the traditional manager in terms of profit yardsticks, productivity, strategic outlook, efficiency of inputs, etc. Under the old system, economic activity was controlled and guided according to the social good. Profit and competition as motivating forces for enterprise production and quality were secondary to the enormous task of rebuilding the industrial infrastructure that was so devastated following World War I.

After World War I, there were no longer independent enterprise activities in a competitive environment where firms would undercut one another. With central planning, production was centrally determined with the yardstick of enterprise performance being the fulfillment of production quotas. Economizing on inputs to generate maximum efficiency was not an immediate concern given the fact that prices were now administratively set to ensure the "proper" flow of resources to the industrial sector. Resources for all enterprises were guaranteed (in theory) so that all economic activity was coordinated to ensure maximum industrial development.

Motivating the labor force was not considered to be a serious concern, since building socialism was a morally fitting prescription to ensure a better life for the worker, under whose name the march was being undertaken. If anything, workers were organized by the party to intimidate recalcitrant managers, many of whom protested the inherent inefficiencies of such organization.

The manager, per se, was no longer a desirable economic agent. He was no longer there to organize the use of capital since the workers now "owned" the means of production and could now ensure "rational production" to meet societal needs. The manager had no real place in planning the output or future activity of his enterprise since these activities were administratively harmonized from the center with all other economic activity in the country. Managerial culture was unsurprisingly devastated by this system.

The new skills necessary for the building of the socialist state were not managerial but technical in nature given the prerequisites of industrialization. Furthermore, these technical, largely engineering, skills were to be developed from the ranks of the workers, a social class which itself had to be rebuilt in order to build a "workers' society" and a proper constituency for the political climate.

It is from these roots that first the Soviet and then the East European HRD programs would draw their overly technical or engineering bias, with later additions to the system geared to cybernetic or computer skills. However, even this new technological move was designed more for input-output analysis by central planners than by enterprise managers who should have been using the computer to make production decisions.

HRD PROGRAMS IN EASTERN EUROPE

❦ *McDonald's (Russia)*

Given the economic and HRD environment of this region, most Western and local corporations have to begin from scratch in developing their employees. McDonald's is a case in point. Aside from the well-documented necessities of establishing a vertically integrated operation and having to import products from potatoes to seeds, McDonald's has had to break all the rules on HRD matters. In everything from hiring to firing to motivating, Russian practices have not been adequate for their needs. The system had simply not prepared Soviet workers, either in skill or work ethic, to enter into a free-market corporate work environment.

Following the standard wisdom on operating a joint venture in Russia, McDonald's first sought as much advice from local sources as possible. It maintained Westerners in the top management positions in the short run, trained the Russians at all levels of the operations in every conceivable skill, introduced them to their corporate culture, and provided excellent financial incentives to retain them.

McDonald's first considered the traditional recruiting processes. However, the majority of the jobs require hard work, a positive attitude, and customer-friendly approaches, and the Soviet economic process had been geared in different directions. Russian managers are generally not adequately trained in profit and loss calculations, market analysis and planning, or motivational managerial techniques. Since the economy had been based upon a conglomeration of monopolies, product quality and customer service were also not primary concerns to employees.

After assessing the HRD environment, McDonald's decided to break from the normal recruiting system. It bypassed the traditional bureaucratic routes by advertising in local newspapers and youth journals. The response was overwhelming, with over 25,000 applications for only 630 positions—at a time when Soviet enterprises could not find enough workers for their operations.

By recruiting mostly college students, McDonald's was able to gain motivated young people from top schools, often possessing multilingual skills and willing to work part time. All employees were then trained through a variety of in-house training programs. Speed, quality of fast food, and quick and friendly service were stressed—all qualities in short supply in the Soviet economy.

Following the training, all employees were sent to Hamburger University outside of Chicago for training and brief internships at American McDonald's restaurants. Top managers stayed in Toronto for an intensive ten-month training program.

McDonald's has discovered that, by adopting these HRD approaches and properly paying its staff, the company has been very successful with high productivity and profits. By isolating itself from the uncertainties of the Russian economy and HRD practices, McDonald's has been able to attract a high quality work force and train them to become highly productive employees.

❦ *Tungsrum and General Electric (Hungary)*

Unlike McDonald's in Moscow, GE did not have to face the problem of finding well-trained managers. Tungsrum, the light bulb factory that GE purchased, was a major exporter to Western Europe and was noted for good quality and low prices. GE saw a perfect fit for its attempt to enter the East European market.

While export activity was aided by favorable government tax incentives and a convoluted structure of exchange rates for Hungarian exporters, production methods in Tungsrum were terribly inefficient with much waste.

Recent economic reform in Hungary meant labor mobility, the right to work second jobs, and the right to self-employment. As a result, Hungarian managers in other enterprises properly complain that workers often relax on the job, collect an easy paycheck which is insufficient to live on given high inflation, and then place all of their energy into their second jobs, where they often make the bulk of their income. Moonlighting, and its consequent effects on worker productivity, existed on a scale in Hungary that was unknown in the rest of the region.

Another potential problem faced by GE was that of employees pilfering supplies from the enterprise in order to run these side businesses. The necessity to protect supplies was spreading throughout the region due to general shortages created by falling output, lack of demand constraint policies, and price disparities between the official and second economy which directs resources through legal and illegal means to the black market.

GE had no choice but to deal directly with the problem. Since there were reasons to shirk work due to low wages and high costs of living, the answer lay in increasing wages and having workers agree to give up the practice of moonlighting if they were to retain their jobs at Tungsrum. They were expected to work to GE standards. In return, GE had to compensate the loss of the second source of income by increasing wages substantially.

Given the fact that possible unemployment and dismissal were not only troubling but also unknown to Hungarian workers, GE took special care to ensure that employee morale was not destroyed by these "free-market" features of the workplace. Those positions eliminated have been eliminated through attrition and early retirement, both induced by generous compensation packages.

GE did not want to antagonize employees by turning the plant upside down in an attempt to bring production methodologies in line with its normal worldwide practice. GE's American managers for Tungsrum were chosen on the basis of length of service, overseas experience, and cultural sensitivity.

American managers prepared strategic marketing and business strategies for the firm, ensured product quality, and generally served as educators providing on-the-job training to Hungarian managers who were still learning the GE way. Hungarian managers were expected to eventually take the place of the American managers once the firm had been reorganized.

GE has also sought to make workers part of the team by encouraging worker input on production, the work environment, and company development plans. To the initial surprise of the workers, GE management has listened and taken steps to implement suggestions when possible. Such practices have helped increase worker morale and productivity.

GE has tried to communicate to its Hungarian employees that no one in the operation is unimportant and that neither GE nor Hungarian business culture will be totally sacrificed. Instead the two cultures have been merged to ensure a smooth transition. In addition, GE has used its resources to make the general incentive problems inherent in the Hungarian labor force work to its advantage. GE is confident that these various HRD strategies will make Tungsrum-GE a global success story.

☙ ABB Zamech (Poland)

Asea Brown Boveri (ABB), the world's largest producer of industrial equipment, is the result of a 1987 merger of the Swedish Asea and the Swiss Brown Boveri, both 100-year-old companies. ABB now generates annual revenues of more than $25 billion and employs nearly 250,000 people around the world, including 10,000 employees in India, 10,000 in South America, and a rapidly growing number of employees in Eastern Europe.

In 1990, ABB formed a joint venture with Zamech, Poland's leading manufacturer of steam turbines, transmission gears, marine equipment, and metal castings. The joint venture had significant HRD implications since ABB needed to change the corporate culture of Zamech as well as provide large-scale training. ABB instituted four key changes into the Zamech corporate culture:

1. Reorganization of operations into profit centers with well-defined budgets, strict performance targets, and clear lines of authority and accountability
2. Identification of a core group of change agents from among the local managers, giving them responsibility for championing high-priority programs and then closely monitoring the results
3. Transferral of ABB expertise from around the world to support the change process, without interfering with it or running it directly
4. Maintenance of high standards and demanding quick results

Following a structural reorganization along business lines and the installation of a standard finance and control system, ABB identified key managers and then began an intensive training process. A team of high-level ABB experts from around the world—authorities in functional areas like finance and control, quality and marketing, as well as technology specialists and managers with strong restructuring experience—was brought in for frequent short-term consultations.

Since most of the Polish managers spoke little or no English, ABB initiated an intensive English language training program. Even more challenging for ABB, however, was the "second language barrier"—the language of business. To introduce Zamech to basic business concepts, ABB created a "mini MBA program" in Warsaw that covered five key modules—business strategy, marketing, finance, manufacturing, and human resources—and was taught by faculty of INSEAD, the French business school.

ABB's Barbara Kux, who oversaw the turnaround process and HRD efforts, recently commented: "I have worked with many corporate restructurings, but never have I seen so much change so quickly. The energy is incredible. These people really want to learn" (Taylor, p. 107).

❦ *International Center for Public Enterprises in Developing Countries (Yugoslavia)*

The International Center for Public Enterprises in Developing Countries (ICPE) was founded in 1974 as a Yugoslav institution for providing technical assistance to developing countries. In 1978, in response to requests from developing countries, ICPE was formally established as an intergovernmental institution for promoting scientific and technical cooperation among these developing countries and for improving the performance of their enterprises.

ICPE cooperates with the United Nations and its agencies, with regional and national institutions of member countries and other developing countries, and with the developed countries interested in public enterprises in developing countries. The working languages of ICPE are English, French, Spanish, and Arabic.

Since 1976, ICPE, jointly with the United Nations Industrial Development Organization (UNIDO), has been organizing seminars on Management of Training in Public Enterprises and Training of Public Enterprise Management Trainers. It has also sponsored workshops with institutions such as the Pakistani Institute of Management, Caribbean Center for Development Administration, the Development Academy of the Philippines, the Guyanan Management Development Training Center, Asian and Pacific

Development Center, and the National Institute of Productivity in Dar es Salaam.

Training is also offered to practicing public enterprise top and middle managers and trainers who are nominated by their respective governments. ICPE, in cooperation with the Economic Development Institute (EDI) of the World Bank, organizes four-week management development courses for top managers of public enterprises and organizations related to them (ministries, banks, etc.).

❦ *Uysoka Skola Ekonomicka/Cornell University (Czechoslovakia)*

In the first HRD program between a U.S. university and an Eastern European training institution, Cornell University and Prague's Uysoka Skola Ekonomicka (Higher School of Economics) have entered into a partnership to exchange faculty and students who specialize in HRD and HRM in industry. Cornell will help the Czech school develop its newly established Department of Human Services "by training faculty, helping with curriculum development, training students, and designing enterprise management programs" (Steinburg, p. 13).

Corporations that have already established operations or seek to establish ties in Czechoslovakia are sponsoring this HRD program. They include AT&T, Chevron, Colgate-Palmolive, Exxon, General Electric, IBM, Kodak, 3M, Sony, Union Carbide, and Xerox.

SUMMARY

This chapter examined the HRD environment in Eastern Europe and the new republics of the former USSR in terms of the region's geography, demographics, languages, religions, history, and cultural beliefs. The economic environment for HRD and the evolving role of HRD, as Eastern Europe transforms itself in the wake of the collapse of the Soviet Union, were considered in detail.

We identified the special HRD activities which McDonald's implemented in Russia, General Electric undertook with Tungsrum in Hungary, and Asea Brown Boveri (ABB) carried out with Zamech in Poland. The training programs of the International Center for Public Enterprises in Developing Countries (Yugoslavia) and the exciting collaborative HRD effort between Cornell University and Prague's Higher School of Economics were also discussed.

REFERENCES

NELSON-HORCHLER, JOANI. "Desperately Seeking Yankee Know-How." *Industry Week* (March 4, 1991), pp. 52–56.

SCHARES, GAIL *et al.* "Reawakening—A Market Economy Takes Root in Eastern Europe." *Business Week* (April 15, 1991), pp. 45–58.

STEINBURG, CRAIG. "HRD Goes to Czechoslovakia." *Training and Development Journal* (February 1992), pp. 12–13.

TAYLOR, WILLIAM. "Change Comes to Poland—The Case of ABB Zamech." *Harvard Business Review* (March—April 1991), pp. 102–3.

❦ ❦

CHAPTER 12

Middle East and North Africa

INTRODUCTION

Nobody knows who discovered the ocean; but it certainly wasn't a fish.

Ancient Arabic Proverb

The fish in this old proverb, like almost all of us, has little chance of understanding the culture in which we live except by contrast and comparison with other cultures. The Middle East and North Africa, although diverse in many ways, are largely united in terms of cultural and religious beliefs that have an enormous impact on the conduct of business and on HRD.

In this chapter, we will explore the HRD environment in this important region of the world and then consider the evolving practice of HRD in a business setting much defined by culture and religion.

❦ *Learning Objectives*

After studying this chapter, you should be able to:

1. Understand how the geography, demographics, languages, history, religions, and principal cultural beliefs of the Middle East and North Africa affect HRD activities

2. Recognize the key economic factors in the region that have an impact on the practice of HRD
3. Outline the role of HRD in light of the unusually strong and pervasive influence of religious and cultural beliefs on business practices and everyday life
4. Give examples of successful HRD programs in the private sector, as well as in government and education projects

CULTURAL FACTORS IMPACTING HRD

❦ *Geography, Demographics, and Language*

Stretching from the Atlantic Ocean through North Africa to Western Asia, the former Arab Empire is now a region tied more by a common culture and language than by geography, economics, or even politics. The region is an elusive one to define; for our purposes, we've tried to include those countries that represent the mainstream of the area both culturally and in terms of business. Obviously we've left out countries like Iran, Iraq, Israel, Sudan, and parts of Turkey that might be considered were we addressing different factors. So in this chapter, we will focus on some, but not all, of the countries of three geographic regions: North Africa, the Middle East, and the Gulf states. In North Africa, we are including Algeria, Libya, Morocco, and Tunisia. Our Middle East group includes Egypt, Jordan, Lebanon, Syria, and the West Bank. The Gulf region is composed of Bahrain, Kuwait, Oman, Qatar, Saudi Arabia, the United Arab Emirates, and Yemen.

With a population approaching 275 million and some of the highest birthrates in the world, this region is expected to have well in excess of 550 million people by the year 2025. Although the vast majority of the residents speak one of the many dialects of Arabic, there are also substantial communities speaking the Berber dialects as well as Coptic, Armenian, Kurdish, and Aramaic. Even in those communities, however, written Arabic, which is considerably more standardized than the spoken forms, is almost always the medium of written communication in education and government. French and English are strong second languages among the educated population and, in some cases, official second languages of government. The region is overwhelmingly Islamic with percentages ranging from 75 percent in Lebanon to virtually 100 percent in Saudi Arabia, Libya, and Yemen. Among the believers in Islam, there are at least five major sects, so a surface unanimity is, in fact, built upon a diverse foundation, and relations among the various sects are often quarrelsome.

❦ History

It was the Muslims from Arabia who, during a series of invasions in the sixth and seventh centuries, carried Islam and Arabic to the shores of the Atlantic on the west and into Central Asia on the east. Gradually, an enormous empire was built up that included parts of Europe as well. Although many of its cultural leaders were not ethnically Arabs, the growing civilization reflected Arab values, tastes, and traditions. Education and philosophy flourished as did medicine, the arts, literature, and mathematics; the beginnings of modern Western science were derived in part from the Arab civilization. The decline of this powerful civilization in the eleventh century marked the end of political unity, but the common culture and language have held on remarkably.

❦ Religion

Perhaps in no other region of the world, certainly in none this large, does religion play such a prominent role not only in family life but in the affairs of community and state. Islamic philosophy is deeply rooted in the minds, hearts, and behavior of the people, and Islamic scripture is considered the final and complete word of God. The principles of the religion are very much a part of the region's laws, business relations, and social customs. Friday is the Islamic day of worship, but the religion is practiced daily through dress and dietary codes as well as prayer. Muslims pray five times daily, facing the large sacred mosque in Makkah, Saudi Arabia; they hope, at least once in their lives, to make a sacred journey to Makkah as part of their religious duties.

In most of the countries of the region, a body of religious law stands alongside civil codes and is often the source of resolution of disputes or punishment for crimes. In the more conservative societies like Saudi Arabia, the clergy has a police function recognized and supported by the civil authorities. Even in certain of the Gulf states that have been historically more liberal, punishment of criminals under the guidelines of Islamic law is not unusual. Religious beliefs about the prohibition of alcohol and the possession of printed material that is sexually revealing or suggestive are strictly enforced by local authorities with very little consideration given to either cultural differences or ignorance of local standards.

❦ Family

In Islamic culture, the family is the basic unit of society and the center of an individual's life. One's family is the source of reputation and honor, and any personal achievement reflects on the entire family. Extended families with two or three generations living in the same household are the norm, and even where urbanization has resulted in nuclear family units, a son and his family will usually live close to the home of his father. Children are cherished and indulged by the entire family and frequently socialize with aunts, uncles, and cousins. They also commonly have responsibilities in caring for elderly members of the family. Grandparents are respected by all family members, and it is taken for granted that grown sons and daughters will provide for their parents in old age.

Much has been written about the role of women in Islamic society, and it is safe to say that, from a Western point of view, they are subservient to men. Within the culture, however, the differences in roles seem to be seen by both men and women more as a natural consequence of gender differences than as evidence of discrimination or oppression. Men are held totally responsible for the protection of, and provision for, the women within their family. Although the family is usually a strong, male-dominated unit, women do exercise considerable influence in the home, especially in educating and socializing both sons and daughters. Although the practice is dying out, polygamy is still found in some communities. But even there, the ability to provide equally for each wife and the agreement of earlier wives to later marriages are traditional features. Infidelity and adultery are illegal and almost always severely punished; divorce, allowed only at the instigation of the husband, is largely frowned upon.

❦ *General Attitudes*

Islamic culture, with its focus on the family and its long history, is generally more relaxed and slower paced than many modern cultures. Patience is much valued, and more importance is given to relationships than to time; in business situations, trust and confidence need to be established before anything can be accomplished. A strong sense of fatalism often mixed with an equally strong sense of humor is characterized by two popular expressions: *Insha'allah* ("if God wills") and *Ma'alesh* ("don't worry" or "never mind").

Despite the wars and disputes that have rocked part of the region for the past forty years, the people are for the most part generous and hospitable, even with strangers. Their long history of struggle with a harsh climate has perhaps encouraged a sense of interdependence. Although the men enjoy lively conversation and socializing in public places, they are private with regard to their family and family matters. When HRD professionals are invited into the home, the occasion should be taken as an honor and will likely be formal.

ECONOMIC ENVIRONMENT FOR HRD

Although the region is culturally connected by the Arab language and the Islamic religion, it is separated by vast economic differences ranging from the extreme poverty of Egypt and Jordan to the tremendous riches of the Gulf states.

The wealth of the OPEC countries has attracted millions of immigrants not only from the poorest Arab countries but more recently from non-Arab countries (Philippines, Pakistan, India, Korea, Bangladesh), which now comprise a majority of the nonnationals in some countries. This situation has created huge cultural, religious, and language barriers among these employees and their Arab managers. This large foreign population (e.g., 70 percent of the people in the United Arab Emirates are nonnationals) contributes to volatility and a tremendous challenge to HRD practitioners. A significant effort of Gulf HRD professionals has been their attempt to transfer skills to local nationals and decrease their dependence on foreigners to manage and implement both government and corporate programs. For example, Saudi Arabia's recent five-year development plan aimed to reduce foreign labor by 22 percent through staffing positions with Saudis. Graduates of training programs in health care, agriculture, and teaching are steadily replacing foreigners.

Although most Arab countries have fine universities, the top present and future leaders are generally trained in the U.K. or in the United States. Leading engineers and technicians have been educated primarily in the United States. This biculturalization of key organizational executives and technicians has enabled them to more easily understand and utilize the services of outside trainers and consultants.

In order to be less dependent on Western technology as well as less exposed to Western values, the countries of North Africa and the Middle East have made a strong commitment to HRD as the means for economic and social development of their countries. Numerous national and technical institutes have been established throughout the region. A recent study of Gulf organizations by the Middle East Institute for Research and Consultation (MEIRC) shows that they spend two to three times more on HRD than does the United States.

The impact of the Gulf War in early 1991 cannot be underestimated in examining the economic climate for HRD. Millions of workers from Egypt, Jordan, Sudan, and Yemen left Kuwait and Iraq. In addition to severely decreasing productivity in those countries, the exodus caused tremendous economic strains on the workers' home countries since they were no longer sending remittances back for their families. Egypt's largest export by far was its workers.

CULTURAL CHARACTERISTICS OF ARAB MANAGEMENT AND ORGANIZATIONS

Mahmoud Al-Faleh has identified the following characteristics of Arab organizations and managers:

- Within an organization, status, position, and seniority significantly outweigh ability and performance in importance.
- Organizations are centrally controlled with a low level of delegation. Subordinates act with deference and obedience to the formal hierarchy of authority.
- Authoritarian management style is predominant. Decision making is constantly pushed upward in the organization.
- Most decisions and commitments are renegotiable at a later time.
- Consultative styles of decision making are pervasive and dominant. This consultation is usually carried out on a person-to-person basis, thus avoiding group meetings. Moreover, decisions are often made in an informal and unstructured manner.
- Organization members are motivated by affiliation and power needs rather than by performance objectives. Social formalities are extremely important.
- Innovation and risk taking are activities that may be punished rather than rewarded.
- There is a strong preference for a person-oriented approach rather than a task-oriented approach in managerial activities.
- Nepotism is regarded as natural and acceptable. Arab managers view their organizations as family units and often assume a paternal role in them. They value loyalty over efficiency.
- There is a strong adherence to the open-door tradition. It is an integral part of the "unwritten" or "informal" organizational structure.
- Punctuality and time constraints are of much less concern than in Western cultures.

HRD FOR GULF MANAGERS

The Middle East Institute for Research and Consultation recently conducted a study of 177 Gulf region (Bahrain, Kuwait, Oman, Qatar, Saudi Arabia, and the United Arab Emirates) managers, HRD specialists, and expatriate managers to list what they perceive as the most effective ways to develop managers. The ten most important elements for management development and success identified were:

1. Experiencing of a quality education and skills gained in problem solving, analysis, conceptual thinking, and communication.

2. Learning from, and being mentored by, successful, experienced managers.
3. Receiving early career responsibilities.
4. Learning and practicing ethics and values such as hard work, integrity, and quality.
5. Improving one's skills and knowledge through self-development.
6. Attending training courses as well as structured on-the-job training.
7. Receiving feedback and recognition.
8. Developing a solid technical knowledge base.
9. Planning a formal career development program.
10. Being encouraged to problemsolve and allowed to make mistakes.

Al-Sane, a leading HRD specialist in the Middle East, proposed eight strategies for Gulf leaders to consider in training managers:

1. Link training and educational systems with real, practical business and industry requirements.
2. Hire managers who have been trained to "think," to be innovative and creative.
3. Invest more in human resources.
4. Market training services more effectively and thereby gain broader use and quality.
5. Ensure CEO commitment to and involvement in the training programs of the organization.
6. Use individual development programs more extensively.
7. Recognize best training programs nationally.
8. Provide greater opportunities for sharing training experiences and ideas among Gulf HRD practitioners.

HRD Programs in Middle Eastern and North African Organizations

❦ *ARAMCO (Saudi Arabia)*

One of the largest, most unique, and most dynamic training programs in the world is the Vocational English Language Training program at the Arabian American Oil Company (ARAMCO). Over 15,000 employees of varied educational backgrounds and job titles are currently enrolled in these training programs where, in some locations, classes are offered continuously for twenty-four hours a day, 365 days a year. Depending on the needs and capabilities of the employee, the duration of the English instruction may vary from ten weeks to seven years, with training generally lasting from two to eight hours each day. These arrangements can accommodate employees who are released for training before, during, or after their eight-hour shifts.

This Vocational English Language Training (VELT) program was developed specifically for ARAMCO with the objective of providing employees with the language skills necessary to pursue other training programs as well as perform as skilled operators and technicians in jobs related to maintenance and gas-oil operations.

Dialdin, general manager for ARAMCO's training operations, identified several features which account for the success of the VELT program.

- *Functional.* One of the main innovations of VELT is its focus on functional competence. The twenty terminal objectives identified in the needs analysis phase were broken down into enabling objectives and specific teaching points for each lesson.
- *Integration.* The practice of all the skills—listening, speaking, reading, and writing—are integrated and functionally tied to objectives.
- *Action Participation.* The program was carefully developed for a learner-centered approach. The trainees learn by doing, and the material is filled with pairs and group work to maximize the trainees' active participation.
- *Variety.* In order to maintain trainee interest and motivation, each lesson contains a variety of exciting activities. There are lots of flash cards, wall charts, picture cards, tapes, and games used throughout the program.
- *Quality Control.* The performance of the trainees is carefully monitored during and after the program.
- *Culturalizing the Instructors.* Special intensive orientation programs are held to assimilate the large influx of newly hired teachers into the ARAMCO and Saudi culture. In addition, nineteen teacher-trainer workshops were held in areas such as computer-assisted instruction, communicative approach to language teaching, systematic approach to improving reading comprehension, and the teacher as motivator. The training staff also arranged for team meetings and cadre support for the new instructors.

❦ AMIDEAST Regional

Founded in 1951, AMIDEAST has trained over 35,000 people throughout the Middle East and North Africa. In addition, tens of thousands of Americans have utilized AMIDEAST's training materials to guide them in their professional and educational encounters with the Arab world.

AMIDEAST collaborates with numerous governmental and private agencies to develop and implement technical assistance projects in the region. These projects seek to build the technical and administrative capabilities of Arab institutions and to promote self-reliance.

Examples of recent or current HRD programs include the following:

- *Yemen.* Coordination of training for Yemeni teacher trainers, curriculum specialists, and educational administrators and planners.

- *Tunisia*. Career development and job-seeking guidance for Tunisians educated in the United States.
- *Jordan*. In cooperation with the University of Jordan, design of agricultural training programs in Arabic and marketing them throughout the Arab world.
- *Egypt*. Organization of a U.S. study visit for Egyptian Supreme Court judges.
- *Lebanon*. Development of an intensive business English and office communications program for a Lebanese company.

❦ *Kuwait Institute for Scientific Research (Kuwait)*

One of the many tragedies of the Gulf War was the dismantling of the training facilities and other resources of the Kuwaiti Institute for Scientific Research (KISR) by the Iraqi army. Thousands of valuable books and training materials, computers, video and audiotapes, and projectors were hauled away.

KISR, however, has rapidly rebuilt itself to what many global HRD professionals describe as one of the most impressive training programs in the Middle East.

Scientists and engineers from all over the world conduct research on areas such as desertification, agricultural production, petrochemicals, technoeconomics, environment, food technology, and marine culture. Top global experts in the various fields are recruited to conduct courses and provide consultations for the professional staff.

❦ *Saudi Arabian Airlines (Saudi Arabia)*

Saudi Arabian Airlines, founded in 1943, serves over 100 cities in fifty countries and carries nearly three million passengers per year. Like many corporations in the Gulf region, it has expanded rapidly over the past ten years while experiencing an acute shortage of qualified local nationals to fill its management positions. Major HRD efforts are required to develop a Saudi management cadre. These training programs need to relate to the unique culture of both the organization and the country.

Hakki describes a recent HRD program for training marketing managers that serves as the model for all Saudi Airlines HRD programs. After identifying the competencies needed and selecting the candidates, the training staff developed a thirty-month management program containing the following subjects: marketing and economics, business management, financial accounting, English language, cross-cultural training, job-specific training, reservations, ticketing, aircraft weight and balance, and customer services.

After completing the theoretical training in each area, each trainee was required to complete a specific on-the-job training experience. During this part of the training program, feedback was received from the managers and supervisors with whom the candidate had worked. The training program was based on the "whole-part-whole" principle in which the trainees were initially exposed to the whole operation, then worked closely on individual tasks in a real job situation, and finally overviewed the entire operation once again.

An important reason for the success of the management program, according to Hakki, was the extensive evaluation component, which ensured a high quality learning experience for each trainee. Feedback was provided to the trainees and their bosses as well as to the training administrators with regard to the training needs of the candidate, progress, program/course revision, and the identification of qualities for future assignments.

SUMMARY

This chapter examined the HRD environment in the Middle East and North Africa in terms of the region's geography, demographics, languages, history, religions, cultural beliefs, and economics. The cultural characteristics and behavior of Arab organizations and managers were also presented. Four highly successful HRD programs—ARAMCO (Saudi Arabia), AMIDEAST (regional), Kuwait Institute for Scientific Research, and Saudi Arabian Airlines—were discussed.

REFERENCES

AL-FALEH, MAHMOUD. "Cultural Influences on Arab Management Development."*Journal of Management Development* (Vol. 6, No. 3), pp. 19–33.

DIALDIN, ALI M. "Large-Scale English Language Training at ARAMCO." In *Corporate Culture: International HRD Perspectives*, edited by Michael Marquardt. Alexandria, Va.: ASTD Press, 1987.

HAKKI, MUSLEH. "Training and Culture at Saudi Arabian Airlines." In *Corporate Culture: International HRD Perspectives*, edited by Michael Marquardt. Alexandria, Va.: ASTD Press, 1987.

MIDDLE EAST INSTITUTE FOR RESEARCH AND CONSULTATION. *Gulf Managers*. Athens: MEIRC, 1988.

CHAPTER 13

Africa

INTRODUCTION

If I know a song of Africa, of the giraffe, and the African new moon lying on her back, of the plows in the fields, and the sweaty faces of the coffee pickers, does Africa know a song of me? Would the air over the plain quiver with a color that I had on, or the children invent a game in which my name was, or the full moon throw a shadow over the gravel of the drive that was like me, or would the eagles of Ngong look out for me?

Isak Dinesen (Karen Blixen)
Out of Africa

In her evocative memory of what was then British East Africa, Karen Blixen focuses on the stunning beauty of the continent. As Africa has emerged from colonialism and been faced with the enormous task of adapting to the modern, industrialized world, conditions for the peoples of that continent have become increasingly more desperate.

This chapter explores the business and HRD environments of Africa and then considers the evolving practice of HRD as her peoples struggle to gain the skills and technology to survive in the age of globalization.

❦ *Learning Objectives*

After studying this chapter, you should be able to:

1. Understand how the geography, demographics, languages, religions, history, and principal cultural beliefs of Africa affect HRD activities
2. Recognize the key economic factors in the region that have an impact on the practice of HRD
3. Outline the role of HRD, especially on-the-job training, apprenticeship, and basic skills development programs
4. Give examples of successful government and private sector HRD programs

CULTURAL FACTORS IMPACTING HRD

❦ *Geography and Demographics*

The second largest continent, Africa is certainly the most culturally diverse by almost any measure. Its 700 million people, one-eighth of the world's population, are citizens of fifty-three independent countries, four homelands declared independent by the Republic of South Africa, and several island dependencies. The number of ethnic, cultural, and linguistic divisions is uncertain but is surely much larger than the number of political entities.

The population is unevenly distributed, with the highest densities along the coast of the Gulf of Guinea, in the lower reaches of the Nile, in the highlands of East Africa and Madagascar, along the northern coast, and in the urban and mining areas of South Africa, Zimbabwe, and Zaire. The Sahara Desert forms a great divide between ethnic groups with Caucasoid peoples, among them Arabs, Berbers, and Tuaregs to the north (this region is covered in greater detail in Chapter 12) and a large number of Negroid peoples, among them Hausa, Wolof, Somali, Dinka, Yoruba, Ibo, Kikuyu, and Masai, to the south. South Africa's Afrikaners are of Dutch and French descent and live among ten indigenous groups including the Zulu and Xhosa. There are also substantial populations of British, Italian, and Spanish descent. Indians are an important minority in many coastal towns of south and east Africa.

❦ *Language*

The peoples of Africa speak more than 800 languages, and five major divisions are generally recognized: Afroasiatic, Khoisan, Niger-Congo, Sudanic, and Malayo-Polynesian. Some fifty of these tongues have a half million speakers each, and unlike those of the Americans, these indigenous spoken languages are very much alive. With notable exceptions, most African languages did not historically have a written form. This, along with their large diversity, has resulted in much of the written mass media being produced in French or English. Both Arabic and Roman letters are now being used increasingly to represent native African languages, and the International African Institute has also had some success in promoting the use of original African written forms in languages other than those for which they were created.

English is one of the official languages, if not the only one, in all the former British colonies except Tanzania, where Swahili has been adopted. French is the official language in most former French possessions south of the Sahara, and Arabic is the official language of the seven Saharan states. Numerous lingua franca such as Lingala in Zaire and Manding in West Africa are used for commerce in mixed-language areas.

❦ Religion

With an estimated 155 million believers, Islam is the dominant faith in northern Africa and the fastest growing religion on the continent. Some 140 million Africans are Christian, with 55 percent of those affiliated with Protestant churches. Forty percent of the population practices traditional religions and animism.

❦ History

Africa is the site of the earliest known protohuman fossils, and the continent was also the home of one of the world's oldest known civilizations, that of ancient Egypt. North Africa first came under European influence during the Roman Empire, and beginning in the seventh century, Arab culture and Muslim faith spread across the Sahara. During the Middle Ages in Europe, a number of African kingdoms flourished, including Ghana, Mali, Ashanti, Benin, and Dahomey. European colonization was begun by the Portuguese, who established trading posts on African coasts during the fifteenth and sixteenth centuries. European explorers began to venture into the interior of the continent in the nineteenth century, and by the early twentieth century, nearly all of Africa had been subjected to European rule. Since World War II, forty-eight nations have gained independence, but the colonial experience has left a legacy of arbitrarily defined borders, a diversity of political systems and problems, and economies dependent upon the industrial world.

❦ *Values*

Given the ethnic, cultural, and linguistic diversity outlined above, it would be unwise to try to make cultural generalizations about Africans. Yet we can identify some characteristics that, if not universal, are certainly evident in many of the continent's societies.

Africans tend first to identify themselves as members of a group, usually defined in terms of village, region, ethnicity, race, or language. They are proud of the group with which they identify and see other groups as potential, if not actual, enemies. The long history of antagonism and violence among neighboring groups struggling under harsh circumstances has made identification with the group one of the principal requisites of survival. The imposition of colonial rule and creation of artificial borders exacerbated the already fragmented situation. As the peoples of Africa struggle with twentieth century economic and political realities, nationalism has been added to the ways of defining group membership. In the same way they are proud of their village or ethnic heritage, they are, for the most part, proud of their country.

❦ *Class*

Along with this pride comes a strong sense of caste and class. Africans are very aware of differences in prestige or status and take for granted any perquisites and powers that are connected with class differences. The less privileged accept their lot, for the most part, passively. The more blessed are not shy about wielding their authority. This is but one aspect of the fatalism that is common to many African cultures. In some cases, it is the fruit of religion; in others, of history, environment, and circumstance. In any case, there is an acceptance of one's lot that to the Western mind is remarkably passive.

ECONOMIC ENVIRONMENT FOR HRD

Sub-Saharan Africa is the poorest region in the world. Many countries have an annual GNP of less than $500 per capita. Rapid population growth, political dictatorships, corruption, droughts, and huge bureaucracies have caused these countries to become even poorer over the past twenty years.

Adding to this dire situation is the fact that AIDS is now devastating Africa's work force and weakening the continent economically. People ages twenty to forty—mainstays of the family and economy—account for 70 percent of AIDS deaths. Critically needed professional engineers, educators, and managers are dying in high numbers, and this has led, according to Mutembi, to lower industrial output and serious socioeconomic problems (*San Francisco Examiner*, December 18, 1991).

The recent political changes in Africa, however, are beginning to bear economic fruit. Western firms are showing new interest in Africa, drawn by the continent's widespread moves toward democracy and economic reforms. The U.S. Overseas Private Investment Corporation (OPIC) in late 1991 organized an investment mission to West and South Africa with more than forty corporations participating, the largest mission OPIC had ever put together.

The World Bank and International Monetary Fund are also more optimistic about Africa's economy. The World Bank has increased by over 50 percent its loans to African governments in the past five years. Improving the quality of education and training is one of the bank's highest priorities. Likewise, the Fund has expanded its portfolio in Africa.

In order to understand HRD in Africa, it is first necessary to briefly examine the five major sectors of employment in Africa:

1. *Government and the Public Sector.* The central and local governments in Africa employ from 30 percent to 75 percent of all employees in the formal sector! Public sector jobs are the goal of most educated Africans because of prestige and, until recently, security. Today civil service administration in most of Africa is bloated, inefficient, and a tremendous drain on the economy. Many state enterprises are being cut back or privatized, although they still remain, according to Roberts, a substantial provider of jobs and HRD in Africa.

2. *Industry.* Industry provides less than 10 percent of Africa's gross domestic product with most manufacturing focusing on import substitution. Government policies still too often hinder the free-market economy, and the difficulties in international financial and trading markets have created additional huge obstacles.

3. *Agriculture.* Agriculture remains the basic work and livelihood for nearly 70 percent of Africans. A food crisis exists, however, since population growth greatly exceeds food production growth. Government subsidy policies have discouraged agricultural production.

4. *Commerce and Finance.* With rapid urban growth and the global integration of many enterprises, Africa's commercial and financial sectors are expanding rapidly. The quality and sophistication of these institutions vary greatly and, in most cases, are still dependent on expatriate financial firms and management. HRD is critically important to Africanize this sector.

5. *The Informal Sector.* Much of Africa's economy lies beyond formal government control and in the hands of "millions of small manufacturers, traders, service providers and self-employed business people who make up the informal sector" (Roberts, p. 6). As the economies of African countries continue to stagnate, the informal sector will gain even more importance. Apprenticeships and on-the-job training in small enterprises will be critical for economic growth, if not survival.

CULTURAL CHARACTERISTICS OF AFRICAN ORGANIZATIONS

Much of the African business life has been influenced by the Western colonial experience (primarily British and French), by African tribal customs, and by the poverty in the region. Jones lists the following attributes of African organizations:

1. Organizations function in an environment of acute resource scarcity, economic uncertainty, and highly centralized political power.

2. These organizations tend to retain the major characteristics of structure developed in the colonial era, namely, rather rigid bureaucratic, rule-bound hierarchies.

3. The local people view organizations as having a wider mission than is generally understood in the West in so far as they are expected to provide socially desirable benefits such as employment, housing, transport, and assistance with social rituals and ceremonies; consideration of profit maximization and efficiency may be viewed as secondary or incidental.

4. Workers have high expectations of organizational benefits to the worker and his family.

5. Many African societies place high emphasis on prestige and status differences, creating relationships of dependency, wide differentials between managers and workers, extreme deference to and dependence upon one's boss, and a paternal but strict style of management.

6. Managers have a high regard for their subordinates as human beings (not as human "resources"). They emphasize maintaining relationships rather than providing opportunities for individual development and ritualized interpersonal interactions rather than accomplishment of work-related tasks.

7. Managers regard their authority, professional competence, and information as personal possessions rather than a part of their organizational role. They are, therefore, reluctant to delegate authority, share information, or to involve subordinates in decision-making processes.

8. The management style tends to push decisions upward in the organizational hierarchy, involve managers in trivial activities, limit information sharing, encourage highly dependent subordinate behavior, and create dissatisfying relationships between managers and employees.

9. African managers require highly developed political skills and well-developed diplomatic skills.

HRD IN AFRICA

African governments have always placed a high priority on HRD for developing skills for the workplace. Roberts notes that "mobilizing professional, managerial and technical skills was seen as vital to replace foreign experts and turn independence into a reality....Developing the workforce was akin to nation-building" (p. 7). Governments established vocational education centers in every African nation, which produced well-trained workers for whom no skilled jobs existed. Now governments and international donors are turning their HRD efforts to the informal sector, especially developing small-scale entrepreneurs. Ministries of Education in most African countries coordinate national training systems and adult vocational centers. Many governments have also set up centers to train small entrepreneurs in bookkeeping, marketing, and other essential skills.

According to Roberts, there are thousands of nonformal HRD centers throughout Africa, mainly in the small craft industries. One example is the Kenya Village Polytechnics, in which 200 low-cost, village-managed centers teach technical skills to educate dropouts.

Agricultural training is a great need in Africa. Most of Africa's fifty-seven universities offer agricultural degrees. Kenya, Ethiopia, and other countries have networks of farmers' training centers that offer courses. Many countries have training and visits by agricultural extension agents which have proved to be highly effective.

Most African countries have established national institutes for public administration to train civil servants in basic management fields, as well as on the usually complex civil service procedures and rules. Low wages, poor management, and poor prospects for advancement, however, drive the better HRD officers from these training centers.

TRAINING AFRICAN MANAGERS

Acknowledging the cultural and organizational milieu in which African managers operate, there are a number of points which HRD professionals must consider when training managers in Africa:

- It is important to acknowledge regional sociocultural values and the fact that Western management practices and techniques might contradict them. For example, performance appraisal and management-by-objectives often fail in African organizations since it is a sign of weakness to admit incompetence or ignorance. And mistakes and inadequacies are *beyond* the control of individuals anyway.

- Many management development and HRD concepts reflect Western values, e.g., individual responsibility for development, the value of self-discovered knowledge as opposed to prescribed knowledge, the teacher-learner relationship that involves interdependence and assumed equality, and development as involving risk and change for learners. For many African learners, there is a greater need for clear and unequivocal direction, regular face-to-face contact, and a perception of training as a way to enhance status rather than for personal growth and as a way to avoid risk by acquiring additional information which is hoarded and protected as a source of power.

Jones suggests the following criteria for management training in Africa:

1. The organizational policy should state that managers have a major responsibility in developing employees and that training does not imply personal inadequacy. The HRD program should be seen as supportive.
2. Learning strategies should reflect the collectivist nature of African society. This would imply that methods should be avoided which focus on individual performance (especially shortcomings); small-group methods and other supportive methodologies would be more appropriate.
3. There should be an explicit focus on continuous learning from experience which will demand that attention be given to developing skills in analyzing successes and failures in a conscious, structured way.
4. Managers should be trained in coaching skills so as to be more effective in developing their subordinates.
5. Since organizational structures tend to be rigidly bureaucratic and slow moving in an environment of accelerating change, it is important that all employees, especially managers, understand the processes of organizational change.

ON-THE-JOB AND APPRENTICESHIP TRAINING IN AFRICA

A recent World Bank report on human resources in Africa states that the increase in investments in human resources needed over the next twenty or thirty years will endanger the budgetary and economic health of most African countries. African countries simply lack the financial resources for providing education and training for their citizens. For many African leaders and HRD professionals, renewed emphasis upon on-the-job training, especially apprenticeship, is seen as the best solution, at least for the near future since it can be provided to large numbers of people and requires less heavy investment.

The apprenticeship system is firmly rooted in the African culture and is particularly well suited to the conditions of African life. The placing of the apprentice is negotiated by the master craftsman and the parents. The small entrepreneur assumes considerable responsibility toward the parents over and above the purely professional training of the young person. He has to attend closely to his apprentice's education in the broadest sense of the term. All parties benefit from the system: the government has nothing to pay (the parents usually pay a sum amounting to about $150) and can at the same time use it as an alternative to unemployment and juvenile delinquency; the parents "place" their child in good hands; the young apprentice can hope one day to emulate the success of his master; the master craftsman at the cost of one or two small sacrifices (a little of his time, a little more in board, and lodging, and sometimes a little pocket money) obtains cheap labor and a certain standing (Bas).

The period of apprenticeship varies in length and is roughly fixed at the start. For the manufacture of rattan furniture, it is only two years. It is over five years on an average in carpentry and six in jewelry.

The principal defect of the traditional apprenticeship system is insufficient theoretical training. This is due both to the low level of knowledge of the master craftsmen and to the number of apprentices in relation to the number of skilled workers.

Governments have begun to pass laws for the "adaptation and renovation" of apprenticeships in Africa which seek to provide for alternate periods of theoretical training by giving entrepreneurs themselves proficiency courses and pedagogical support in their training function. Examples are the 1977 law in the Ivory Coast, the 1983 law in Togo, and the 1981 law in Algeria creating the National Institute for the Promotion and Development of Vocational Training in the Enterprise and Apprenticeship.

NONFORMAL EDUCATION PROGRAMS IN AFRICA

According to Hamilton and Asiedu, nonformal educational programs have a substantial history in most African countries. These programs are designed to handle a number of community problems ranging from literacy to family planning. In recent years, the bulk of the activities of nonformal education has been devoted to skills training for employment. There are three main categories of activities that characterize the skills-training approaches—preemployment training for industry, skills upgrading for small business and industry, and training for farmers and craftsmen in rural areas.

Many of these preemployment programs have been developed by nongovernment or private agencies. The YMCAs and YWCAs have for many years operated programs in Sierra Leone, Ghana, Kenya, Tanzania, and Zambia. Skills-upgrading programs are mostly sponsored by governments.

A skills-training program that appears to be increasing in popularity and demand is based on the Opportunities Industrialization Center (OIC) model created in the black ghetto of Philadelphia in 1964. Similar skills-training programs have been replicated in Cameroon, Nigeria, Ghana, Ethiopia, Liberia, Sierra Leone, Togo, Lesotho, Guinea, Ivory Coast, Kenya, Zaire, and the Central African Republic. The OICs offer vocational-technical training in a variety of areas (e.g., accounting, air conditioning, auto mechanics, carpentry, electricity, computer technology, and farm management). The OIC model consists of seven program components: recruitment, counseling, prevocational training, vocational training, job development, placement, and agricultural resettlement.

HRD PROGRAMS IN AFRICAN ORGANIZATIONS

❦ Pan-African Institute for Development (Regional)

The Pan-African Institute for Development (PAID) was founded in 1964 as an international, nonprofit, and nongovernmental organization dedicated to promoting integrated and participative development of both rural and urban peoples throughout Africa.

The objectives of the Pan-African Institute for Development are to further the economic, social, and cultural development of the countries of Africa and to promote the people's development and improve their levels of living.

There are four regional institutes:

- PAID Central Africa, founded in 1965 in Douala (Cameroon)
- PAID West Africa, founded in 1969 in Buea (Cameroon)
- PAID Eastern and Southern Africa, founded in 1978 in Kabwe (Zambia)
- PAID West Africa-Sahel, founded in 1977 in Ouagadougou (Burkina Faso)

PAID's training focuses on the areas of rural and periurban socioeconomic development; small- and medium-scale rural-based business enterprises and other income-generation activities; promoting participation of women in the development effort; and promoting the well-being of disadvantaged or vulnerable groups such as women, nursing mothers, children, disabled persons, and old people. In 1983, PAID won the Maurice Pate Prize from UNICEF for its contribution to the development of the Third World.

❦ Eskom (South Africa)

Eskom, one of the largest utility companies in the world, supplies more than 60 percent of the electricity used in the entire African continent. Its twenty-five power stations have an installed capacity of over 36,000 MW.

Despite the economic and political isolation of South Africa, Eskom has been able to maintain its international links. In determining the role of HRD within the company, Eskom first developed a clear vision as to where the corporation wished to go based upon its values as to what the future of the country should be.

If the country was to be multiracial, then Eskom had to develop multiracial leadership and employment within the company. If the country was to be more export driven and to be a leader for all Africa, then Eskom was determined to support such HRD efforts. As a result, Eskom decided on three key visions:

1. To be one of the best performing power and electrical companies on a world-wide standard
2. To provide electricity for all, in urban and rural areas, in rich and poor areas
3. To create economic wealth through the provision of energy in South Africa

Eskom has undertaken numerous HRD activities to develop the corporate leadership to meet these goals. In adding people of color and women to their leadership positions, the company decided to become risk takers, to get a "mind shift" away from the attitude that people first must have the experience (not heretofore available) before they are put into positions of responsibility. An advisory group of senior Black staff regularly meet with executives to discuss progress and additional HRD and organizational activities which can enable them to better serve and lead Eskom. There are also cultural-awareness programs to help change attitudes and bridge the cultural gaps among employees.

Internal management development programs are taught which expose managers to the wide challenges in Eskom and South Africa. In addition, senior managers are sent to top business schools in the United States, U.K., and South Africa to acquire additional leadership skills and experience.

✌ *Work Force and Skills Training Project (Botswana)*

Despite a decade of strong economic growth from 1973 to 1983 (9.3 percent annually), Botswana lacked the human resources required for sustained economic growth. Looking to the future, the government of Botswana faced three critical conditions: (1) a high rate of unemployment for unskilled workers, (2) a lack of educated personnel for managerial positions in the government and the private sector, and (3) a high number of expatriates still in such positions fifteen years after independence. In 1982, the government of Botswana and the U.S. Agency for International Development designed a ten-year HRD project to address these conditions through the provision of technical assistance and training to the four government ministries and private institutions with primary responsibility for generating employment in rural areas.

The project included three major components: technical assistance, training, and the management of training. The project provided expert personnel who assumed line positions in participating government ministries, training institutions, or private-sector associations. In addition to performing the responsibilities of their positions, these experts provided training and support for the local counterparts.

Training included long-term academic training in degree programs, short-term training in specific technical areas, and internships or study tours with U.S. businesses. The project developed a computer tracking system for all in-country, U.S., and third-country trainees to monitor and assess their progress.

The project has worked closely with the training officers of the ministries to create a professional cadre of training specialists able to assess training needs, determine training priorities, and manage and evaluate training programs. The ministries were thereby better able to issue requests for training and technical assistance that matched their most critical requirements.

By the end of the project, systems for the management of training were well established in both the public and the private sectors, so that government ministries and private firms were able to identify and assign priority to their training needs, and the training institutions of Botswana were able to respond to those needs. With adequately trained personnel, both the public and private sectors were able to formulate and carry out policies and programs that effectively stimulated expansion of the private sector, thereby generating employment for the growing population of job seekers.

SUMMARY

The cultural factors of geography, demographics, language, religion, history, and class have all impacted HRD activity in Africa. African governments have always placed a high priority on HRD which was seen as "akin to nation-building." Unfortunately, few skilled jobs existed for the trained Africans. HRD has been refocused to the on-the-job and apprenticeship forms of training. Nonformal education programs, based on the Opportunities Industrialization Centers in the United States, have become popular in Africa.

The chapter examined four successful HRD programs of Africa—the Pan-African Institute for Development (Regional), Eskom (South Africa), and the Work Force and Skills Training Project (Botswana).

REFERENCES

BAS, DANIEL. "On-the-Job Training in Africa." *International Labor Review* (Vol. 128, No. 4), pp. 485–96.

HAMILTON, EDWIN AND KOBINA ASIEDU. "Vocational-Technical Education in Tropical Africa." *Journal of Negro Education* (Vol. 56, No. 3), pp. 338–55.

JONES, MERRICK L. "Management Development: An African Focus." In *International Human Resource Management.* Boston: PWS-Kent Publishing Company, 1991.

MUTEMBI, J. *San Francisco Examiner,* (December 18, 1991), p. 2.

ROBERTS, LEE. "HRD in Africa." In *The Handbook for Human Resource Development,* 2nd ed., edited by Leonard Nadler. New York: John Wiley and Sons, 1990.

THOMPSON, A. R. *Education and Development in Africa.* Harare, Zimbabwe: College Press, 1981.

CHAPTER 14

ॐ ॐ

South Central Asia

INTRODUCTION

> If I were asked under what sky the human mind has most deeply pondered over
> the greatest problems of life and found solutions for some of them, I should
> point to India.
>
> *Jean Houston*
> *The Religions of Man*

In South Central Asia, the age of globalization is running headlong into
the legacies of countless dynasties (and ages) stretching back for at least
sixty centuries, and we can anticipate that damage from the collision,
although it has the potential of being serious, will not be fatal.

In this chapter, however, our focus will be considerably more narrow.
First, we will outline the cultural, business, and HRD environments of South
Central Asia and then consider the evolving practice of HRD as many of the
region's countries enter the HRD arena.

ॐ *Learning Objectives*

After studying this chapter, you should be able to:

1. Understand how the geography, demographics, languages, history, religions, and
   principal cultural beliefs of South Central Asia affect HRD activities

2. Recognize the key economic factors in the region that have an impact on the practice of HRD
3. Outline the role of HRD in the region as it moves toward industrialization
4. Give examples of successful government and private-sector HRD programs

CULTURAL FACTORS IMPACTING HRD

❧ *Geography and Demographics*

The Indian subcontinent, stretching from the Himalayas in the north to the Indian Ocean in the south, is composed of some of the most densely populated countries in the world. Even with its enormous size, India's population density of 692 per square mile is two to three times that of most European countries. The population for the five countries we will consider—Bangladesh, India, Nepal, Pakistan, and Sri Lanka—is currently estimated at 1.2 billion and is expected to grow to 2 billion by the year 2025.

The region is a complex mosaic of cultures and ethnic groups with Indo-Aryans the most populous group and large populations of Punjabi, Sinhalese, Bengali, Dravidian, Tamils, Sindhi, Baluchi, Sherpa, and others. Throughout the area, however, caste and religion tend to be more important than ethnic identity. The creation of Pakistan in 1946, the secession of Bangladesh in 1971, and the continuing religious strife throughout the region speak to the strength of religious convictions and differences.

❧ *Language*

In India alone, there are at least 300 known languages, twenty-four of which have more than one million speakers. Fifteen languages are recognized in the Indian constitution, but Hindi and English are the official languages. Pakistan's official languages are Urdu and English, but the former is mainly known only to those with formal education, and only 7 percent of the people speak the latter; regional provinces most commonly use their local languages, whose total number is unknown. In Nepal, there are as many as twenty major languages spoken; in Sri Lanka, 74 percent of the population speaks Sinhalese, 18 percent, Tamil; in Bangladesh, the majority speaks Bengali, but there are numerous local tongues as well. Regional estimates of languages and dialects are in wide dispute, but the total is certainly in excess of 1,500.

❦ *History and Religion*

The earliest known civilization in the region grew up in the Indus Valley from 4000 to 2500 B.C. Beginning about 1500 B.C, Aryan invaders swept into India from the northwest and began to mix with the local Dravidian population. Over the next two thousand years, the Aryans developed a religious philosophy and social caste system that has evolved as Hinduism. In the sixth century B.C., Buddhism was established, and it spread and prospered to reach a golden age under King Ashoka in the third century B.C. From the fourth to the seventh centuries A.D., North India experienced a golden age under the Gupta dynasty, when Hindu art, science, literature, and theology flourished. Arab, Turk, and Afghan Muslims ruled successively from the eighth to the eighteenth centuries and saw the first wave of European traders arrive in the seventeenth century, lured by India's fabled riches. From 1746 to 1763, India was a battleground for France and Great Britain, with the latter finally emerging as the colonial power under terms of the Treaty of Paris in 1763.

Although it was not formally established as an independent country until 1947, the seeds of modern Pakistan date to Arab traders, who in the eighth century introduced Islam to the area. Muslim warriors captured much of what is now known as Pakistan in the tenth century, and Muslim power reached its peak under the sixteenth and seventeenth century Mogul empire. Although many Indians were converted to Islam, the majority of the population remained Hindu. The last Mogul emperor was deposed in 1859, and the British continued to rule the area as a single empire. An independence movement begun after World War I, led to the creation of Pakistan and India as sovereign states in 1947. Pakistan was divided into East and West Pakistan, the latter gaining independence as Bangladesh in 1971.

With some exceptions, the early histories of Nepal and Sri Lanka parallel those of their neighbors. Sri Lanka was well known in its own right to civilizations dating back to the Romans, and was ruled by the British as the Crown Colony of Ceylon, until it gained independence in 1948. The known history of Nepal dates to the sixth century B.C., when Buddha was born into a wealthy family in the plains of that country. Nepal was unified under a single king in the eighth century. The Nepalese successfully resisted British attempts to conquer the small kingdom in the early nineteenth century and never became a British colony. Nepal is a constitutional monarchy with considerable control of the legislature vested in the king.

❦ *The Culture of Hinduism*

Hinduism is unique among the world's major religions in that it had no single founder and has no well-defined ecclesiastical organization. It has grown over a period of 4,000 years by incorporating or living alongside of the many religious and cultural movements of the subcontinent. Hinduism is composed of innumerable sects, but its most general features include the caste system, acceptance of the Veda, the sacred scriptures of Brahmanism, and a belief in karma, according to which an individual reaps the results of good and bad actions through a series of lifetimes.

The *Laws of Manu* are the basis of an elaborate Hindu social system that applies to every aspect of life, describing in detail the roles of the four classes and four stages of life. The entire system was designed to ensure not only the proper functioning of society as a whole but also the fulfillment of the individual's needs through his lifetime. The universe is seen as undergoing an eternally repeated cycle of creation, preservation, and dissolution. A single individual in the midst of one of countless lives is seen as relatively insignificant.

❦ *General Attitudes*

The Hindu peoples are religious, philosophical, and family oriented. They value the ideals of humility and self-denial, believing more in physical purity and spiritual refinement than in comfort and luxury. In light of their belief in reincarnation and karma, they are strongly fatalistic and see their lot in life as a result of their former actions and a manifestation of God. Indians are proud of their long and rich heritage, as well as their current status as the world's most populous democracy.

❦ *Family*

The elaborate caste system has an enormous impact on family life, dictating everything from eligible marriage partners to food handling and preparation. Hindu families are large and take precedence over the individual. Extended families live under the same roof or close together; sometimes entire villages are made up of several generations of only a few extended families. Social mobility between castes is severely limited, and more than 600 million belong to the lowest caste.

Marriages are typically arranged by the family with others of the same caste and subgroup. For women, premarital chastity is an essential part of the marriage contract. Marriage ceremonies are often elaborate as marriage is considered to be a sacred bond that endures beyond death. The wife manages the affairs of the household and has influence in all family matters. The elderly are accorded deep respect with younger family members often yielding to their advice and counsel. Children are expected to take care of their elderly parents.

ECONOMIC ENVIRONMENT FOR HRD

The fastest growing region in the world, South Central Asia has a total literacy rate of 30 percent, less than 15 percent for women from rural areas. Over two-thirds of the labor force of nearly 500 million workers in the region is in the agricultural sector, with tea, coffee, fish, and processed foods being the chief exports. The countries are all very poor with a regional GNP of less than $400 per capita. Eighty percent of the population is rural, and most villages are still primitive in that they lack pure water supply, sewage, drainage, and electricity. All the countries in South Central Asia are committing major expenditures in training small farmers through agricultural extension workers. Several agricultural institutions have been established to impart practical, skill-oriented training.

Although India and Sri Lanka have had democratic elections since their independence in 1947, Pakistan and Bangladesh have generally toiled under military rule. The Kingdom of Nepal, a constitutional monarchy, recently created a parliament, and prodemocracy forces are growing. Ethnic and religious conflicts have plagued India and Sri Lanka for centuries. The British colonial system left a number of influences which impact on HRD:

• Strong desire and respect for government work
• Elite private educational system
• Search for opportunities outside India, causing a tremendous "brain drain".

EMERGING HRD TRENDS IN INDIA

India, with an estimated population of one billion people by the year 2000, perceives itself as an emerging industrial power. It has already attained self-sufficiency in the manufacture of machinery for its major industries— aircraft, ships, automotive, heavy vehicles, locomotives, construction machinery, and machine tools. Consumer goods like refrigerators, TV sets, and household appliances are all manufactured indigenously. India is now placing particular emphasis on new technological areas such as electronics, computer sciences, telecommunications, and space and ocean development.

This economic transformation has been made possible by the tremendous HRD efforts within India, which have increased the country's capabilities in science and technology. In the years since independence in 1947, some 120 universities, 150 engineering colleges, five institutes of technology, and 350 polytechnical training centers have been established. Each year, India produces nearly 200,000 qualified technical and professional personnel. As a result, India has the world's third largest reservoir of trained manpower. Unfortunately, many of these highly trained professionals leave India to work in both developed and developing nations around the world.

The Indian government has also placed a renewed emphasis on the production of handicrafts, which is seen as a source of employment opportunities and an earner of foreign exchange. Over 150,000 people were recently trained in the four major export crafts of hand-knotted woolen carpets, art metalware, hand-printed textiles, and woodware.

In 1986, the government of India adopted a new educational policy, coordinated by the Ministry of Human Development, that placed special emphasis on vocational training linked closely to workplace needs and specific occupations. The emphasis is on attitudes, knowledge, and skills for entrepreneurship and self-employment. All students, regardless of caste, creed, location, and sex are to have access to education and training of a comparable quality. The old examination system has been replaced by one which focuses on evaluation of performance. The new education policy also has brought about changes in instructional materials and methodology. HRD programs are implemented through various ways and channels including:

- Establishment of centers in rural areas for continuing education
- Workers' education through the employers, trade unions, and concerned agencies of government
- Postsecondary education institutions
- Wider promotion of books, libraries, reading rooms
- Use of radio, TV, and films, as mass and group learning media
- Creation of learners' groups and organizations
- Programs of distance learning
- Organizing assistance in self-learning
- Organizing need- and interest-based vocational training programs

In order to increase the relevance of management education, particularly in the noncorporate and undermanaged sectors, the management education system will study and document the Indian experience and create a body of knowledge and specific educational programs suited to these sectors.

According to Frank, there has been "a massive growth in training programs in India. They are offered by all kinds of institutions, from the most prestigious Indian institutes of management and universities to small technical and vocational schools, and by thousands of individuals" (p. 38).

India's HRD campaign is already under way on a massive scale and is likely to have growing impact in the coming years. If the campaign succeeds—and there is every indication that the government is determined to provide all the necessary direction and resources to make it do so—India of the early twenty-first century may well have overcome its many problems and become one of the most successful economies of the world.

The government of India is seeking to improve the role of women. The Committee on the Status of Women has stated forcefully that the training of women is critical for India's development. Government policy has encouraged women's access to training. The large-scale training of Rural Youth for Self-Employment Program reserves a minimum quota of women trainees.

NATIONAL PRODUCTIVITY ORGANIZATIONS

National Productivity Organizations (NPOs) are active in all the countries of South Central Asia and serve to increase labor productivity and quality on a national scale. NPOs are either part of the government or are quasi-governmental. India's Productivity Council, for example, has a governing board that includes representatives from the government, employees, and employers and operates through forty-eight local productivity councils and regional directorates. The NPOs have focused much of their activities on HRD, including training and education courses, observational study tours, provisions of technical and expert consulting services, HRD research, conferences, and developing HRD publications (Ramchandran).

HRD PROGRAMS IN SOUTH CENTRAL ASIA

❦ *Nepal Administrative Staff College (Nepal)*

Founded in 1982, the Nepal Administrative Staff College is the official training unit of the government and has four specific objectives:

- To provide necessary training for the employees of His Majesty's government and public enterprises in Nepal
- To identify means for enhancing the managerial capability of Nepalese public enterprise management and thereby support the country's development program
- To conduct problem-oriented research with a view to preparing training materials and making training more useful

- To provide consultancy and information services to public and private agencies of Nepal

The college undertakes various programs including preservice training for new entrants to civil service, in-service training for senior government officials, management training for government managers, foreign officer training, and training and seminars on current issues and problems.

The college has conducted a variety of HRD-related research on issues such as motivating the Nepalese Civil Service, local administration in Nepal, manpower utilization in the government, and development of the Boards of Public Institutions.

❦ *Biman Bangladesh Airlines (Bangladesh)*

Biman Bangladesh Airlines was established upon Bangladesh independence in 1972 with only 2,300 employees inherited from Pakistan International Airlines and with very few other resources. Its growth during the past two decades to a modern, efficient international airline, is attributable to its long-term commitment to training and organization development.

Starting with a single instructor and seven courses in 1972, Biman now has a team of instructors teaching over 100 courses per year. The airline realizes that human resource development is the "key to attainment of organizational objectives" (Ashraf, p. 23). The triangular approach places an emphasis on knowledge, attitude, and skills. Each department develops annual training priorities for its staff. The Biman training philosophy entails:

- Practical, job-focused training
- Development of interpersonal skills so people can work in teams and with the entire organization
- Provision of career opportunities to enable people to move upward in the organization

Nearly 90 percent of all the training is conducted at the Bangladesh Airlines Training Center. Over 15,000 people have been trained in four major areas of aviation training:

- Technical operations
- Engineering and maintenance
- Marketing, sales, and customer service
- Secretarial science management

An Apprentice Training School was inaugurated in 1986 in collaboration with the International Civil Aviation Organization and the United

Nations Development Program. The school also serves personnel of other airlines in the region.

❧ *Bangladesh Management Development Center (Bangladesh)*

Bangladesh Management Development Center (BMDC) came into existence in 1961 as a result of a tripartite agreement between the government of Pakistan, the United Nations's Special Fund, and the ILO under the administrative control of the Ministry of Labor. The institute, as a national management training center, has the overall objective of training and developing professional skills of senior- and middle-level managers, as well as providing services furthering the development of productivity in the nation's business, commercial, and industrial sectors. The institute is responsible for the development of professional managers for all levels of private- and public-sector industries and the provisions of management training and development in other sectors of the economy such as transport, communication, and agriculture.

BMDC is recognized throughout Asia as a leader in HRD research and the development of quality training programs. BMDC has provided consultancy services for every major Bangladesh organization including banks, telecommunications, minerals, food processing, transportation, and manufacturing. It has collaborated with international organizations such as the International Telecommunication Union, UNICEF, Asian Productivity Organization, and the International Center for Public Enterprises.

❧ *Sheraton and ITC Limited (India)*

ITC Limited, one of the largest corporations in India, and Sheraton first began their joint hotel venture in 1971. ITC entered this sector because tourism was consistent with the priorities of the government of India and was open to private investment.

Sheraton provided all the technical and management expertise necessary to develop and establish all systems required in setting up a new hotel division with ITC. In addition, Sheraton provided training to the Indian managers in Sheraton hotels spread all over the world.

The cornerstones of the ITC-Sheraton HRD program were the Hotel Executive Training Institutes. Designed to be equivalent to a hotel management degree anywhere in the world, the objective of these training institutes was to produce skilled hoteliers who would contribute effectively to the running of a deluxe hotel with the latest systems and technology. The training encompassed all aspects of operations. Extensive training in departments like front office, food and beverage, and housekeeping ensured complete comprehension of each function. The hotel executive trainees were trained to eventually take the mantle from U.S. Sheraton managers as general managers and regional directors.

When Sheraton began operations in India in the early seventies, a majority of the forty-six managers were expatriates. By mid-1985 there were only seven Sheraton manager positions in India filled by expatriates, with the balance taken by Indian managers—the bulk of whom were the products of the earlier training institutes.

Sheraton's entry into India led to a rapid maturing of the hotel industry. It has made the business more competitive with discernible improvements in quality of service. The Sheraton management program assumed the role of a formal vocational degree and has to date trained over 1,800 Indian hotel managers. The training programs of ITC-Sheraton have been among the most sought after in the hotel industry.

❦ *Pakistan Institute of Management (Pakistan)*

The Pakistan Institute of Management (PIM) was established in 1954 by the government of Pakistan to impart training to the managers of business and industry in Pakistan, especially those from public enterprises. The Institute soon developed into a full-fledged training institution for the executives of all sectors of business and industry.

At present, the institute offers nearly 140 short courses of one to five weeks to senior-, middle-, and junior-level managers from public, private, and multinational enterprises. The areas of training include general management, financial management, production management, marketing management, personnel management, and supervisory development. So far, the institute has organized and conducted over 3,000 short courses and trained over 50,000 executives. The institute also offers in-company training and consultancy on request according to the need of a particular enterprise. The PIM has also organized international and regional conferences, seminars, and workshops on various aspects of management in collaboration with international agencies.

SUMMARY

South Central Asia, with a population of 1.2 billion people which is projected to exceed 2 billion within the next thirty years, is a region with a complex mosaic of cultures and ethnic groups. Poverty and illiteracy are major obstacles, but HRD is being seen by all the countries in the region as critical for national economic development.

National Productivity Organizations (NPOs), which serve to increase economic output and quality, are active in all the countries of South Central Asia. Each has provided extensive training and technical assistance to key industries in their country.

In this chapter, we examined five of the top HRD institutes in the region, namely, Nepal Administrative Staff College, Biman Bangladesh Airlines Training Center, Bangladesh Management Development Center, Sheraton-ITC Executive Training Institute, and Pakistan Institute of Management.

REFERENCES

Ashraf, K. A. M. "Organization Development & Training at Biman Bangladesh Airlines." *Air Asia* (February 1988), pp. 23–25.

Frank, Eric. "HRD in India." *Journal of European Industrial Training* (May 1988), pp. 32–38.

Ramchandran, Vankatram K. "HRD in Asia." In *The Handbook for Human Resource Development*, 2nd ed., edited by Leonard Nadler. New York: John Wiley and Sons, 1990.

❦ ❦

CHAPTER 15

East Asia

INTRODUCTION

Man has three ways of gaining wisdom. Firstly, on meditation, this is the noblest; secondly, on imitation, this is the easiest; and thirdly, on experience, this is the most difficult.

From The Teachings of Confucius

Confucianism remains one of the dominant influences throughout East Asia. The high pedestal on which Confucius placed teachers and his high value of learning causes managers as well as parents to promote and prize education and development. HRD in East Asia is growing at a rate unrivaled in the rest of the world.

This chapter explores the cultural, business, and HRD environments of East Asia and then considers the evolving practice of HRD as a number of the region's countries evolve into global industrial and economic powers.

❦ *Learning Objectives*

After studying this chapter, you should be able to:

1. Understand how the geography, demographics, languages, history, religions, and cultural beliefs of East Asia affect HRD activities

2. Recognize the key economic factors in the region that have an impact on the practice of HRD
3. Outline the role of HRD in the region as its countries become even more important industrial and economic powers
4. Give examples of successful government and private-sector HRD programs

CULTURAL FACTORS IMPACTING HRD

Because of the vastness and diversity of this region, we have divided the geography, demographics, languages, and history into two subregions: (1) China, Korea, Taiwan, and Hong Kong, and (2) Southeast Asia. Japan is covered in Chapter 16.

❦ *Geography, Demographics, and Language*

China, Korea, Taiwan, and Hong Kong. The population of China (the third largest country in the world), along with that of its neighbors, Taiwan, Hong Kong, and South Korea, exceeds 1.2 billion. Although China itself is a multiracial state, about 94 percent of the people are Han Chinese; the remaining 6 percent is spread among some sixty other ethnic groups, the largest being Huis, Mongols, Uighurs, Chuangs, Yis, and Tibetans. In both Hong Kong and Taiwan, approximately 98 percent of the population is ethnic Chinese, although the vast majority of the Chinese in Taiwan are descended from eighteenth and nineteenth century immigrants from Fukien province. Non-Chinese aborigines constitute about 2 percent of the population of Taiwan, and there are substantial Filipino, American, and European populations in Hong Kong. The Koreans are ethnically homogeneous Mongoloid people who have shared a common history, language, and culture since at least the seventh century A.D., when the peninsula was first unified.

Although the number of languages spoken in China varies according to one's definitions of language and dialect, they represent in total more than one billion native speakers. The languages and dialects of the Chinese share a single writing system, and standard spoken Chinese is based on the Mandarin dialect native to 70 percent of the population. Korean, a member of the Ural-Altaic language family, was brought to the region by early invaders. The writing system, developed in the fifteenth century, is used in conjunction with borrowed Chinese characters.

Southeast Asia. Southeast Asia is composed of ten independent countries: Brunei, Cambodia, Indonesia, Laos, Malaysia, Myanmar (Burma), the Philippines, Singapore, Thailand, and Vietnam.

These countries are home to 450 million people with a staggering diversity of cultural, religious, and ethnic traditions. The hundreds of languages spoken derive principally from the Sino-Tibetan, Malayo-Polynesian, and Mon-Khmer language families; among those that are written, forms vary considerably, ranging from those of Chinese or Indian derivation through Romanized alphabets adapted from European languages to the Arabic script imported with the spread of Islam. Most of the people live in small villages, with the rest principally in the largest cities: Djakarta, Bangkok, Ho Chi Minh City, Manila, and Singapore.

❦ History

China, Korea, Taiwan, and Hong Kong. China's written history begins during the sixteenth century B.C. with the Shang dynasty. Ruled by a series of dynasties since the Shang, China became a republic after the fall of the Ch'ing or Manchu dynasty in 1912. From 1921 until the communist victory in 1949, a long and bitter civil war raged in China between the communist forces, led by Mao Tse-tung, and those of the nationalists, led by Chiang Kai-shek. Following their defeat, the nationalists fled to the island of Taiwan and established the independent Republic of China. The United Nations recognized Taiwan as the legitimate government of China until 1971, when the People's Republic assumed the UN seat. The sovereignty of Taiwan is still in dispute.

Originally acquired by the British because of its magnificent natural harbor, Hong Kong is still the port of entry and exit for one-third of China's trade. In 1984, China and Britain signed a joint declaration under which China would resume sovereignty over the whole colony in 1997 but would grant Hong Kong a high degree of autonomy.

After more than 1,000 years of Chinese settlements among the indigenous Korean tribes, the first of several kingdoms arose in the north around 100 A.D. However, Korea was not united until 700 years later and had its golden age from the fourteenth to the seventeenth centuries. For the next 350 years, Korea was dominated politically by either China or Japan. Despite this long history as a cultural bridge between their two neighbors, the Koreans have maintained their identity as a separate and distinct people. Partition of the country after World War II into two zones occupied by the Russians and the Americans was followed by the establishment of the separate states of North and South Korea in 1948. The Korean War (1950–53) marked the beginning of almost forty years of enmity between the two governments. In 1990, talks were initiated in an effort to reduce tensions, open relations, and possibly seek reunification.

Southeast Asia. The ancestors of the peoples who now occupy Southeast Asia began leaving China and Tibet 2,500 years ago and migrated down fertile valleys and alluvial plains toward the tropics and the sea. Continuing this migration for centuries, they pushed aside or incorporated the small aboriginal cultures they encountered along the way. Many settled on the mainland, becoming the Khmers and Chams of Cambodia and Vietnam, the Pyus and Mons of Burma and Western Thailand, and the Malays farther down the peninsula. Others built boats and spread through the Indonesian archipelago, becoming the forbears of the Dyaks of Borneo, the Bataks of Sumatra, and the Filipinos. Agrarian for the most part, they worshiped ancestors and spirits whom they believed inhabited the fields and streams. Their descent and inheritance systems were mainly matrilineal, and over the centuries, they devised a body of social tradition and custom that survives today as an equivalent of Western common law.

❦ Religion

The principal religions of East Asia include (in order of historical appearance) Hinduism, Buddhism, Taoism, Confucianism, Islam, and Christianity. With the exception of China (where 60 percent of the population considers itself nonreligious), the governments of the area subscribe to the notion of freedom of religion, but among the people, there are periodic hostilities and disagreements. Islam is the predominant religion in Indonesia, Malaysia, and Brunei, while Myanmar, Thailand, Laos, Vietnam, and Cambodia all have Buddhist majorities. Although close to 30 percent of South Koreans are Christian, the Philippines remains the only East Asian country that is predominantly so. Hong Kong and Singapore show strong Chinese influence with more than half the population practicing Buddhism, Taoism, Confucianism, or some combination of the three. In each of the countries, strong indigenous, mostly animist religions continue to have followers as well.

❦ Family

It is safe to make at least one generalization about the people of the region, whether they be native to Beijing, Manila, Djakarta, Taipei, or Mandalay: they have strong loyalty and attachment to their families. The rules and regulations vary somewhat depending upon the history and religious influences, but in all of East Asia, an individual exists principally as a member of a family. Families are large, typically with three or more generations living together, the young taking care of the elderly. Elders are respected, and the word of the father is usually law. In the Philippines especially, a mother's advice is also taken very seriously. Cooperation among family members and assistance in times of need are enlisted and expected. Even when businesses are not family owned, they are often family based; certainly business throughout the area is a family affair.

❦ The Importance of Correct Behavior

Loyalty to family is extended also to community, ethnic group, and nation. To speak badly of another brings shame upon his family. To refuse the request of a friend brings shame upon one's own family. There is much concern in all of these cultures with losing face. As a result, the people tend to be reserved in public, discreet in their social relations, and reluctant to make pronouncements about others. They're often shocked by the ease with which Westerners voice opinions about others and also by how seriously they take these opinions and, for that matter, themselves. They appreciate a quiet voice, an unassuming manner, and a sense of discretion.

Problems will be handled in time. Conflicts must be addressed quietly by the appropriate people at the right moment. Family and friends are always more important than being on time or resolving a conflict immediately. East Asians rarely disagree in public, seldom say no, and generally have time for others.

❦ An Emphasis on Education

We can see in the people's attitude toward education a common thread of their cultural histories. The almost universal veneration of books for the learning contained in them is common to all of the cultural currents of the region. In addition, from India, China, the Middle East, and Europe came strong traditions of learning and education and along with them writing systems through which people could encode and decode the wisdom of the past.

ECONOMIC ENVIRONMENT FOR HRD

East Asia is the emerging economic region of the world with a total population of nearly two billion and a rapidly increasing GNP. There are four primary subregions in East Asia—each with its own unique economic characteristics, levels of development, and HRD needs and capabilities.

1. *China*. China has one-fifth of the world's population and one of the last state-managed economies. There are tremendous needs for technological and manage-

rial training. The state-run industries which have become an albatross to economic development are gradually being replaced by privately run industries. In 1992, for the first time in forty years, the private sector will produce more than 50 percent of the industrial output.

2. *Singapore, Hong Kong, Taiwan and South Korea.* The "Four Tigers," or newly industrialized countries, are rapidly approaching the industrial levels of Japan and the industrialized countries of the West. HRD is highly advanced, and much can be learned from their training technologies.

3. *Indonesia, Malaysia, the Philippines, Thailand and Brunei.* These are lesser developed nations that will grow the most rapidly—economically and in terms of population—throughout the nineties. HRD is seen as critical for national development.

4. *Vietnam, Myanmar, Cambodia, Laos.* These poor, war-torn countries are just beginning the transition from military-dominated, state-planned economies to free-market democracies. HRD is desperately needed, but few resources or skills are available.

HRD PROGRAMS IN EAST ASIA

❦ *Hong Kong Bank (Hong Kong)*

Hong Kong Bank is one of the world's largest and most successful banks with 16,000 employees and assets of over $150 billion. The bank has offices in fifty-five countries strategically located in Asia, Europe, and North America to take advantage of time zone changes and thereby create a global network where transactions are processed twenty-four hours a day. And just as the sun never sets on work at the Hong Kong Bank, so does it never set on training, which is seen as a never-ending employee requisite.

Much of Hong Kong Bank's success can be attributed to its strong commitment to human resource development. Bryan Neal, director of training, describes the employees' prevailing attitude toward training:

> We keep up quite a pace here. Nearly everyone works a 12-hour day: eight hours at a job and another three or four in training. Our staff seems to be on a never ending search for knowledge, and we like to work and train together. We've made a massive investment (more than $1 million per year) in training because we want to take advantage of new technology, be more customer oriented and improve our staff's English. [Piturro, p. 40]

An important aspect of the bank's HRD efforts is to carefully train top executives with the skills and attitudes to operate anywhere. An international cadre of several hundred senior managers have been trained together and then posted in three-year assignments around the world. Recently, a group of 200 Europeans were trained and, according to Piturro, received "special attention that is possibly unparalleled in the financial services industry" (p. 43).

Another special HRD emphasis of Hong Kong Bank is on improving customer service, so that the bank will be perceived as a friendly bank, not just as an efficient one. Based upon the American Management Association's training program, Hong Kong Bank has implemented a plan to reach front-line managers who, in turn, can train their subordinates. The courses are offered in English and Cantonese, and those who sign up for the English version are looked upon favorably by peers and managers. The customer service courses include such subjects as understanding customer service, telephone courtesy, better customer relations through leadership, and basic selling skills.

A key challenge for the HRD staff in conducting the customer service courses is to help the trainees change attitudes and values. Typically, a Chinese employee looks first and always to his boss for approval and takes no action until it is clear what his boss wants. Customer service requires being immediately responsive and sensitive to the customers' needs and wants. Coming up with ideas spontaneously, responding quickly, and acting assertively are difficult for Asians, but Hong Kong Bank employees are gaining these competencies with the HRD staff serving as prototypes for the bank employees.

❦ *Distance Training Program (Indonesia)*

The Indonesia archipelago consists of 5,000 islands stretched across nearly 3,000 miles of ocean. This combination of great distances and vast expanses of water has served to isolate the islands from one another for much of their history.

Soon after independence in 1949, the government of Indonesia began to search for ways to link its peoples and provide training and education to its vast rural population. Indonesia was well aware of the inability of its existing training institutions and university to meet the country's constantly expanding need for trained manpower. Only about 18 percent to 20 percent of those who apply for entrance into higher education are able to be accepted due to shortages of staff, materials, and infrastructure. With the development of satellite technology in the sixties, the government recognized that a satellite system might solve the problem of reaching its scattered citizens in a relatively inexpensive way. By placing earth stations at remote sites, the entire country could be reached, and, from an HRD standpoint, this network would allow for a comprehensive two-way delivery system.

In the mid seventies, the decision was made to install a national satellite system with forty-two earth stations and two satellites. The satellites were named Palapa A-1 and Palapa A-2 (the name Palapa was chosen because of its connection with a quote by a famous Indonesian historical leader, Prime Minister Gadjah Mada, who vowed that he would not eat palapa—a popular food dish of that era—until the islands of Indonesia were united into one nation). The HRD impact of these new Palapas indeed has served to carry out that vow and to make Indonesia one nation.

The Palapa A-1 satellite was launched in 1976, and Indonesia became the first developing nation to have its own domestic satellite system. Over the next ten years, the Palapa system was expanded to 120 earth stations that provide telephone, telex, radio, facsimile, and television coverage to all twenty-six provinces of Indonesia.

The telecommunications system utilizes a two-channel dedicated, audio-graphics system. The first channel is an audioconferencing system connecting eleven training sites in an open network. All learners are tuned into the same satellite channel at all times; thus anything said at one location is heard at all locations simultaneously. The second channel provides (a) graphics in support of the audio via facsimile and telewriting machines, (b) private conferencing telephone facilities, and (c) emergency backup to any failure of the audio channel.

Courses being taught in the Distance Training Program are adult education, agriculture, forestry, animal husbandry, fisheries management, nutrition, management and organizational behavior, and poultry management.

The initial learning results from the Distance Training Program were so impressive that the Ministry of Education requested additional World Bank loans to expand the satellite training system. The governments of Australia and Canada have also added development projects that can effectively utilize the satellite communication for training and educational purposes. The Indonesian project, according to Shaw, has demonstrated that satellite technology and audioconferencing networks can meet important learning needs of the Third World, especially in the development of remote areas.

❦ *Vocational Training (China)*

Vocational training is an immense undertaking in China, a nation with over 1.1 billion people. More than 400,000 vocational training teachers work with an estimated five million trainees.

The Cultural Revolution (1966–69) virtually destroyed China's educational system, and Chinese leaders realize the critical importance of rebuilding it. The number of secondary students enrolled in specialized technical and vocational schools has risen from 5 percent in 1978 to over 50 percent in the early nineties.

China's vocational training system has three components:

1. *Specialized secondary schools.* Nearly 3,000 specialized secondary schools train 1.2 million students with an emphasis on engineering, agronomy, forestry, health services, and finance.
2. *Workers' Training Schools.* These schools, which are under the jurisdiction of an industrial unit rather than the State Education Commission, provide part-time training to secondary students and include technical theory and production practice for numerous trades. Politics and physical education are also part of the curriculum.
3. *Vocational Schools.* These trade and agricultural schools enroll nearly three million students for a period of three to four years. The major specializations are agronomy, agricultural machinery, accounting, garment making, preschool education, textile skills, architecture, chemical industry, electricity and electronics, machine making, and benchwork.

Full-time vocational training instructors generally teach five fifty-five-minute classes per day, six days per week. They must also spend half a day per week in organized political activity. Each class has thirty to forty students (compared to the fifty to sixty in academic schools). The State Education Commission compiles the training materials. Instructors may supplement the state-provided materials, but they must first obtain approval from the school's Communist party secretary. The state assigns jobs to graduates based on the needs of the national economy and the skills of the trainees.

Because of the need for large numbers of vocational training instructors, the government has assigned many college graduates to be instructors and has set up training classes for them.

The limited resources force administrators and teachers to play many roles—typist, driver, custodian, delivery person. Supplies and modern equipment are at a premium. For example, computer programming is usually taught for the first several months without access to computers, and then students may have to travel to another school to share their three or four computers.

Like other developing nations, China needs large numbers of skilled technicians and service personnel as it enters the twenty-first century. And it is clear that China is depending heavily on its vocational educators to lead the effort to modernize the country's industry and service sector.

❦ *Singapore Institute of Education (Singapore)*

The Singapore Institute of Education, among other HRD activities, trains and develops school principals. After an extensive analysis of the most effective HRD methodologies which could be used to develop these educators/administrators, the institute chose mentoring. It has since established a highly successful Mentoring Model which includes four components as shown in Figure 15.1.

Preattachment Seminar. Prior to serving as mentors and protégés (mentees), the participating principals attend a preattachment seminar. The selection of principals who will attend is a well-planned and highly selective process. They must be people "who are efficient and effective, open-minded and secure with a strong commitment to the profession and a willingness to share" (Chong et al., p. 7).

The preattachment seminar runs for five mornings, four hours each morning. The seminar consists of simulations that are actually developed and facilitated by the mentors themselves. Through the simulations, the skills are practiced as they will be in the real world when the protégés are attached to the mentors. The seminar also covers such topics as the roles of principalship and skills transfer. It ends in a pairing-off session and the negotiation of key tasks the protégés would like to learn, see, or do during the practicum following the seminar. Eng, deputy director of the institute, calls this preliminary stage-setting phase "crucially important in setting in motion the beginnings of a relationship that can serve to ease the trainee-principal (protégé) into the school of the mentoring principal. It ensures that certain key tasks get done with the support of the mentor whose trust once gained can open up [key] cultural elements of the school" (Chong et al., p. 7).

FIGURE 15.1
Singapore Mentoring Model

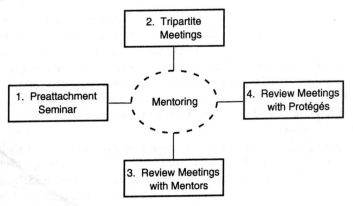

Tripartite Meetings. The eight-week practicum is divided into two four-week periods. At the beginning of each period, tripartite meetings are held among the mentor, the protégé, and the Institute of Education staff person to review the learning activities identified, the learning objectives of the activities, and the learning strategies. At the end of each period, the three people evaluate the gains made in mastering skills relevant to principalship and the extent of leadership behavior demonstrated by the protégé. These tripartite meetings include a candid evaluation to determine the protégé's development in six critical aspects:

- Relationship with people
- Communications
- Problem solving

- Decision making
- Self-confidence
- Supervision

Review Meetings with Mentors. All mentors meet periodically with the institute's staff who are coordinating the programs. Mentors are encouraged to share with each other innovative ways of helping the participants to learn, as well as difficulties they have encountered. Mentors work on clarifying roles and developing mentoring skills. The skills obtained from these review meetings are documented and then incorporated into a training manual for use by future mentors.

Review Meetings with Protégés. The protégés also meet regularly with institute staff throughout the eight-week practicum and are encouraged to share innovative learning, clarify standards of performance expected, and overcome learning difficulties.

🐝 *Cathay Pacific (Hong Kong)*

Cathay Pacific is recognized as one of the world's best airlines—one that combines efficient operations, sophisticated technology, and traditional Asian service. One of Asia's largest airlines, Cathay Pacific carries over eight million passengers a year to thirty-six destinations, including the Hong Kong to Los Angeles route, the largest scheduled nonstop service in the world. In 1990, the *Business Traveller* readers' poll voted it best airline.

The Staff Development and Training Center of Cathay Pacific offers a highly renowned leadership program for executives and managers. This sequential program is developed to help managers prepare for key transitional points in their career as they move toward competent management positions. There are three developmental stages as shown in Figure 15.2.

FIGURE 15.2
Cathay Pacific Leadership Program

Stage I—Entry-Level Programs. The "Welcome Aboard" program provides new executives with both an overview of the company and customer service training. The purpose of this program is to give executives an understanding of the company's goals and the role they will play in contributing to these goals.

Stage II—Performance-Management Skills for Managerial Staff. This course provides information and skills needed by senior managers to conduct appraisal reviews when assessing members of their staff of "E2" grade and above.

Stage III—Managing the Cathay Pacific Way Program. The focus here is on airlines commitment, management practices, work unit climate, team building, values clarification, and the application of diagnosis. It is composed of two modular residential workshops.

Cathay Pacific has established three Business Academies for the purpose of providing opportunities for "increased awareness and personal growth, and most importantly, a chance for managers to acquire the business acumen to lead Cathay Pacific into the twenty-first century."

The First-Level Academy is tailored for employees who have been with the company for more than five years and is offered in conjunction with the University of Hong Kong Business School. It includes action learning projects, the development of critical management tools, and examination of key business issues faced by Cathay Pacific.

The Second-Level Academy is a two-year program for executives and managers that results in a diploma in business studies. The objectives are to build a foundation for continuing self-education and development, provide graduate-level management training, and develop participant confidence in making strategic and tactical decisions.

The Third-Level Academy is made up of business degree programs in collaboration with appropriate universities.

Cathay Pacific's HRD department also offers customized training courses in the areas of customer focus, teamwork, communications, leading and motivating staff, decision making, commitment, contribution to innovation, and professional development programs. Among the professional development workshops are train the trainer, beyond classroom instruction, designing experimental learning skills, and facilitating skills.

SUMMARY

East Asia, home to nearly two billion people and to several major religious and cultural groups, consists of four primary subregions—(1) China, (2) Singapore, Hong Kong, Taiwan, and South Korea, (3) Indonesia, Malaysia, the Philippines, Thailand, and Brunei, and (4) Vietnam, Myanmar, Cambodia, and Laos—each with their own unique economic characteristics, levels of development, and HRD needs and capabilities.

There are many excellent HRD programs in East Asia. Hong Kong Bank is a world leader in the financial services field. Indonesia has developed a highly valued distance learning program utilizing satellite technology. China's vocational training program reaches an estimated five million trainees each year and employs over 400,000 vocational training teachers. The Singapore Institute of Education has developed a powerful mentoring program for school principals. Cathay Pacific's HRD programs have helped it achieve many best airline awards.

REFERENCES

BOTT, PAUL A. "Vocational Education in China." *Vocational Education Journal.* (April 1988), pp. 26–28.

CHONG, KENG CHOY et al. *Mentoring—A Singapore Contribution.* Singapore: SIE Press, 1989.

Piturro, Marlene C. "Hong Kong Bank Builds a Global Network and Braces for 1997." *Management Review* (Vol. 78, No. 9), pp. 40–43.

SHAW, WILLARD D. *Distance Education.* Washington, D.C.: AED Press, 1987.

CHAPTER 16

❦ ❦

Japan

INTRODUCTION

Knowledge power is something Japan understands. The knowledge-density of its work force has been skyrocketing.

Alvin Toffler
Powershift

Japan has quickly become the second largest economic power in the world. As a result, Japanese business practices—group consensus, long-term planning, quality orientation, organizational learning—are all seen as essential in the emerging global economy. In this chapter, we will examine the unique elements of Japanese corporate culture and how HRD is practiced in the Japanese workplace.

❦ *Learning Objectives*

After studying this chapter, you should be able to:

1. Understand how the geography, demographics, languages, history, religions, and key cultural beliefs of Japan and the Japanese affect HRD activities
2. Outline the economic environment in Japan and relate it to the practice of HRD

3. Identify the key cultural constructs that have an impact on HRD in Japan and describe the principal training strategies that are employed in Japanese business
4. Provide examples of HRD programs in the corporate and education sectors

CULTURAL FACTORS IMPACTING HRD

❦ *Geography and Demographics*

Japan is made up of more than 3,000 islands extending some 1,300 miles northeast to southwest in eastern Asia between the Pacific Ocean and the Sea of Japan. Four large islands, Honshu, Hokkaido, Shikoku, and Kyushu, account for 98 percent of the land area and are home to virtually all of the population.

By the year 1700, Edo (now Tokyo) was already the largest city in the world; today, it is home to an estimated eight million people. Although Japan's total area is comparable to that of California, its 125 million residents are concentrated in an area about the size of Indiana. Overall, 80 percent of the population lives in urban areas with most of the rest living on the scant 11 percent of the land that is arable.

The people are 99.4 percent Japanese with a small number of Koreans and Chinese comprising almost all of the remainder. The native Ainu, thought to be descendants of the Caucasoid people who once lived in north Asia, live mainly on the northern island of Hokkaido.

❦ *Language*

Japanese is the official language, but its remoteness from other world languages, the complexity of its written form, and the fact that there are relatively few speakers of Japanese as a second language have combined to make it a domestic rather than an international language. English is universally taught in the public schools and is seen as a basic requirement at the university level. Although the many spoken dialects of Japanese are more or less mutually intelligible, the Tokyo dialect is, not surprisingly, the standard for textbooks and media. The written language, initially borrowed from the Chinese and augmented by two native phonetic alphabets and a third based on Roman letters, has been standardized and is accessible to the 99 percent of the population that is literate.

❦ *History and Religion*

Modern Japanese culture has its roots in migrations from Northeast Asia beginning in the fourth century B.C. Evidence of the earlier Jomon civilization can still be seen in the traditional beliefs, rituals, and customs known under its Chinese name, Shinto. A religion without a recognized founder or basic scriptures, Shinto, with its emphasis on honor, courage, politeness, and reserve, has been an important influence in the development of Japanese social values. By the tenth century, Japanese culture had also woven in the threads of Buddhism, with its emphasis on harmony, flexibility, adaptation, and compromise, as well as of Confucianism, with its virtues of frugality, hard work, and respect for elders. More recently, the simplicity and austerity so valued in Zen philosophy have been adapted to the Japanese culture.

Historically, geographically, and culturally, Japan has been first and foremost an island, but it was never more so than during the period from the beginning of the seventeenth through the mid-nineteenth centuries. For 250 years, Japan's rulers effectively isolated the country from all but a handful of Dutch traders, who were limited to a small trading station in Nagasaki, and occasional visitors from mainland Asia. Japan's forced emergence from this self-imposed isolation began in 1854, when Commodore Matthew Perry sailed his "black ships" into lower Tokyo Bay and successfully pressured the Japanese into establishing commercial and diplomatic relations with the United States. The next century saw Japan's rise as an industrial, commercial, military, and, finally, imperial power; and since its utter military defeat in 1945, Japan has risen from the ashes of war to become one of the major players in global business and economics.

❦ *Family*

The family, and by extension the company, community, and nation, is the foundation of Japanese society. The Japanese are bound together by a strong sense of obligation to, and responsibility for, the group. Historically, their identity, their honor, and in some ways their survival has depended upon membership in, and protection by, the groups that define them. The Western notions of independence, self-determination, and individualism are alien and largely misunderstood by the Japanese, who have historically seen family, class, village, and ethnic identity as both determining their fate in life and assuring their livelihood. In return for lifelong loyalty and obedience to the group, the individual expects and receives protection against the forces that would otherwise certainly overwhelm him.

This role as a benevolent protector, historically assumed by family and village elders and, by extension, the emperor or shogun, is largely taken on today by the company. Since employees usually stay with a single company for life, there is a mutual commitment between employer and employee that is seldom present in the West. Length of tenure is often valued over specific contribution. Employees are neither hired nor fired on the basis of their ability to aggressively produce short-term results; in fact, laying off an employee is seen as a disgrace for all parties concerned. Accordingly, Japanese management practices tend to focus on process improvement and long-term human resource development rather than on short-term numbers and results.

❧ Lack of Privacy

The practice of individual subordination to group needs taken together with the extreme population density has resulted in an absence of individual privacy. The Japanese, in effect, have learned to live as if those around them are not there. Paper walls are somehow soundproof, and close neighbors focus on their miniature gardens and overlook the proximity of their houses. In business, the "open" office, so much disliked by Americans, is a natural extension of this ability to ignore one's surroundings.

❧ Consensus and Organizational Design

In a society that anticipates long and close relationships, both planning and conflict resolution are best accomplished through consensus gathering. If people are going to stay together for the duration, and if they are going to do so in close proximity, it would make sense for them to gather consensus on the conditions under which they will do so.

The organizational structure of modern Japanese companies can easily be seen as a reflection of the historical structure between the great feudal landholders of Japan (the Daimyo) and their advisers, samurai, and other vassals. Such companies have relatively flat organizational structures compared to their Western counterparts but, more importantly, are organized into groups or clusters of individuals rather than along the more familiar Western management lines. Each group, in turn, has a leader, who is responsible for communicating on behalf of the group to other peer groups and to the leaders of groups above and below.

The result is that, while strategic planning and policy making certainly take into consideration the wishes and desires of upper management, in a very real way, decisions evolve and are influenced from the bottom up. Ideally, they are then articulated and implemented with resources provided from the top down. Cooperation, flexibility, and polite acquiescence to the will of the group are necessary enabling requirements for this process. No is hardly ever an acceptable response to a request from a superior or group, and when unavoidable, it comes in the form of an apparent yes.

❦ *Communication Styles*

Japanese communication styles tend to be implicit, nonverbal, and, therefore, highly contextual. The language, itself, encourages vagueness and ambiguity; it is for this reason that Japanese haiku poetry most often fails in English and other Western languages when the translator is reduced to rendering a single reading from the many contained within the characters of the original text. Communication is further affected by the Japanese reluctance to be too direct or blunt. Movement in a conversation often takes the form of a slow spiraling toward the main idea or conclusion. This strategy, of course, works well with the process of consensus gathering; it is likely that the will of the group will be developed and understood through indirect reference long before it is stated for all to hear.

ECONOMIC ENVIRONMENT FOR HRD

During the past half-century, Japan has risen from destruction to become an economic global giant. With modest beginnings in the late forties, Japan quickly began shifting its industrial base. It centered on the textile industries in the late fifties, on steel and shipbuilding in the sixties and began moving toward automobiles, electronics, and cameras in the seventies. The eighties and early nineties have seen Japanese industry diversify to other high-technology industries such as semiconductors, computers, and robotics. Japan now has global dominance in video cassette recorders (95 percent), copiers (85 percent), and facsimile machines (70 percent).

Japan is a leader in spending on Research and Development (R&D), and the percentage of GNP devoted to R&D is targeted to reach 3.5 percent by 1995. For many companies, such as Hitachi, Honda, and Matsushita Electronic, R&D expenditures are now greater than capital spending on plant and equipment.

Japan's status in today's world is impressive. Some examples of Japan's economic influence include the following:

- Japanese banks control over 40 percent of the world's financial assets; seven of the eight largest banks in terms of assets are Japanese.
- Over 300 of the largest global 1,000 corporations are Japanese.
- The Japanese automotive industry has grown from 1.8 percent of the world market in 1953 to over 25 percent by 1992.
- Japanese trade surplus exceeds an embarrassing $50 billion per year.

The economic interaction between Japan and the United States continues to flourish. Over 750 manufacturing plants in the United States are owned or partially owned by Japanese and employ over 200,000 Americans. By the year 2000, it is estimated that 840,000 Americans will be working for Japanese companies (Fucini and Fucini).

The U.S. economic role in Japan also continues to grow. U.S. companies now create and sell in Japan nearly $100 billion in goods and services annually. In 1990, there were 126 joint ventures between American and Japanese companies in the auto industry alone. One U.S. company, Texas Instruments, now employs over 5,000 people in its Japanese plants.

HRD IN BUSINESS AND INDUSTRY

Lindberg, in her comprehensive study on training and development in Japan, suggests that the development of human resources is seen as "crucial to the nation's survival" (p. 113). Training has been and continues to be necessary to ensure that the small country, devoid of natural resources, can industrialize rapidly and compete with other nations around the world. Given this challenge, Japan recognizes its people as its greatest resource.

In order to understand Japanese HRD activities and the impact of these activities on Japanese business and industry, it is important to understand how Japanese culture has shaped HRD assumptions and practices, for it is these cultural constructs that prescribe "who gets the training, who does the training, what the content of training is, how long it lasts, where it occurs and why it occurs at all" (Lindberg, p. 113).)

Lindberg identifies eleven cultural constructs that have shaped HRD in Japan:

1. *Philosophy of Egalitarianism.* Japanese companies strongly believe in the value of their employees. Employees across a wide spectrum of social and economic stratum are given the opportunity to advance their positions. Japanese organizations practice a more egalitarian distribution of resources throughout the organization than do organizations in Western countries. Participatory management fits with the Japanese *ringi* system, a form of consensus building and problem solving based on the circulation of data and group decision-making processes (Ishida). This sense of participation is strong even at the lower levels in the organization.

2. *Groupism.* One of the most noticeable characteristics of the Japanese is their strong sense of group identity, group loyalty, and the belief that the whole is more than the sum of the parts. This belief creates a level of interdependency in the workplace where group ties among employees become so strong that there is a collective sense of responsibility for one another's actions. This groupism causes Japanese to center on how work is divided among groups, in contrast to

the United States where jobs generally embody individual discrete tasks and responsibilities. In this ambiguous, interdependent division of labor, employees need to be able to change roles and assignments as circumstances change in the group.

3. *Relationships.* The relationships among employees, like all human relations in Japan, are both highly personal and formal. The role of the older, senior-ranking employee toward a junior employee is similar to that of a father who would guide and assist his son in the organization by providing him with protection, securing favorable assignments, and advising him on problems and difficult circumstances.

4. *Leadership.* Whereas in the West leaders are "individual stars," in Japan they are "group-minded team players." Group harmony comes before competition. "Japanese followers are relatively docile, but the leader must be skillfully unassertive" (Hayashi, p. 117). The leadership style includes warmth, sociability, and concern for the employee.

5. *Long-Term Orientation.* Japanese managers have a more long-term perspective, ten to twenty years in the future, than American managers. Rewards are given for long-term accomplishments—market share and growth—rather than for short-term profits.

6. *Generalist Orientation in Education.* The Japanese education system is broad based and general and emphasizes theoretical and unspecialized studies. It inspires a lifelong interest in learning and provides a "high learning readiness" for Japanese organizations (Lindberg, p. 105).

7. *Generalist Orientation in Business and Industry.* Japanese employers have historically paid little attention to prospective or new employees' educational background for several reasons:
   • They are most concerned with their personality, dedication, general ability, and openness to new knowledge.
   • School-acquired knowledge will soon be obsolete with the speed of technological change.
   • The corporation will be able to teach the new employees everything they need to know.
   • People are being hired not just for specific positions for this year but for the company for the remainder of their lives.

8. *Government Policy.* In Japan, the government has been minimally involved in HRD. Historically, the Japanese school system did not prepare students for the industrial economy. As a result, Japanese businesses were required to develop an internal labor training system. Since the private sector had done such a splendid job in training workers, there was little incentive for the government to develop public vocational training institutes.

9. *Hierarchy within a Duel Economy.* There are two distinct groups of organizations in Japan: (1) the large industries that pay better wages and benefits, offer lifetime employment, provide substantial training, and offer employees personal status; and (2) the small and medium-sized organizations (e.g., suppliers, vendors, satellite firms) that cannot guarantee lifetime employment, provide fewer or no chances for training, and are likely to employ women, part-time laborers, and males in job transition.

10. *Lifetime Employment System.* Although only about 25 percent of the work force is protected by the guarantee of lifelong employment, it does represent "a national ideal, the fullest expression of the company as family" (Smith, p. 28). This system has served as a major foundation for continuous training for employees in Japan's major enterprises since the early 1900s. The employers' commitment to ongoing training results in the following:
    - High versatility and adaptability of workers
    - Employment dependent on length of service rather than on current value
    - Upper-level managers and technicians who, knowing they will not be replaced until retirement, are more willing to train and develop their subordinates
    - Virtually no turnover

11. *Internal Labor Market.* The final Japanese construct within Japanese culture impacting HRD is the internal labor market, which includes all hiring being done at entry-level positions, skill hierarchies, internal promotion, continuous training, and lifelong development of careers.

These eleven constructs within Japanese culture have created a "unique environment for learning" in Japan which is intricately woven into Japan's approach to human resource development (Lindberg, p. 108). They affect the HRD environment in the following ways:

- *Broad Scope of Training.* Training in Japan tends to be more general and broad in nature, unlike training in Western organizations, which stresses expertise in specialized areas. In Japan, the primary goal of HRD is to develop a flexible, multiskilled work force capable of adapting to technological change at any time.

- *Company-Specific Training.* The skills and knowledge learned by Japanese employees are company specific. HRD objectives focus on employees (1) gaining a thorough knowledge of the organization, (2) having their behaviors, attitudes, and values shaped to those desired by the organization, and (3) acquiring and developing skills which the organization needs.

- *On-the-Job Training.* The major component of all Japanese HRD programs is on-the-job training.

- *Employee as Trainer.* Every staff person, especially supervisors and managers, is considered a trainer in Japanese organizations.

- *Long-Term Development.* Just as the Japanese organizations have long-term business perspectives, so do they maintain a long-term perspective relative to the training and development of their employees. Employers expect that skills, knowledge, and abilities will steadily accumulate over the years.

- *Self-Development and Volunteerism.* Japanese employees are encouraged to volunteer to participate in group activities such as quality circles in order to learn about quality control. Employees develop programs for self-learning in nonjob-related subjects such as history, English conversation, cooking, and flower arrangement. Besides receiving training within the company, employees are encouraged to seek self-development programs outside of work. Recent studies reveal that, in some companies, up to 70 percent of the employees pursue self-development through correspondence courses, in-house study groups, and television and radio courses.

- *Performance-Based Training.* In contrast to the West where the focus is often on the future skills needed for a promotion, HRD in Japan is focused on improving present performance. The reason for the Japanese approach is the fixed, hierarchical progression in an organization based on years of employment. Since promotions are routinely made by seniority, employees can concentrate on improving their performance within their present positions with little concern about future promotion.

- *Human Relations–Based Training.* Japanese employers value human relations skills as much or more than talent and technical skills. HRD programs therefore encourage the development of the total person.

Japanese culture impacts HRD learning activities for (1) new employee orientation, (2) training of blue-collar workers, and (3) training of white-collar workers.

1. *New Employee Orientation.* According to Weber, Japan provides the most complete orientation of any country for new employees. This is due to the internal labor market cultural construct mentioned earlier in which companies hire unskilled, inexperienced young recruits for entry-level positions.

   The orientation program may last for weeks or even months with a thorough indoctrination into the culture of the organization, including history, policies, practices, and management philosophy. The orientation discusses how to be "cooperative, committed, and loyal to the employer" (Lindberg, p. 110). The orientation program may also include theoretical and practical course work in the professional area of the employee and the employee's industry.

2. *Training of Blue-Collar Workers.* After orientation, the formal, technical training of the employee begins. This may be accomplished through on-the-job training and/or attending the company's vocational training center. The vocational training center, which is of very high quality, trains the new employees in basic industrial skills and prepares them to take national trade skill tests.

3. *Training of White-Collar Workers.* Since they enter the corporation with little experience and a lack of specific job descriptions, the white-collar workers spend their first years in an apprentice-type capacity. The jobs for the new white-collar workers are relatively easy and are assigned not so much on a match of skills but rather on the worker's personality and relationship to the peer group. The trainee's supervisor serves as a tutor in a wise elder–junior learner type of relationship.

The primary manner in which training is provided and information is shared is through the process of consensus building and after-hours socializing. Learning by osmosis is just as important as specific training for a specific job.

A major technique used in HRD for Japanese managers is job rotation in which a person is rotated through a variety of positions, functions, and departments in the corporation. Overseas experience is considered important for those working in global organizations. The job rotation provides the prospective manager with a general overview of the organization.

The OJT process of job rotation also provides the employee with the opportunity to practice different technical and managerial skills, as well as to experience the joys and difficulties of the business. Also, by temporarily serving in some of the subordinate positions in the corporation (e.g., making beds for a hotel company), they will have a greater sensitivity to the feelings and experiences of these employees later on when they are managers.

The final benefit of job rotation as a training technique for Japanese companies is that it helps to create more homogeneity and conformity among the workers in the company, which would be more difficult to develop if managers and technical staff did not understand the activities and operations of the entire company. Also, by rotating staff throughout the organization, communication processes and consensus building is improved.

Larger Japanese firms also send their white-collar workers to external HRD training programs. In increasing numbers, these companies are sending top managerial candidates to the United States for advanced degree programs, as well as the development of contacts for future business opportunities.

HRD Programs in Japan

❦ *Hitachi*

Hitachi is a global corporate giant with annual sales of over $50 billion. It is one of the world's largest manufacturers of electrical equipment, producing as many as 20,000 different products and systems ranging from nuclear power to microelectronics. By character and tradition, Hitachi considers the training and development of its employees (now numbering over 300,000) as "one of its most important business commitments." The company's strong commitment "to respect, develop and make the most of each individual is the basis of employee education and that business progress and growth cannot be realized without such a philosophy" (Tanaka, p. 12). Hitachi's principles of education include employees learning the "Hitachi spirit," and having "good sense, noble character, high creativity and a strong sense of responsibility and performance capability." As can be seen by these principles, training, for the Hitachi professional, is seen as a means of cultivating the personality of each person.

This long-standing commitment to the training and development of its employees is reflected in the establishment of the Hitachi Training Center of Apprentices in 1910, the year the Hitachi company itself was incorporated. In that year, the training center began a five-year program for training technicians and skilled workers who were to assume key positions in the manufacturing work force.

The most important of a Hitachi manager's various responsibilities, according to Tanaka, is to "educate, lead and develop subordinates" (p. 17). The manager is to be a mentor in a teacher-student relationship.

In addition to the Hitachi Institute of Management Development, which trains over 5,000 managers annually, Hitachi also has an Institute of Technology, technical colleges, and an Institute of Supervisory and Technical Training.

A unique element of the Hitachi Training Program is seen in the cultural courses, which are designed to give employees self-motivation and to help them live and work better. Topics include:

- *Haiku.* A short poem of Japanese literature, comprising three stanzas of five, seven, and five syllables, depicting various seasonal phenomena that happen in nature and to people. This course is designed to help trainees appreciate nature better, express themselves in pure and concise literary form, and experience a world existing away from day-to-day business. Trainees actually write *haiku* poems, which instructors may correct, and then the most refined examples are left in the meeting room as a record of the writers' participation.
- *Chado.* The tea ceremony of Japan cultivates the mind and teaches rules of decorum in presenting a guest with a cup of *matcha* green tea. To live simply and quietly is said to be the ceremony's essence. Trainees actually practice the tea ceremony in a *chashitsu* (tea house) located in a wooded area at the institute.
- *Book Briefing.* This is a session wherein trainees give a briefing on books they have read. By doing so, they can also learn about others' interests, discuss up-to-date themes and various issues. This briefing also provides an opportunity for developing presentation skills.

❦ *SANNO Institute of Management*

Founded in 1950, SANNO Institute of Management is one of the largest HRD organizations in Japan, training over 500,000 Japanese company employees annually. In addition to a graduate business school and college, SANNO has a General Management and Research Center which provides public training seminars, consulting services, in-house training, and correspondence courses to over 20,000 organizations from Japan and around the world. To better respond to the needs of Japanese business and public service organizations, SANNO conducts extensive research in the areas of management, business, finance, marketing, sales, interpersonal skills, personnel development, information processing, and computer applications.

SANNO also regularly sponsors a number of national and regional management conventions and trade fairs. The Computer Applications and

Communications Show in Tokyo is attended by over 300,000 people each year.

In 1990, SANNO helped establish the Japanese Society for Training and Development (JSTD). In addition to an annual conference, JSTD, with SANNO support, has a monthly forum and publishes the JSTD *Journal,* supports international exchanges with the International Federation of Training and Development Organizations (IFTDO) and various national training associations, and carries out research and study programs.

SANNO also coordinates a Euro-Japan cooperative program involving business education in topics such as creativity and group dynamics, HRD administration, production and manufacturing management, executive development, and computer application.

The International Projects Division of SANNO manages the international services—consultations, seminars, research and international exchange programs—that the company offers to Japanese and foreign companies and governmental organizations. Four programs of particular HRD interest are:

1. *International Seminar on Japanese Business and Management.* This is a five-week summer program for overseas business students which provides a behind-the-scenes look at contemporary Japanese business. The seminar includes lectures by academicians, business and government leaders, tours of top Japanese corporations, and visits to major cultural and historical centers in Japan.

2. *Executive Development Program.* The one-month Executive Development Program is designed for foreign managers of global subsidiaries in Japan and includes business simulations, case studies, and company visits. Its primary purpose is to provide participants with a better understanding of the Japanese style of management and corporate disciplines as well as a mastery of the tools to do business successfully in Japan.

3. *Lecture Series.* SANNO conducts an extensive series of lectures and seminars—in both English and Japanese—designed to prepare companies for the global marketplace.

4. *Study Tours.* Every year SANNO organizes and sponsors study tours for Japanese business personnel to visit countries around the world. Recently, they arranged for sixty NEC managers to visit telecommunications companies in Canada and the United States.

❦ *Toyota*

Toyota, Japan's largest industrial corporation, employs 100,000 people and has annual sales of over $70 billion. By 1993, Toyota could pass Ford and trail only GM among the world's largest automakers. A key reason for Toyota's steady and rapid growth has been its commitment to high-quality training.

College graduates embarking on a Toyota career begin with a nine-month training program. During this time, they spend four weeks working in a factory and three months selling cars. They get lectures from top management and instruction in problem solving. Their supervisors make them keep rewriting solutions until they produce one that is suitable.

Employees are trained to work with less supervision, accept more responsibility, and move projects along more quickly. Instead of getting up to ten approvals on a new program, in many cases they now need only three. Decision making by consensus and teamwork, however, remain important.

Like most Japanese companies, Toyota uses the godfather system of training managers, called the Advisory System. Managerial candidates who are entering Toyota are assigned to group leaders who are two ranks above them. These group leaders are responsible for the training of these new managers for the rest of their careers. Training revolves around actual work situations and problems on the job. Approximately 500 Toyota employees are officially appointed as advisers (DeMente).

Toyota also conducts ongoing training seminars for its managers. In-house executives as well as outside management specialists serve as trainers. The president and chairman regularly participate as speakers at these training programs.

In addition, Toyota teaches foreign languages and provides courses on international issues for these managers. They learn the Toyota management style and how to transfer their technology competencies to their subordinates.

Administrative and technical personnel are rotated every three to five years. This constant rotation and new on-the-job training is aimed at "enhancing the individual development of employees and continuously reenergizing the workplace" (DeMente, p. 29).

A primary objective of Toyota's collective HRD programs is to ensure employees' familiarity with company policies and understanding of performance expectations and responsibilities. Another important aim is to assist employees in developing new skills and learning new technologies. Toyota differs from most other Japanese firms insofar as it allows employees who had been recruited as factory workers to be promoted to white-collar management positions.

SUMMARY

Japan has quickly emerged as an economic superpower, and the cultural factors supporting high quality HRD are important reasons for this success.

According to Lindberg, the cultural constructs positively affect HRD in the following ways—broad scope of training, company-specific training, OJT, employee as trainer, long-term development, self-development and volunteerism, performance-based training, and human relations–based training.

Three globally acclaimed HRD programs were identified and discussed. Hitachi's long history as a leader in HRD in Japan includes its Institute of Management Development and Institute of Technology. Holistic human development programs include training in poetry, tea ceremony, and book reading. SANNO Institute of Management, which trains over 500,000 people annually, helped establish the Japanese Society for Training and Development. Toyota, rapidly becoming the world's largest automaker, successfully uses an extensive advisory system in training its staff.

REFERENCES

DeMente, Boye. *How to Do Business in Japan*. Lincolnwood, Ill: NTC Publishing, 1990.

Hayashi, S. *Culture and Management in Japan*. Tokyo: University of Tokyo Press, 1988.

Ishida H. "Transferability of Japanese Human Resource Management Abroad," *Human Resource Management* (Vol. 25, No. 1), pp. 102–120.

Frank, Eric. "HRD in Japan." *Journal of European Industrial Training* (March, May 1988), pp. 42–49.

Fucini, Joseph J., and Suzy Fucini. *Working for the Japanese*. New York: Free Press, 1990.

Gordon, Meryl. "Japanese Lessons." *Working Women* (March 1992),. pp. 72–74.

Lindberg, Karen. "The Intricacies of Training and Development in Japan." *Human Resource Development Quarterly* (Summer 1991), pp. 101–14.

Smith, L. "Divisive Forces in an Inbred Nation," *Fortune* (March 1987), pp. 24–28.

Tanaka, Toyoshige. "Developing Managers in the Hitachi Institute of Management Development." *Journal of Management Development* (Vol. 8, No. 4), pp. 12–21.

Taylor, Alex. "Why Toyota Keeps Getting Better and Better and Better." *Fortune* (November 19, 1990), pp. 66–77.

Toffler, Alvin. *Powershift*. New York: Bantam Books, 1990.

Weber, D. E. "An Eye to the East: Training in Japan," *Training and Development Journal* (October 1984), pp. 32–33.

CHAPTER 17

South Pacific Region

INTRODUCTION

Remember, just as we trainers in the South Pacific start the day earlier than you in the rest of the world (because of proximity to international dateline), so are we willing to be the first to start trying out new HRD ideas and strategies.

New Zealand HRD Professional

HRD in the South Pacific is rich in innovation and economic impact. The national training and development societies of Australia and New Zealand have been among the most dynamic in the world, and their members have implemented highly successful HRD programs in the surrounding island-nations of Papua New Guinea, Fiji, Tuvalu, and Tonga. In this chapter, we will explore the interesting array of cultures and HRD programs of the South Pacific.

❦ Learning Objectives

After studying this chapter, you should be able to:

1. Understand how the geography, demographics, languages, religions, history, and key cultural beliefs of the South Pacific region affect HRD activities

2. Describe the economic environment in the region and relate it to the practice of HRD
3. Outline the evolving role of HRD in the region
4. Provide examples of HRD programs in the corporate and public sectors

CULTURAL FACTORS IMPACTING HRD

❦ *Geography and Demographics*

The South Pacific region includes the smallest continent, Australia, and the large islands of New Zealand and Papua New Guinea, as well as Oceania, consisting of some 25,000 islands scattered across the South Pacific and usually divided into three major groups: Melanesia, Micronesia, and Polynesia. Except for New Zealand and the southern part of Australia, the entire region lies well within the tropics and enjoys continuous warm temperatures.

It is home to an estimated twenty-seven million people, more than twenty million of whom live in Australia and New Zealand. The vast majority in these two countries is Caucasian, most of Anglo-Celtic descent. As a result of recent immigration, Australia has growing populations from many European and Asian countries, as well as some from Latin America. The Asian population has grown from 1 to 4 percent since 1975. The original inhabitants make up 1 percent of the current population of Australia and 9 percent of New Zealand. Papua New Guinea has two major population groups, Papuans (84 percent) and Melanesians (15 percent). Approximately 70 percent of Oceania's 1.2 million people are Melanesian, Micronesian, and Polynesian peoples native to the islands, 20 percent are of Asian origin, and 7 percent have European ancestry. In some cases, such as that of Fiji, there is a large population descended from Asian Indians brought as laborers during the British colonial period.

❦ *Language*

With more than 700 distinct languages, Papua New Guinea is one of the most complicated linguistic areas in the world. Pidgin English and Motu are the most widely spoken languages and are used for trade throughout the country. The number of native Australian languages is thought to be more than 500, with more than fifty of them broadcast regularly on the radio. There are an estimated 500 Eastern Malayo-Polynesian spoken in Oceania. Hindi is widely spoken in Fiji as a result of earlier migration from India.

English is the official language of Australia and (with Maori) New Zealand and is used as a lingua franca throughout the region.

❦ Religion

Christianity is professed by the vast majority of the people, with Catholicism and Protestantism both well represented in Australia, New Guinea, New Zealand, Fiji, and many smaller island groups. An estimated 50 percent of those living in Oceania practice indigenous religions. Newer immigrants, especially in Australia, include substantial numbers of Buddhists, Hindus, and Moslems.

❦ History

Little is known of the early history of the South Pacific region. Early migrations from the Asian continent are reflected in some of the languages of the region, but many others are of unknown origin. The islands we now call Fiji were apparently settled more than 3,500 years ago by people now known as the Lapita and thought to be of Asian origin. Maori migrations from Polynesian islands to New Zealand probably began around 900 A.D. and continued to increase until the historical "great migration" of the thirteenth and fourteenth centuries. Except for Antarctica, Australia was probably the last continent to be inhabited by man, certainly the last to be explored and settled by Europeans. An estimated 300,000 aborigines distributed among some 500 tribes lived in Australia when the Europeans arrived.

The Dutch thoroughly explored the South Pacific region in the early seventeenth century but never returned to colonize the lands they found. In 1769 and 1770, Capt. James Cook visited New Zealand and then took formal possession of the eastern coast of Australia for Britain. The British established penal colonies in 1788 in what have become Sydney, Hobart, and Brisbane. Free settlements were established in Melbourne, Adelaide, and Perth, and with the discovery of gold in 1851, the number of free immigrants to Australia increased considerably. In 1840, the Maoris ceded sovereignty to the British in return for legal protection and rights to perpetual ownership of Maori lands. The six colonies of Australia became a member of the British Commonwealth in 1901 with New Zealand following in 1907. Papua New Guinea was governed under various British, Australian, and U.N. territorial and trust arrangements until its independence in 1975. The king of Fiji voluntarily ceded the islands to Britain in 1874; Fiji gained its independence in 1970. A military coup in 1987 resulted in Fiji withdrawing from the commonwealth.

❦ *Cultural Characteristics*

The peoples of the South Pacific region are friendly, outgoing, and hospitable. The pace of life, even in those urban areas that are not tropical, is slower than that of most of the industrialized world. Leisure activities and family events play an important part not only in life but also in everyday conversation.

❦ *Family and Leisure*

Families continue to play a more central role in the non-European communities where extended families are common, women are usually at home, and the family unit is likely to be male dominated. In these communities, three or four generations may live together in one house, and extended family connections are important in both work and leisure activities.

Australians and New Zealanders are avid sports enthusiasts and enjoy rugby, field hockey, cricket, sailing, and football. Weekends spent on the beach or excursions to the "outback" are common.

ECONOMIC ENVIRONMENT FOR HRD

This expansive area of the South Pacific has a high GNP, vast mineral resources, and diverse topographical terrains. Ten of the largest 500 industrial corporations are located in Australia and New Zealand, as well as two of the most active HRD associations—Australian Institute for Training and Development and the New Zealand Society for Training and Development.

Australia is the world's fourteenth largest trading nation, and export earnings are approximately 14 percent of the gross domestic products. It is also the twelfth largest market for U.S. exports. Australia's market reflects the demands of an urban population with tastes and life styles similar to those of the United States. The country's growing economy is diversified, with strong mining, agricultural, manufacturing, transport, financial, and service sectors.

HISTORY OF HRD IN THE SOUTH PACIFIC

The role of HRD has changed drastically during the past twenty-five years as the South Pacific region has entered the global marketplace as part of the Pacific Rim. According to Frank, the status of HRD professionals in Australia, prior to 1970, was not high. Trainers lacked any professional association, and employers "saw their incumbency as a short interlude" while they looked for a better position. It was even considered "fatal" to remain too long in the HRD role (p. 50).

It was the National Conference on Training, convened by the government in Canberra in 1971, that focused widespread attention within Australia on the country's poor performance relative to other industrialized countries in the providing of HRD programs for the work force. The 300 leaders from corporate and government organizations recognized the "critical links between training and productivity performance" (p. 51). The Australian National Training Council was formed with the purpose of improving the quality of training in Australia. (Similar training councils were later established in New Zealand, Papua New Guinea, and Fiji.)

Today Australian and New Zealand HRD professionals not only are highly respected in their own countries but have served in major leadership roles in the International Federation of Training and Development Organizations (see Chapter 8). Also, two global conferences of the federation have been held in Australia (1976 and 1984). Finally, the importance of HRD in promoting self-reliance and improved living standards in developing nations is fully recognized by the Australian International Development Assistance Bureau which recently stated:

> The lack of suitable qualified human resources is recognized as a significant obstacle to economic and social progress in most developing countries. Training and education is the main way in which aid donors can contribute to enhance human resources in these countries, and such aid is therefore seen as a priority form of assistance (Frank, p. 52).

HRD PROGRAMS IN THE SOUTH PACIFIC

❦ *Broken Hill Proprietary Company Limited (Australia)*

BHP, Broken Hill Proprietary Company Limited, is Australia's largest corporation with sales of over $12 billion per year and more than 50,000 employees throughout the world. Operations include oil and gas exploration, production and refining, mining and mineral processing, steel making, manufacturing, and worldwide trade in these and other products. More than 50 percent of their business is to customers outside Australia.

BHP prides itself on the company's managerial and technical excellence, both in the field and at all levels of planning, development, and operations, which include over 1,000 geoscientists and engineers. Computer technology is well utilized with nearly 1,200 information systems staff covering the whole range of computer-based applications, including commercial, technical process control, mining, planning, and exploration activities.

To develop its managers in the rapidly globalized enterprise, BHP offers three management courses:

1. *BHP Organization and Management Theory.* This is a one-week residential course for managers who are in their first supervisory position. The focus is to introduce BHP's global business culture and management expectations.
2. *Management Development.* The objective of this program is to improve the managers' competencies and effectiveness. Topics include Managing Yourself, Managing the Company's Resources, and Managing Competitive Strategy. This course is conducted in collaboration with the Australian Management College and includes outside experts and college instructors as well as BHP executives. The participants are purposely drawn from all the business units of BHP to allow for cross-fertilization of ideas and the building of networks.
3. *Advanced Management Program.* Designed for selected senior managers, this program emphasizes global strategic management skills.

The HRD staff also builds the concept of continuous learning into the job so that employees see that their challenging jobs provide opportunity for valuable, practical learning.

❦ Westpac Group (Australia)

The Westpac Group is a financial services group headquartered in Sydney with nearly 50,000 employees. Spending on training is approximately 8 percent of the total payroll.

Its renewed emphasis on training began in 1987 when a comprehensive review was made of the effectiveness of Westpac's training efforts. It was discovered that there was a wide disparity of quality in design and delivery as well as inefficiencies where training was done for training's sake or areas where very little training was done at all. Although there was an efficient staff of professional trainers, the managers tended to abrogate their responsibilities for identifying training needs and acquire training solutions by simply regarding these matters as functions that the training people should address.

Based upon these discoveries, Westpac decided to create a separate business entity, called Westpac Training Pty, Limited, which would manage the provision of training services to the Westpac Group as a business in itself.

Westpac Training quickly developed a system for identifying training needs and determining training strategies for all the business units of the Westpac Group. They required that the training strategies be linked to overall human resource strategies, which in turn were linked to corporate business objectives. Each business unit now sets the training budget it feels is necessary to support its staff development.

By serving in a facilitative role in determining training needs and strategies, Westpac Training gets involved at the early stages as each unit examines training solutions. This enables coordination throughout Westpac and brings efficiencies such as the elimination of duplication of development or acquisition of similar training products by different areas. Westpac is also able to optimize the use of its excellent training people.

Westpac Training has to be serious about marketing itself to the various units of the company and raising awareness of the value of investing in the cost-effective training of the Internal Training Business Unit relative to outside training providers. Westpac Training is involved in the evolution of training strategies, and because of the natural synergies which arise through the use of an in-house provider, it is generally the preferred provider. Westpac Training also evaluates the effectiveness of training within the organization, which includes pretesting of the trainees as well as subsequent follow-up back in the workplace to determine if behavioral change and performance improvement have taken place.

The latest thrust of Westpac Training has been the establishment of the Westpac Manager Training Institute, which provides structured training in various management skills at key stages of employees' careers. Customer service and technology training have become key training programs of the institute.

❦ *Vocational Training and Apprenticeship (New Zealand*

Vocational training in New Zealand, until recently, was based on a British model that evolved through the craft guilds and was modified during the industrial revolution. Jointly controlled by unions and employers, this traditional system may have served New Zealand well in the past but was not sufficiently responsive to the fast-changing needs of industry caught up in the information age.

In the early eighties, legislation was introduced which provided for young people to be apprenticed to groups of firms or to industry as a whole and not just to individual employers. The new legislation promoted the concept of competency-based training both off and on the job, provided for improved training opportunities for women and adults, and encouraged the development of broad-based initial training in collaboration with other industries with common or similar skill requirements.

The respective trade areas assessed the skill requirements of their trade in light of the needs of the remaining years of this century and beyond. Each trade had to determine the required level of preentry skill, identify ways to include women and those of non-European background (Maori and Pacific Island groups), and address the issue of assessed rather than assumed competence.

These far-reaching changes affected all the various stakeholders in the system—in all, fourteen different groups, including employers, technical training institutes, unions, and examining and certifying bodies. The New Zealand government encouraged change by providing greater reimbursement to employers for wage losses for those apprentices who were involved in off-job, institution-based training.

There was also a need for complete job analysis, which not only had to be done in an internationally recognized manner but also made usable on a local basis in New Zealand. The skills listed had to cover the range needed across the whole of New Zealand—from, as Burleigh describes it, "the subtropical north to the cooler, harsher south, [for] the sunset industries as well as those where sunrise technology was in use" (p. 37).

A critical element in the transformation of vocational training and apprenticeship training in New Zealand was the collaboration among industry, government, and training institutions. Once it was accepted that the "what" of vocational training would be determined by industry and the "how" was to be in the hands of the HRD professionals, significant progress was made.

Special attention was also paid to working with the tradesperson supplying on-the-job training, where perhaps up to 85 percent of the learning takes place. To improve this training, the New Zealand Vocational Training Council developed training materials which were highly applicable and understandable for tutor and learner.

New training manuals were also developed for the network of technical institutes throughout New Zealand. These manuals, which have significantly improved the training standards, were developed through consultation with expert incumbent workers in specific occupations and have been validated by industry as a whole. The industrial employers have also provided better support to the tutors by supplying state-of-the-art equipment and full precourse preparation of the apprentice that maximizes the impact of the course content.

According to Burleigh, the result of this reform of vocational training in New Zealand has been positive. Attitudes have changed, training programs have been more effective, and competencies have improved.

❦ *New Zealand School for Training of Trainers (New Zealand)*

With centers in Wellington, Auckland, Rotorua, Napier, Palmerston, Christchurch, and Dumedin, the New Zealand School for Training of Trainers conducts a wide array of courses for individuals and organizations throughout the country. The school was recently recognized as a "Center of Excellence" by the *Journal of European Industrial Training*. Their highly acclaimed, multistaged "Training and Development Program for Trainers" consists of nine modules designed to provide training officers from both the corporate and government sectors with practical HRD skills (see Figure 17.1).

The Training and Development Program for Trainers has the following important features:

- The courses develop practical skills.
- Trainers can elect to proceed through the modules according to their needs.
- The majority of modules include a work-based project to give participants an opportunity to practice new skills in their own organization with the support of a mentor.
- The course staff closely supervises the progress of each work-based project to ensure maximum benefit is gained for both organization and participant.

❦ Institute of Social and Administrative Studies, University of the South Pacific (Fiji)

The Institute of Social and Administrative Studies was established in 1977 and performs three basic functions—training, research, and consultancy work—for eleven nations of the South Pacific region: Cook Islands, Fiji, Kiribati, Nauru, Vanuatu, Niue, Solomon Islands, Tokelau, Tonga, Tuvalu, and Western Samoa. The institute is part of the University of the South Pacific, which was established in 1968 to serve the educational and training needs of the region.

The institute offers several types of training programs in social welfare, project planning, financial management, auditing, personnel management, training of trainers, health administration, and rural development. The participants in the courses are middle- and senior-level executives and administrators from governments, public enterprises, and private firms. Most of the courses are for participants from all the countries of the region. On special request from some governments, courses have been organized for administrators and executives of a particular country.

Research is being undertaken by staff members of the institute in issues such as local administration in Solomon Islands, election studies, rural development in Fiji, government and administration in small island states, government of plural societies, and working and training needs of small businesses.

Consultancy work is undertaken for governments and private bodies in the areas of rural institutions, employment and administration, local government, transportation, and social development and welfare services.

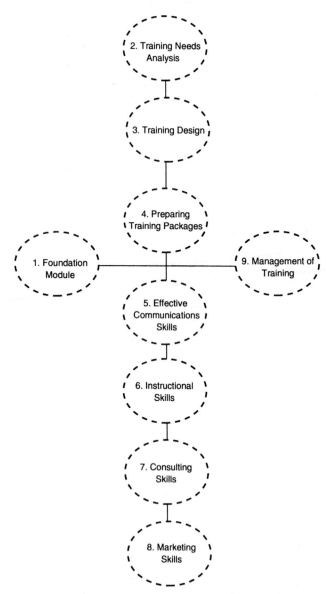

FIGURE 17.1
Training and Development Program for Trainers

SUMMARY

The South Pacific consists of over 25,000 islands ranging from the world's largest—Australia—to many a few hundred yards in circumference. The cultural milieu includes European, Asian, and indigenous elements. HRD has rapidly become a significant factor in the economic development of the region. This chapter examined five successful HRD programs— Broken Hill Proprietary Company Limited (Australia), Westpac Group (Australia), New Zealand's training and apprenticeship programs as well as its School for Training of Trainers, and Institute of Social and Administrative Studies (Fiji).

REFERENCES

BURLEIGH, ADDRIENNE. "New Zealand Updates Apprenticeship." *Vocational Education Journal* (April 1988), pp. 36–38.

FRANK, ERIC. "HRD in Australia." *Journal of European Industrial Training* (May 1988), pp. 49–56.

HUEY, R. J. "Financial Services Training—The Westpac Experience." *Journal of Management Development* (Vol. 8, No. 3), pp. 50–54.

MARTIN, COLIN. "Centers of Excellence—New Zealand Programme for the Training of Trainers." *Journal of European Industrial Training* (January 1987), pp. 23–25.

CHAPTER 18

❦ ❦

Canada

INTRODUCTION

The global environment is changing before our very eyes, and our productivity is not keeping pace. We must change the way we think, the way we learn, and the way we work.

Michael Wilson
Canada Industry Minister

Despite its long border with the United States, "guarded only by neighborly respect and honorable obligations," perhaps the most important thing to understand about Canada is that it is *not* the United States.

Even with their long history of cooperation and friendship and the many superficial ethnic and cultural similarities, the two countries are distinct in a number of important ways. Within Canada's vast borders, there are also equally important differences of culture, belief, attitude, and practice that must be understood by the HRD practitioner if she is to be successful. In this chapter, we will consider the HRD environment in Canada and explore the many faces of this variegated country.

❦ Learning Objectives

After studying this chapter, you should be able to:

1. Understand how the geography, demographics, history, languages, religions, and key cultural beliefs of Canada and the Canadians affect HRD activities
2. Describe the economic environment in Canada and relate it to the practice of HRD
3. Outline the historical development of HRD in Canada and identify the principal challenges facing HRD professionals in Canada
4. Provide examples of HRD programs in the corporate and education sectors

CULTURAL FACTORS IMPACTING HRD

❦ Geography and Demographics

Extending over an area of 3.85 million square miles, Canada is the second largest country in the world, exceeded in size only by the newly established Russian republic. Canada's 26.5 million people are scattered across ten provinces, but almost 40 percent live in Ontario, and most of the population lives within 100 miles of the country's southern border with the United States. Much of the north is uninhabitable because of the arctic climate and permanently frozen ground. Even so, if Canada's population density were applied to Manhattan, there would be 154 residents sharing the island.

More than 40 percent of the population is of British descent, with another 30 percent of French origin. There are also sizable German, Italian, and Ukrainian populations in Ontario and the western provinces. British Columbia, on the Pacific, has large Japanese and Chinese communities as well. Native peoples comprise 1.5 percent of the population and live largely in the two northern territories.

❦ Language

Although Canada has a great deal of cultural diversity, the two dominant cultures are those of the British and the French. Native Canadian culture continues to play an important role in the north but has relatively little impact on the cultural identity of the vast majority of Canadians. English and French are the two official government languages, and legislation supports their equal status throughout the country in matters of business, education, and culture. Other European languages are spoken locally as well; in addition to the language spoken by Canada's 17,500 Inuit, it is estimated that some 500 other languages are spoken by the descendants of native Canadians. A recent Canadian government decision to grant 770,000 square miles, an area equal to a fifth of the whole country, to the Inuit of the Northwest Territory will certainly bring that culture to greater prominence in national affairs.

❦ *Religion*

Christianity is the predominant religion with 47 percent of the population practicing Roman Catholicism and 41 percent Protestantism of one type or another. Not surprisingly, the vast majority of the residents of French-speaking Quebec are Catholic, while Protestantism dominates in the English-speaking provinces. The majority of the remaining 12 percent report no religious preferences, with the rest being of Eastern Orthodox, Jewish, or other persuasions.

❦ *A Dual Identity: French and English*

For almost four centuries, the British and the French have either directly or indirectly had competing visions of what Canada was and was to become. What was originally a colonial struggle over land and wealth has lately taken the form of competition between the two cultures and languages. Quebec, overwhelmingly French, and the rest of Canada, predominantly English in origin and attitudes, are in a struggle that has had enormous political, economic, and cultural costs.

Behind the historical and political facts lie significant differences in cultural beliefs, attitudes, and behaviors. Principal among these have been differences in religious belief. Although there is official separation of church and state in Canada, religious organizations have always played a large role in politics and daily life. Communities tend to be defined along religious lines, and state support of private religious schools is widespread.

Differences in philosophy between the Catholic and Protestant world views have tended to be played out in government policies regarding not only family and community matters but also economic and political policy. For example, all business-related materials, including sales and marketing brochures, advertising, customer-support materials, and even some internal records, must be published or otherwise made available in both French and English. This represents an enormous cost of doing business and makes little sense to those who observe that French is seldom needed outside of Quebec and English is, for the most part, redundant within that province. Nonetheless, Canadians of both English and French descent are sensitive to policies, attitudes, or remarks that seem to favor one culture over the other.

❦ Common Values

Despite the French/English rivalry, Canadians share a great deal of common beliefs and values. They are typically warm and friendly, although the people of Ontario have the reputation of being more reserved and formal. Dress and appearance are considered important, especially at business or cultural events. Canadians are proud of their country, their province, and their cultural heritage. Despite the many cultural similarities with the United States, Canadians are quick to point out that they're not Americans in disguise.

❦ Leisure

Modern Canada was carved from a vast, trackless wilderness by explorers, trappers, miners, and settlers who faced enormous obstacles and challenges. This sense of adventure and challenge continues today; in Canada, nature is never very far away. From the Vancouver Sea Festival to the Calgary Stampede in Alberta and the summer dance festivals of Nova Scotia, the people of Canada enjoy the abundant natural world around them. Outdoor sports such as hockey, curling, rugby, skiing, tennis, and golf are enjoyed by millions. Throughout the country, museums and galleries are also favorite centers of attraction, and the larger cities such as Montreal host world-class film and music festivals.

ECONOMIC ENVIRONMENT FOR HRD

Canada's population and economy are approximately one-tenth those of the United States. However, because of the close economic links between Canada and the United States, their economic cycles have been similar. Canada's labor force has grown at a faster rate than that of the United States, and, partly related to this, the unemployment rate, on average, has been slightly above that of the United States.

Canada ranks seventh in the world in gross domestic product and is one of the world's largest producers of minerals. The significant growth of Canadian manufacturing in the fifties transformed the nation from a rural agricultural society into an industrial and urban society. A number of changes have opened Canada to world market conditions—the Canada–U.S. Free Trade Agreement, privatization, and tax reform. In addition, a number of positive efforts have been made to reposition and restructure the Canadian economy.

The U.S.–Canada trading relationship has been enhanced by the bilateral Free Trade Agreement (FTA) that became effective on January 1, 1989.

Over a ten-year period, the FTA will remove all tariffs and virtually all import and export restrictions and liberalize rules in areas of agriculture, services, energy, financial services, investment, and government procurement.

Canadian workers are well educated, highly skilled, and well paid. They have clearly defined employment rights protected by social and labor relations legislation. Thirty percent of the labor force has some secondary education, and one-half of the employees are in white-collar occupations. The management style, philosophy, and compensation of business managers is like that in the United States.

In late 1991, the Canadian government and the Business Council of National Issues, an Ottawa-based group of 150 leading chief executives, released a study entitled "Canada at the Crossroad: The Reality of a New Competitive Environment." The study examined the business reality of Canada and was based largely on an examination of twenty-five major Canadian industries.

The major conclusions were as follows:

- Productivity growth in Canada is the lowest among the group of seven major industrialized countries making Canada increasingly vulnerable to competition from the United States and Japan, as well as from Germany and other members of the European Community.
- Labor costs in Canada have risen so steadily that hundreds of manufacturing firms are moving to the United States to take advantage of lower American wages, more modest personal and business taxes, and less onerous regulatory and social policies. In 1987, the average hourly manufacturing wage in Canada was slightly below that in the United States but now is about $2 higher.
- Private-sector investment in research and development is far behind that of most industrialized countries. A recent government study showed that only 1,700 of 40,000 manufacturing firms in Canada do any research and development at all.
- Only one-third of Canadian companies provide training for employees to upgrade their skills. German firms spend eight times as much on training and U.S. firms twice as much.
- While more than half the jobs in the nineties are expected to require more than a high school education, 30 percent of Canadian students drop out of high school and 40 percent have no postsecondary education.

The study also cited the Canadian government's "paternalistic outlook in their management of the economy," through such mechanisms as high tariffs, subsidies, government ownership, and other interventionist policies. The distinctly Canadian economic system is one based on overreliance on government and sheltered markets and a low grade of domestic rivalry that has hindered the development of world-class industries. The report criticized organized labor, which includes 37 percent of Canada's labor force, for hindering competitiveness. It called on unions to seek a broadening of workers' skills and more cooperative labor-management relations to accommodate changes in production.

Despite the 1989 U.S.–Canada free-trade agreement, protectionist trade barriers still exist, not only in global markets but between provinces within Canada. In fact, Prime Minister Brian Mulroney has complained repeatedly that there are more barriers to interprovincial trade in Canada than there are in the European Community.

HRD IN CANADA

Noah Meltz of the University of Toronto, in his study on the history and trends of worker training in Canada, notes that there have been a number of important changes in Canada's HRD efforts over the past thirty years, a primary one being that government funding has shifted away from pure training toward a combination of training and work experience. Canadian policy toward training has begun to link growth, stabilization, and equity.

In Canada, training for employment is a shared responsibility between the provinces (because of their responsibility for education) and the federal government (because of its responsibility for the general state of the economy). As a result, both the federal government and the provinces are free to engage in training. In addition, unlike in the United States, the national employment service is federally run and financed. In practice, the bulk of public expenditures on training have come from the federal government. Canada has always relied on immigrants to provide a significant portion of its skilled and professional work force. Immigrants make up between one-fifth and one-third of the most skilled trades such as those in construction and manufacturing.

In 1989, the Conference Board of Canada conducted a survey to measure the extent and impact of a lack of basic skills among Canadian employees. The purpose of the study was to provide policymakers and educators with a wide range of information on how employee illiteracy is affecting Canadian businesses today. According to preliminary results of the study, over 70 percent of organizations surveyed have experienced difficulty in meeting human resource objectives because of a lack of basic literacy and numeracy skills among employees. It appears that illiteracy is having a significant negative impact on Canadian business objectives, management, and operational processes. Some companies have implemented training programs as a result of new processes or the introduction of new technology in the workplace. These programs have heightened the awareness of functional illiteracy issues.

Over the past thirty years, there have been four major government initiatives for worker training: the Technical and Vocational Act (1960), the Adult Occupational Training Act (1967), the National Training Act (1982), and the Canadian Jobs Strategy (1985). The Canadian Jobs Strategy seeks to combine work experience with training in order to enhance the long-term ability of people to acquire skills and enter or reenter the work force and to link training with ongoing economic activity and real jobs. The new programs are directed toward the long-term unemployed, young people out of school and unable to find work, women entering the labor market, workers needing skills training to avoid layoffs, employers needing assistance to train employees in skills for which there is an existing or anticipated shortage, communities suffering severe economic decline, and innovative pilot projects.

In terms of numbers, employers are training many more people than the federal and provincial governments. Formal training programs, however, are much shorter in corporate than in government settings. Meltz sees as a major issue in the nineties the need for improved relations between government funding and corporate HRD activities, especially with the pressures to decrease government spending in order to reduce the deficit.

HRD PROGRAMS IN CANADA

❦ *Royal Bank of Canada*

Royal Bank of Canada is the largest bank in Canada and the third largest in North America. It has more than 7.5 million customers, 1,600 branches, and 3,100 cash machines. Royal Bank is one of the most profitable, and its return on assets and equity is consistently among the highest in North America. Much of this success can be attributed to its extensive HRD programs.

Royal Bank offers employees over 230 different workshops and seminars, as well as sixty self-study courses covering areas of management, computers, and banking. In addition, the bank encourages staff to take advantage of outside training and education programs. For example, the bank has enrolled more than 60,000 employees in the past twenty-five years with training programs at the Institute of Canadian Bankers.

The Royal Bank sees learning and development as a three-way partnership between the employee, the manager, and the bank. Training has become much broader, more flexible, more accessible, and more individualized than in the past because of the rapidly changing banking environment. In such an environment, success depends on the ability of all bank people to learn quickly and continuously.

As a result, the Royal Bank's HRD program enables staff to acquire knowledge and skills through a wide variety of means—audiotapes, self-completing workbooks, computer-based training courses and videos, as well as on-the-job and classroom training.

In all these activities, the bank places the focus on the learners as being responsible for their own training and development. Each employee is given a *Learning Resource Guide* listing hundreds of courses and self-development materials. Using this as a base, the employees develop with the manager their learning action plan.

In order to remain competitive and to recruit and retain its quality people, the human resource planning and development department has developed a comprehensive work and family program which includes numerous handbooks to guide the employee and manager on such Royal Bank policies as flexitime, flexiplace, job sharing, childcare, maternity leave, elder care, and access to professional consultation for employees experiencing financial, marital, or legal problems. The *Childcare Handbook*, for example, provides educational guidance on type of childcare, selecting the caregiver, and strategies for work and parenting in the nineties.

At a recent Royal Bank leadership conference, 350 Royal Bank managers developed a long-term strategy to improve the performance of bank branches. To accomplish this organizational transformation, a number of HRD measures were set into motion:

1. Creation of formal mechanisms (conferences, newsletters, computer systems) to allow managers to share expertise more systematically
2. Guarantee of fifteen days of training per year for area managers and launching of Area Manager University, which would include an intensive series of courses and training modules

As a result of its excellent array of HRD programs and activities, Royal Bank of Canada was selected by the American Society for Training and Development as the top international (non–U.S. headquartered) corporation in 1992.

❦ Manitoba Institute of Management

The Manitoba Institute of Management (MIM) was established in 1965 as a private, nonprofit corporation. Its mission is to be a center of excellence for management development in Manitoba and western Canada. It has grown beyond that, and MIM programs are now run in Canada, in several states of the United States, and in several countries of the eastern Caribbean. MIM activities fall into the following categories: management consulting, in-house management training programs, publicly offered seminars and work-shops, small enterprise programs, and creative writing on a contract basis.

The institute also has associates in several universities in Canada and the United States who participate in MIM programs on an as-needed basis. The professional staff is multidisciplinary, and their qualifications range from resource management to industrial engineering.

The main areas of cooperative interest involve expanding MIM's small business programs to interested countries other than Canada and those in the Caribbean. MIM's small business management development program has been institutionalized in four provinces in Canada and in Barbados. MIM has worked on a cooperative basis with the Barbados Institute of Management and Productivity (BIMAP) for the past ten years and is presently cooperating with BIMAP to expand these programs (originally introduced to Barbados) to eight other countries in the Caribbean.

MIM conducts over 100 short-duration seminars and workshops across Canada on a variety of management topics. MIM's professional staff is also involved in in-house training programs that are specifically designed. A management development needs survey has been developed which enables MIM and an organization's management to identify the critical areas where management development is required.

❦ *Quebec Telephone*

Quebec Telephone is the recent recipient of an award from the Human Resources Professionals of the Province of Quebec for its comprehensive career planning program. The career planning program consists of five parts:

- Employee file
- Job file
- Career interview

- Individually tailored career plan
- Identification of employee training and development needs

HRD professionals have equipped themselves with a number of tools for gathering information on employees and jobs in order to create a data bank of high quality. Data gathered about individual employees include both per-sonal characteristics (training and experience acquired, languages spoken, work performance, personal interests) and the employee's potential for development. The individual potential is measured by means of several instruments: a self-study questionnaire, psychometric tests, and observations of behavior in the work setting.

With the results of these instruments, the career counselor proceeds to reconcile the individual's own view of his or her potential with the superior's observation-based assessment. From this, an employee profile is developed which is given directly to the employee with a copy sent to the immediate supervisor.

The job file includes both the tasks and the requirements of the job, as well as the psychological characteristics required by the job. Each job file shows the employee's occupational code so as to situate each job within a logical career progression.

The career plan involves the comparison of individual profiles with job profiles in order to obtain the best match between jobs and jobholders. Quebec Telephone has developed a computer program called PLANCA (from its French title *Plan de Carrière*), which enables planners to compare individual and job profiles to the mutual benefit of the employees and of the company. For the employees, the program is useful because it identifies those jobs within the company that are potentially accessible, so that they can plan their training and development efforts more effectively. In this way each person, in cooperation with the supervisor and career counselor, can develop an individually tailored career plan. The obvious advantage to the company is that it can more easily and accurately pinpoint the best-suited candidates for vacant or potentially vacant positions.

❦ Seagram Company Ltd.

The Seagram Company, Ltd. is a leading worldwide producer and marketer of distilled spirits, wines, fruit juices, coolers, and mixers. With affiliates in 30 countries, sales in 1992 exceeded $6 billion.

In line with the organizational pledge to provide equality of opportunity and to maximize the full potential of all employees, Seagram has initiated a number of HRD programs. The Performance Management Program is designed to promote communication between managers and employees with respect to performance and development needs and opportunities. Reinforcing the company's emphasis on training and development, Seagram has established a core curriculum for different job levels throughout the organization. Special training programs for women and minorities have been developed.

Each business unit is required to dedicate a portion of its budget for comprehensive training and development programs. Succession planning is now the responsibility of each manager and is seen as crucial for facilitating career advancement. Managers are expected to identify the potential of employees worldwide and then assure relevant training programs that will position employees for future company opportunities.

SUMMARY

Canada's rich cultural environment includes French, British, and, more recently, Chinese elements. According to a recent study, the country is experiencing a number of difficult economic trends including low productivity, high labor costs, little investments in research and development, high functional illiteracy, and limited investment in HRD (Germany spends eight times as much per employee, the United States twice as much).

The federal and provincial governments are shifting funding away from pure training toward a combination of training and work experience.

Four top HRD programs in Canada include: the Royal Bank of Canada, the Manitoba Institute of Management, Quebec Telephone, and The Seagram Company.

REFERENCES

MELTZ, NOAH. "The Evolution of Worker Training: The Canadian Experience." In *New Developments in Worker Training*, edited by Louis A. Ferman. Madison, Wisc.: Industrial Relations Assoc. Press, 1990.

PORTER, MICHAEL. *Canada at the Crossroads: The Reality of a New Competitive Environment*, Ottawa, 1991.

ROYAL BANK OF CANADA. *Enhancing Your Profession*. Montreal: Corporate Human Resources, 1991.

WIL, THIERRY *et al*. "Human Resource Planning and Quebec-Telephone." *Human Resource Planning* (Vol. 11, No. 4), pp. 255–269.

CHAPTER 19

Latin America and the Caribbean

INTRODUCTION

> We speak of Latin lovers. Latins love their individuality, their families, their friends, life, and business—in that order.
>
> *An American operations manager stationed in Caracas,*
> *quoted in* The World Class Executive *by Neil Chesanow*

The global HRD professional, in order to succeed in Latin America, has to recognize, understand, and come to terms with a unique set of cultural assumptions and beliefs that affect HRD expectations, behaviors, policies, practices, and methods. For the North American, especially, some of the most basic, unconscious beliefs and assumptions about the world must be examined in a new light in order to really function in the "Other America."

In this chapter, we will provide an overview of the HRD environment in Latin America and describe some successful HRD programs throughout the region.

❦ *Learning Objectives*

After studying this chapter, you should be able to:

1. Understand how the geography, demographics, religions, cultures, history, and languages of Latin America affect HRD activities

2. Describe the economic environment in the region and relate it to the practice of HRD
3. Identify the key twenty-first century challenges facing HRD professionals in Latin America
4. Provide examples of HRD programs in the corporate and public sectors

CULTURAL FACTORS IMPACTING HRD

❦ *Geography and Demographics*

Stretching from the Caribbean to Cape Horn, Latin America comprises an enormous land area of over 40 countries with a population approaching 450 million people. They live in a rich number of cultures that variously have indigenous, European, African, and Asian roots.

When the European explorers began to arrive in Latin America in the early sixteenth century, the region was home to an estimated thirty million native people. Ranging from the powerful Mayan and Incan empires to the relatively isolated cultures of the Amazon basin and Patagonia, these people had a wide variety of life styles, languages, beliefs, rituals, and behaviors. While their empires have been eclipsed, the modern descendants of these native peoples remain a major determinant in the social, political, economic, and cultural life of their various countries. Along the Caribbean coast and in northeast Brazil, there are also numerous African influences and traditions brought to the area by the slaves of earlier times. But it must be said that the mainstream of Latin American culture today has evolved principally from the invading cultures of Europe.

The people of the region fall into five general ethnic groups: Indian, Mestizo, mulatto, black, and white, with the latter group in the distinct minority except in Argentina, Costa Rica, and Uruguay. Nonetheless, throughout the region, power, politics, economics, and business continue for the most part to be dominated by people living within the evolved versions of the earlier Spanish and Portuguese colonial cultures.

❦ *Religion*

Roman Catholicism is the predominant and, in many cases, official religion of the countries in the region. Minorities practice other religions ranging from Candomblé and Voodoo with African origins to European Protestantism and indigenous animistic religions.

❦ Family: Roles and Responsibilities

The family, and by extension the group, plays an important role in both the Spanish/Portuguese and the native Latin American cultures. Throughout the region, political and economic power have often stayed for generations in the hands of a few powerful families. As a consequence, Latin Americans are accustomed to deferring decisions and actions to the people in charge. The strong, decisive ruler is a much feared and envied figure in both politics and business. Within the native American communities, however, this imported feature is modified by a strong tradition of family and community consensus gathering, much like that seen in Asia. As a result, these families and communities look outward in one tradition and inward in another. The authority assumed by the strong leader, of course, has its concomitant responsibility and honor. As a result, Latin American men, in those contexts where they are taken to be the leader, are much concerned not only with their ability to provide and protect but also with their honor. The well-known concept of *machismo* is a natural result; for many Latin American men, honor is what matters most. It is sometimes valued over human life; it routinely affects day-to-day life at home, in the community, and in business.

The role of women is, of course, largely circumscribed and defined by this cultural tradition. While in reality Latin American women carry enormous burdens in the family, the community, and the economy, they are often viewed as fragile creatures who need to be protected from the ways of the world. Maidens and mothers, they are to be shielded from the harsh realities of life by their natural protectors—fathers, brothers, and husbands.

❦ Time: Relative and Imprecise

Carlos Fuentes, the Mexican author and educator, observes that North Americans and Latin Americans have trouble understanding each other because they don't have a common place in time. Latin America looks first to its past, while North America lives almost completely in the future. As for the present, it is the scene of constant misunderstanding, disappointment, and irritation. From the North American point of view, Latins are always late. For the Latin Americans, their northern neighbors never take enough time to develop relationships or understand situations.

The one culture is driven by time; the other sees it as a resource to be enjoyed and experienced. North Americans "spend, gain, lose, waste, and invest" time; they are only *in* time when they are "on time." Latin Americans "have" time today, and if that's not enough, there's always tomorrow. There is always time for family and friends, for romance and politics, for a cup of coffee or a long lunch.

🦢 *Social Behavior and Communication Styles*

Latin American culture puts a primary emphasis on relationships. Whenever possible, one does business with friends. When dealing with enemies, one is firm but polite. Form is often more important than content. For example, great attention is given to rank and title, often simply as a matter of respect and not as a reflection of accomplishment. It is common in Latin America to refer to a prominent leader as *doctor* even though he might not have finished primary school. *Don*, *jefe*, and *licenciado* are all titles of respect used with people who might not be patriarchs, chiefs, or licensed practitioners. What is important is the appropriate show of respect to others and the gracious acceptance of it when granted by others.

Latin Americans are typically both warm and effusive. There is much touching, and the distance between speakers is small. Form is again very important, and content is context specific. Business commitments and promises made in a social context need to be revisited in a work environment. Latin Americans, more than people in almost any other culture, take great pleasure in social interaction for its own sake.

ECONOMIC ENVIRONMENT FOR HRD

"Can this really be Latin America?" asks the *Washington Post* (January 13, 1992). *Business Week* (December 30, 1991), headlined "From *Bolsa* (stock market) to *Bolsa*, There's Plenty of Salsa," proclaims that Latin American markets have made a stunning comeback. The *Wall Street Journal* calls South America one of the hottest of the emerging markets after years of economic stagnation.

Inflation is down, investments are up, stock markets are booming, government spending is under control, and economies have begun to grow. Democracies have replaced military dictatorships. Latin American countries have embarked on a fundamental change of their state-dominated economies to free markets. The privatization of government agencies is continuing. The government and corporate leaders have undergone these economic and political changes, "a sweeping revolution," because they realize these actions are necessary to become competitive internationally.

Regionwide problems still remain. Foreign debt is over $400 billion with some countries in arrears in debt payments. Unemployment remains high, productivity capacity is going unused, and the dramatic skew in income distribution still exists. Drug wars and intimidation haunt Colombia, Peru, Bolivia, and Venezuela. Bureaucracies and labor unrests still exist.

Latin American nations, however, are forming regional trading blocs. Brazil, Argentina, Uruguay, and Paraguay have agreed to create a common market, called Mercosur, by 1994. Mexico has joined the North American bloc with Canada and the United States.

Throughout all of these changes and challenges, HRD has served as an important lever for economic development. Nadler points out that most of the countries of the region have some kind of government-sponsored or government-directed national HRD activity.

A long-standing challenge for economic development in Latin America, however, is the lack of adequate schooling. Illiteracy is one of the major obstacles faced by most countries in Latin America. Population growth continues to exceed the ability of most countries to provide the necessary educational opportunities. The end result is a work force unprepared for the technical and managerial jobs required in the global competitive marketplace.

EVENTS AFFECTING HRD IN THE TWENTY-FIRST CENTURY

McGinn suggests a number of major events that are likely to occur as we enter the twenty-first century, each of which would have a profound impact on HRD in this region of the world:

1. *Increasing mobility of labor across national boundaries.* Although the overall flow of less educated people to the United States is likely to slow down as a result of increased capital investment in Latin America and the Caribbean, labor flows among countries in Latin America are likely to increase. Industrial development will be concentrated in a few countries where there has been less investment. The more educated people will flock to technological centers in Argentina, Brazil, and Mexico, as well as to the United States and Canada.

2. *Pressures for proved quality and relevance in the area of education and training.* The increased pressure for relevance in the curriculum will mean less emphasis on teaching of classics and more on mathematics, science, and applied language. The quality of public education programs will likewise be under pressure to improve.

3. *Rapid growth in private education and nonformal training programs aimed at both children and adults.* There will be a rapid growth in private education in Latin America and the Caribbean. McGinn cites three reasons for this:
   (a) The changed attitude toward state-controlled education and the spread of the ideology of privatization have led many people to seek private schools and institutes.

(b) Global firms have found that trainees at the private institutions are more "international" in attitudes and values.

(c) Graduates of private schools have better opportunities to gain admission into higher level educational programs in other countries.

4. *Increased autonomy for school managers.* The sum of the forces described above will be an increased pressure on public education and training "to produce graduates who can be certified to possess certain knowledge, skills and attitudes" (p. 65). To achieve these results, managers will be encouraged to use considerable initiative in the finance, organization, and operation of their schools.

HRD PROGRAMS IN LATIN AMERICA

❦ *Motorola*

Motorola is the largest worldwide supplier of cellular telephone systems, two-way radio systems, mobile radios, and pagers. It is also the fourth largest supplier of semiconductors. The Motorola plant in Guadalajara, Mexico, is a major manufacturer of semiconductor products.

In 1989, Motorola-Mexico won the National Training award of the American Chamber of Commerce of Mexico for implementing the organizational effectiveness change model in its Guadalajara semiconductor plant.

The first step of the model was to develop a vision that would permeate all levels of the organization. After a series of meetings, a program of change was launched which was called "Transformation for Excellence," and the overriding vision was "to become world class in the manufacture and assembly of discrete semiconductors" (Banning and Wintermantel, p. 54).

Objectives were then identified which involved such areas as productivity levels, quality and performance standards, strengthening the overall management systems, and increasing the organization's sensitivity to market changes and reaction speed. Pivotal strategies to achieve these objectives included performance measurement mechanisms, as well as increased quality control systems and staffing levels.

Changes in organizational structures were made to reflect the importance of the multicultural nature of the work force and to reduce management levels to provide for quicker response and more accountability.

The next step was to identify the essential skills needed to implement these organizational changes. Due to the changes in production methods, the installation of new equipment, and the increased emphasis on quality control, the training programs for managers, supervisors, and production personnel were completely revised. Management skills seminars in applied strategic planning were created. Interdepartmental training included the various elements of the Transformation for Excellence program.

The fourth step, competitive staffing, was accomplished by reviewing all the positions within the Guadalajara plant and, when necessary, transferring employees from other Motorola business units or hiring new employees.

The preferred management style was determined to be participative with a heavy emphasis on cooperation and inventiveness. Employees were encouraged to criticize, suggest, and creatively solve problems. The management systems were oriented toward (1) reinforcing the transformation for excellence process, (2) developing greater sensitivity in the marketplace, and (3) rewarding performance.

The results of the organization development efforts have been impressive. The most important change taking place has been the change in mindset and attitude among the employees. Teamwork and pride in the product are widespread. According to Wintermantel, the staff has become more adept in problem solving. Productivity has doubled in some areas with increases averaging 30 percent to 40 percent plantwide. The rate of on-time deliveries is now close to 100 percent, and cycle times have been cut in half. Most important, according to Banning and Wintermantel, is the pride that the employees have in being a world-class operation.

❦ *Organization of American States*

The Organization of American States (OAS), with thirty-five member states, is the world's oldest regional organization, dating back to 1890. One of its purposes is "to promote, by cooperative action, the economic, social and cultural development" of the Latin American/Caribbean region. A large number of (1) national, (2) multinational, and (3) "inter-American" programs of assistance and training are carried out each year to support this objective. Current HRD programs include the following:

1. National Projects
   (a) Bahamas—An HRD specialist trained 150 young people in entrepreneurial development, marketing, and business skills.
   (b) Costa Rica—OAS provided training courses in customs in order to upgrade the national customs system.
   (c) Dominica—Local hospital staff were trained in financial management and computer application. Youth were trained in numerous vocational areas, and over 90 percent were assisted in identifying jobs.
   (d) El Salvador—OAS continued providing technical assistance for expanding exports of agroindustrial products.
   (e) Jamaica—Over 100 participants were trained in crafts involving ceramics, leather goods, and paper products through the National Manpower and Employment Training program.

(f) Paraguay—Training courses have been recently conducted on bee keeping, carpentry, fish farming, water supply systems, health, and nutrition.

(g) Venezuela—OAS is training staff of the National Productivity Center in production, quality control, and management areas.

2. Multinational Projects—Numerous seminars have been conducted throughout Latin America and the Caribbean on tariffs, trade, customs, marketing, tax policies and small enterprise development.

3. Inter-American Centers—The following five regional centers, which are coordinated by OAS, provide training for thousands of Latin and Caribbean leaders each year:

(a) Inter-American Center for Training in Public Administration
(b) Inter-American Center on Social Development
(b) Inter-American Tax Studies Center
(d) Inter-American Marketing Center
(e) Inter-American Statistical Training Center

❦ Latin American and Caribbean National Training Centers

Many countries in Latin America and the Caribbean have vocational training programs that focus primarily on assisting small enterprise managers. Two of the best known and most successful are CEBRAE in Brazil and SERCOTEC in Chile. CEBRAE, which was established in 1972, has a network of twenty-two training centers throughout Brazil and employs over 2,000 people. It works closely with various Brazilian universities and the Brazilian Confederation of Industries. CEBRAE has also been a Brazilian leader in developing culturally appropriate training materials, including visual aids and case studies.

SERCOTEC, established in Chile in the early fifties, is the largest national training center in Latin America. It has designed and delivered comprehensive training programs for entrepreneur-managers of small industries. Thousands of seminars have been offered in techniques of management, marketing, and finance.

Other highly acclaimed vocational training centers include SENA in Columbia, SENATI in Peru, INA in Costa Rica, and INFOTEP in the Dominican Republic. Funding for their training programs has been raised through a training tax on all industries in the respective countries which enables these institutions to offer free training programs.

❦ Central Bank of Guatemala

Central banks in Latin America have not only provided economic and monetary services for the development of their respective countries but also played "an important role in the education and training of their countries"

(Ochoa, p. 1). The Central Bank of Guatemala has long been recognized as one of the top banks committed to developing the society as well as demonstrating an impressive commitment to human resource development.

Maritza Ochoa, a senior training officer with the bank, identifies three characteristics of its training and development program:

1. HRD programs are positioned to change the organizational culture and attitudes from an autocratic, paternalistic, and passive leadership style to a participative, democratic, and active one. Every manager is trained to become a trainer of his or her staff.
2. Since most employees spend their entire careers with the Central Bank, the HRD activities assist employees from induction to retirement training. Opportunities are made available for graduate degree programs in Latin America and the United States.
3. Recognizing the employee as a total person, HRD programs are offered in human and social, as well as management and technical, areas.

The bank has special training programs for secretaries, executives, and financial specialists. French and English languages are offered. Opportunities are offered to attend courses, seminars, and conferences throughout the world.

Employees who have received academic training abroad are highly encouraged not only to teach within the bank but also to teach part-time at local universities and thereby contribute to the development of Guatemala.

SUMMARY

Latin America and the Caribbean represent a rich number of cultures of European, African, Asian, and indigenous roots. The economic climate for HRD has improved noticeably in the past few years. McGinn has identified a number of major events that are likely to affect HRD in the near future including increasing mobility of labor across national boundaries, pressure for improved quality and relevance of training institutes, a rapid growth in private education and training programs, and an increased autonomy for school managers.

Four successful HRD programs in the region were explored including Motorola's Organizational Effectiveness Change program in Guadalajara, Mexico; the diverse technical assistance projects of the Organization of American States; the small enterprise training programs of the National Training Centers of Chile and Brazil; and the comprehensive HRD activities of the Central Bank of Guatemala.

REFERENCES

BANNING, KENT AND DICK WINTERMANTEL. "Motorola Turns Vision to Profits," *Personnel Journal* (February, 1991), pp. 51–55.

CHESANOW, NEIL. *The World Class Executive*. New York: Rawson Associates, 1985.

FUENTES, CARLOS. *A Change of Skin*. New York: Noonday Press, 1968.

MCGINN, NOEL. "Economic Integration within the Americas: Implications for Education." *La Educacion* (No. 106, 1990), pp. 55–69.

NADLER, ZEACE. "Latin America." In *The Handbook of Human Resource Development*, 2nd ed. New York: John Wiley & Sons, 1990.

OCHOA, MARITZA. "HRD in Guatemala: The Case of the Central Bank of Guatemala." Unpublished paper, Washington, D.C., 1992.

CHAPTER 20

❦ ❦

United States

INTRODUCTION

> Our investment in training is a national disgrace. Despite lip service about people-as-our-most-important-asset, we value hardware assets over people, and have done so for the last century.
>
> *Tom Peters*
> *Thriving on Chaos*

Everyone agrees that these are difficult times for American business, and there is a rising consensus that one of the key elements in any plan to improve the situation will be a redefinition of some of the ways in which human resources are valued, trained, and employed. Many of the paradigms that served as the foundations upon which the United States became a world-wide industrial power seem to be crumbling from within.

In order to know where to go next, however, one must first have some sense of the current situation. In this chapter, we will consider the present HRD environment in the United States and describe model HRD programs designed to successfully confront the challenges of the future.

❦ Learning Objectives

After studying this chapter, you should be able to:

1. Understand how the geography, demographics, history, languages, religions, and key cultural beliefs of the United States affect HRD activities
2. Recognize the key economic factors in the United States and relate them to the practice of HRD
3. Outline the evolving role of HRD as it faces increased global challenges
4. Provide examples of successful HRD programs in the corporate and public sectors

CULTURAL FACTORS IMPACTING HRD

❦ Geography and Demographics

The fourth largest country in the world, the United States is the third most populous. With a population of more than 250 million, the United States is an increasingly diverse society, but approximately 75 percent of Americans are descended from Europeans. African Americans are the largest minority with about 12 percent of the population; Hispanic Americans account for another 9 percent. Asians and Pacific Islanders, the fastest-growing minority group, currently make up 3 percent of the population, and native Americans, less than 1 percent.

❦ History

Although North America's history prior to the arrival of Europeans is not fully known, it's clear that the earlier inhabitants had large empires and advanced civilizations. Isolated European explorers probably reached North American shores perhaps as early as the eleventh century, but exploration began in earnest in the late fifteenth century. It has been estimated that, at that time, 1.5 million native Americans lived within the borders of what was to become the United States. England, France, and Spain were the principal nations to establish colonies, but others who took part included the Netherlands, Sweden, and, in the west, Russia. Many of the early inhabitants had fled religious persecution in England and France; others came as part of ventures funded by European commercial companies. The American Revolution of 1776 led to a loose confederation of states that was formalized with the Constitution of 1787.

Throughout the nineteenth century, explorers, trappers, hunters, and settlers spread westward, and the government acquired territory from France, Mexico, and Spain until the country stretched from the Atlantic Ocean to the Pacific. A long and brutal civil war broke out in 1861 between the industrial states of the North and the more agrarian states of the South, which seceded over the issue of slavery and economic differences. The war ended in 1865 with the victory of the northern forces, and the country was reunited politically.

During the twentieth century, the United States has been a major world power, playing significant roles in the outcome of World War I and World War II and in geopolitical events around the world. Lately, its economic and political influence has waned as that of other countries has increased, but it remains today among the most powerful nations on earth.

❦ Language

English is the predominant and official language of the United States and is spoken by most citizens. However, in urban areas there are significant communities where Spanish is the first language and others where any of a dozen European and Asian languages are the principal means of communication. Many first- and second-generation Americans also speak the native language of their parents and grandparents. It has been estimated that no more than 250,000 native Americans speak their native languages, of which approximately 200 languages still remain.

❦ Religion

Fifty-six percent of all Americans give their religious affiliation as Protestant, with another 28 percent identifying themselves as Catholic, 2 percent as Jewish, and a small percentage as Eastern Orthodox. There are also small populations representing other major world religions including Buddhism, Hinduism, Islam, and others.

❦ Patriotism

Although there is a great deal of diversity and lately no small amount of acrimony between cultures and ethnic communities in the United States, Americans, especially when facing outward, continue to be first and foremost Americans. They are extremely patriotic, and although they may be critical of the U.S. government or its policies, they will almost always argue that, even with its faults, the United States continues to be a good place, if not the best place, to live.

❦ *Freedom, Democracy, and Equality*

Americans see themselves first as individuals and only secondarily as members of families, communities, religions, or organizations. It is this pervasive sense of the individual self that accounts for much of what puzzles people from cultures where the individual exists primarily as a unit of the family. Perhaps more than any other single thing, Americans value what they call "individual freedom." As soon as they are able, most leave their family home and community to strike out on their own.

Along with their impassioned commitment to the individual, Americans have an equally strong belief in democracy, which they commonly equate with freedom, believing that one is not possible in the absence of the other.

Although they will quickly cite examples of where it hasn't worked, Americans basically believe in equality. In large measure, they continue to think that theirs is a land of opportunity where any individual may rise to a position of wealth, power, and influence. Even in the face of their own failure to reach the "American Dream," many Americans continue to blame themselves and not question the validity of their notions. With a fervor that often surprises people from other cultures, most Americans believe not only that "all men are created equal," but that there is equal social, political, and economic opportunity for all.

CURRENT HRD ENVIRONMENT IN THE UNITED STATES

The American Society for Training and Development (ASTD) recently conducted an extensive study of HRD in the United States. Among their major findings were the following:

- Over $250 billion per year is spent on training and development, and this figure continues to grow.
- An estimated 200,000 people work as HRD professionals, a majority in corporations.
- Employee training by employers is the largest delivery system for adult education. Two out of three Americans say they learned everything they need to do their job on the job and not in the classroom.
- Over 70 percent of all executives, professional, and technical workers are retrained by companies.
- Salaries for HRD professionals continue to rise. HRD is a growing profession of the nineties.

- The average investment in training by U.S. companies is only 1.4 percent of payroll—only enough to train about 10 percent of the work force.
- 89 percent of the largest companies designate a chief human resource executive at the corporate level.
- Some 250 colleges and universities offer a master's or a bachelor's degree in HRD.
- The big challenge for HRD in America will be to reskill America's workers in an information age and a service economy.

RECENT CHANGES IN THE TRAINING AND DEVELOPMENT INDUSTRY

Several major shifts have been occurring in the HRD field over the past several years.

❦ *Shift of Emphasis*

In addition to providing more training and education programs, corporations are providing a different kind. Companies are shifting from "nice-to-know" courses to needs-driven training. Instead of a patchwork of unconnected training programs, companies are developing training programs tied clearly and closely to their strategic goals.

Training courses are emphasizing the building of practical skills rather than providing information. With the increased concern about higher productivity in the competitive global marketplace, organizations are showing increased concern about corporate goals rather than individual goals. Improving performance rather than providing enjoyable learning experiences is the new emphasis.

❦ *Shift of Status*

The responsibility for HRD within the organization is gradually moving upward as top executives increase their support and recognition of its contribution to corporate success. HRD managers are also increasingly able to prove the effectiveness of the training program.

Human resource managers are now more likely to be involved in strategic planning and to be part of the management team. Trainers are enjoying more organizational status, as well as more decision-making authority, more budget control, and more respect. Compensation studies show a sharp jump in median salaries, especially at the high end of the scale.

❦ *Shift of Provider*

More and more of the training and education being conducted for companies is being contracted to outside instructors and consultants. The outside contractors are often selected either because of their cost effectiveness relative to full-time internal staff or because they possess expertise not available within the organization. In addition, universities and other training institutions are being utilized. Another recent phenomenon is the establishment of corporate training institutes or colleges where degrees can be earned.

Another shift relative to the providing of training is the greater utilization of managers and other staff outside the HRD department to plan and deliver the training. In addition, more and more companies see subordinate development as the most important responsibility of the manager.

❦ *Shift of Content*

As the external business environment has changed—technology, information-based economy, global competition, trade, and finance—so have the corporate strategies and priorities and therefore the content of training and development programs.

In corporate settings where improved productivity is a critical need, the HRD programs focus on team productivity and quality training. Where the corporate goal is to gain competitive advantage, the major training content areas are marketing and sales, as well as customer training and service. To meet the corporate goal of gaining technological superiority, the training programs emphasize the skills and knowledge needed by the technical people. Communication skills training is growing in all companies as they attempt to develop and transmit corporate culture and increase employee motivation. And finally, leadership and management development programs for managers continue to expand as companies change strategic direction or try to manage better with fewer managers.

❦ *Shift of Recipient*

As technological competence and skills updating become more critical in the global marketplace, training for nonmanagerial staff is increasing. Customer service training is also involving a greater range of people in the organization. At the other end of the scale, top executives also realize that they must become continuous learners and be trained in areas such as global economics, competitive benchmarking, culture and marketing, and international finance.

❦ *Shift of Methods*

Methods for the delivery of training programs have also begun to change. Although classroom-based instruction delivered to a group of learners is still common, more and more training is technology based and tailored for individuals or small groups.

Computer-assisted learning is continuing to grow as it allows for individual employees to learn immediately rather than to wait until a group has been gathered; one computer learning approach is utilized by Xerox, where computer-embedded instruction teaches technology to employees and clients.

More and more companies, are making extensive use of companywide TV networking to provide training in new products for sales, update employees on corporate policies and activities, and educate engineers and other technical professionals.

HRD PROGRAMS IN THE UNITED STATES

❦ *Xerox Corporation*

Xerox Corporation is the world's largest provider of copiers, duplicators, and electronic printers with annual revenues of $20 billion. Xerox manufactures more than 250 equipment products supported by software, supplies, and accessories.

Xerox created the copier industry in 1959 when it introduced the world's first plain paper copier. Its dominance of the copier/duplicator market was changed in the mid-seventies, when Xerox lost its key patents and hundreds of Japanese and U.S. firms entered this copying machine market.

To regain its competitive edge, Xerox, under the leadership of Chairman David Kearns, decided to significantly expand its HRD activities and began a companywide Leadership through Quality program in 1983.

All of Xerox's 110,000 employees worldwide received training for the quality program. Over a four-year period, Xerox spent $125 million on this program alone, in addition to the $260 million annual commitment to training.

The procedure for the quality training program was for the top six people in the company to receive the training first. Then the training cascaded down throughout the company; when a manager took a course, he or she, with the assistance of a training facilitator, had to teach it to the next group. In this way, managers got double the training.

Quality training at Xerox not only involves all employees but also is supported by a broad employee communications program that assures ample opportunity for employee involvement, expression, and feedback. Xerox employees and dealers/agents do not interact with customers until they have successfully completed training.

The results of Xerox's quality training program have been remarkable. Its "highly satisfied" customers have increased 38 percent for copiers/duplicators and 39 percent for printing systems. Customer complaints have fallen over 60 percent. And a recent market research survey ranked Xerox copiers first in five out of six market segments.

Presently Xerox spends about 4 percent of its annual payroll for employee training, about $250 million to $300 million a year. Fifty million dollars of this is earmarked for the Xerox International Center for Training and Management Development in Leesburg, Virginia. Programs include sales training, service and technical courses, and management development. The center, which has 120 staff trainers, trains 12,000 employees annually. And 21,000 engineers and other line employees have at least forty hours annually of training at district headquarters.

Much of Xerox's training is done by the top achievers in the company, who are made full-time trainers for a two-year assignment. According to Kearns, training is combined with and integrated into "the strategy of the company, the direction of the company, and the skills and behavior that people need in order to get the job done.... The toughest problem that training professionals have within a company is how to intercept and integrate new ideas into the training and how to do it quickly" (Galagan, p. 42).

Another aspect of the training philosophy at Xerox is to get a change in thinking on the part of everyone at Xerox. Whether one is developing a product or a marketing program, he or she should think of its training aspects. For example, if a new product requires five weeks of training, the engineer should ask if there would be some way to design it so that only one week of training is necessary.

Xerox has recently adopted a set of principles to guide training in the nineties. Among the principles are the following:

- Xerox is committed to providing its customers with training opportunities and product documentation required to ensure their satisfaction and self-sufficiency.
- Xerox is committed to having a work force prepared to meet current and future business objectives by providing its employees at all levels with appropriate education and training opportunities.
- All new Xerox employees will be oriented in Xerox's philosophy, ethics, values, principles, and business priorities, including Leadership through Quality, in their first ninety days of employment.
- Xerox employees will interact with customers only after having successfully completed specified training.

- All newly hired or first-time Xerox managers will successfully complete specified supervisory training within 120 days of appointment.
- Xerox managers will successfully complete functional knowledge and skills
training to properly coach, inspect, and reinforce the work of their employees
(Galagan, p. 50).

❦ Aetna Life and Casualty

Aetna Life and Casualty, ranked fourth in assets and first in revenues
among the Fortune 500 service companies, has 45,000 employees and 10,000
independent agents operating worldwide. Aetna is recognized as a global
leader both in creating innovative employee training programs to meet the
changing needs of the financial services industry and in educational outreach
within its communities to develop employees of the future. The company
invests more than $40 million annually in training employees, independent
agents, and potential employees.

Aetna has made extensive use of technology to deliver training programs to a work force that is located throughout the United States, Europe,
and Pacific Rim. Among the HRD technologies utilized are computer-based
training, expert systems, and a direct-broadcast satellite television network.

Aetna's commitment to HRD is demonstrated by the efforts and activities of the Aetna Institute for Corporate Education located in Hartford,
Connecticut. The institute was founded in 1981 and operates as a residential
learning center for employees and independent insurance agents. Every year
more than 26,000 people are trained both on-site and via the Aetna television
network at seventy-five sites across the United States. Subjects range from
technical skills to management to basic literacy.

The various training and development programs of Aetna include:

1. *Aetna Management Process.* The Aetna Management Process trains managers to
think more clearly and thereby be better able to determine business objectives
and map out critical factors for achieving those objectives.
2. *Office of the Chairman Educational Series.* This series includes a set of training
programs to develop managers and executives in a core of ten specific managerial competencies which Aetna considers critical to successful performance such
as adaptability, communications, computer skills, teamwork, and leadership.
3. *Technical Training.* This consists of courses in the insurance discipline such as
underwriting, marketing, claims, and utilization of information systems.
4. *Effective Business Skills School.* More than 1,500 employees are trained each year
in reading, writing, mathematics, verbal communications, and computer skills.
5. *Learning Design Process Model.* This is a tool used by Aetna to develop new
training methodologies and strategies that are timely, cost effective, and
designed to strengthen the competence of all Aetna employees.

6. *Stepping Up.* Aetna has implemented this three-part HRD program to address the employability gap among the disadvantaged groups in the communities Aetna serves. Stepping Up includes:
• *Saturday Academy,* an innovative program to provide educational enrichment to inner city junior high school students and their parents, serves more than 400 youngsters and adults each year in Hartford, Connecticut, and Washington, D.C.
• *Students at Work* provides work/study opportunities and motivation for high school students who are at risk of dropping out. Students are guaranteed regular full-time jobs with Aetna if they complete the program and graduate from high school. The program is now operating in Houston, Dallas, Philadelphia, Atlanta, Sacramento, Seattle, and Oakland.
• *Hire and Train programs* are aimed at youth and marginally or unemployed adults in Aetna communities who are identified by local community and government agencies. The individuals have their educational needs assessed and receive training tailored to their needs to prepare them for entry-level jobs at Aetna (Galagan, pp. 32–33).

The trend at Aetna is toward more integration of training with business goals. Training is measured in relation to job performance and outcomes on the job. Another trend is to tailor training to small work groups, thereby giving trainees the opportunity for developing skills in planning, performance appraisals, communication, and decision making.

❦ Federal Express

In 1990 Federal Express Corporation, the world's largest air cargo express company, received both the Corporate Award of the American Society for Training and Development and the Malcolm Baldridge National Quality Award. Federal Express, which began operations in 1973, delivers more than 1.5 million express documents and packages to 129 countries around the world each working day.

The company spends 3 percent of the total expenses, or about $225 million a year, on training. Approximately 900 of the 91,000 employees work officially in HRD activities. This number of HRD professionals is expected to increase, especially in skills training where design and delivery is decentralized.

Federal Express provides a wide array of training programs—an interactive video network; an electronic university delivering college courses and degree programs via personal computers; a Leadership Institute for managers; and a Quality Academy utilized to teach the numerous quality processes and tools of Federal Express.

Federal Express considers job knowledge a prerequisite to job performance. Every six months, 35,000 Federal Express carriers and customer service agents must participate in a computerized Job Knowledge Testing program, the results of which become part of the record. Each employee receives a personalized prescription for job training and suggested learning resources. If necessary, employees are taken off the job for remedial training. Those employees performing best in the training often receive merit pay and promotion opportunities.

All new employees also receive intensive training. For example, all Call Center staff receive six weeks of intensive training before they ever take their first call. Couriers spend four weeks of training before donning their navy blue uniforms and jumping into the company's fleet of 30,000 vans.

Federal Express introduced interactive video instruction in 1987 to support the Job Knowledge Testing program. The company has over 1,200 interactive video units in 700 locations, all linked to the mainframe in Memphis, Tennessee, that train the 45,000 customer contact employees, couriers, and ground operations people in 135 countries around the world. The interactive video training system delivers self-paced, adaptive training and testing. A human resources vice-president notes that "things are changing so fast that we have to update the curriculum every six weeks" (Galagan, p. 30).

All of the managers at Federal Express are trained in quality processes. There are thirty-five quality administrators and 100 trainers within the company who facilitate the quality improvement process throughout the company. At Federal Express, it is the employee's responsibility to acquire the training necessary for the job. The company provides all the resources and tools and even pays employees for test preparation time, but they must maintain their training edge.

Federal Express has developed a special HRD program called the Leadership Evaluation and Awareness Process (LEAP) to develop its managers. It is a series of "gates" through which prospective managers must pass to be considered for management positions. LEAP measures the employee's potential against nine leadership dimensions considered most important at Federal Express: charisma, individual consideration, intellectual stimulation, courage, dependability, flexibility, integrity, judgment, and respect for others.

Teaching at the Federal Express Leadership Institute is considered a prestigious thirty-month assignment and is done only by the "cream of the management crop" who receive hefty bonuses and opportunities for promotion. Federal Express is working to establish a requirement of forty hours of training per year for all managers. Since the LEAP program and ongoing management development were begun, front-line management turnover has dropped by 84 percent.

❦ Business Council for International Understanding

Since 1958, the Business Council for International Understanding (BCIU) Institute at the American University in Washington, D.C., has trained over 25,000 American and international managers and technicians to live and operate effectively in 148 countries around the world. Programs are custom designed for each company and are directed toward corporate staff, negotiating teams, departing expatriates and their families, reentering staff and their families, as well as international corporate executives coming to the United States. Eighty percent of the training programs are conducted in Washington, D.C.; the remaining 20 percent are done on-site or overseas.

BCIU's programs cover the following topics:

- Knowledge of how people in other cultures think and make decisions
- Insights into cultural perspectives
- Skills for coping with unfamiliar and frustrating personal and business situations
- Knowledge about the social, political, and economic institutions and customs of the people of a particular country or countries
- Understanding of how to do business in these countries
- Awareness of pertinent international events which affect corporate operations overseas
- Special programs for spouses, children, teenagers, and multicareer families

BCIU's tailored intercultural communications, area and country studies, and language programs of three, four, five, and ten days are conducted for relocating families on an ongoing basis and provide a cost-effective alternative for successful adjustment and performance overseas.

The BCIU Institute supports the complete training cycle through extensive research and graduate follow-up in country. Graduates are visited regularly in country by the BCIU Institute staff and resource persons allowing them insight into the progress of their graduates and their projects worldwide. Knowledge gained on these follow-up trips is then incorporated into future training and development programs for business personnel and their families headed overseas to join these or similar projects.

❦ Meridian International Center

In contrast to BCIU's training of Americans preparing to live and work abroad, the Meridian International Center (MIC) trains foreigners who come to the United States to live and work. Over the past forty years, Meridian International Center has trained 160,000 people from over 150 countries.

Programs are conducted in English, Spanish, French, Arabic, and Japanese at sites in Washington, D.C., Seattle, and Miami. Over sixty current and former heads of state have been trained at Meridian International Center.

Meridian International Center conducts training programs for a variety of audiences:

- *Cultural Training for Managers and Students.* Throughout the year MIC conducts a one-week cultural orientation course for graduate managers from Eastern Europe and Third World nations. This program introduces participants to American cultures and values and prepares them for their work or study experience in the United States. Recently, ninety French-speaking Africans from Senegal, Cameroon, and Zaire participated in an intercultural training program conducted in French.

- *U.S. Study Programs for Senior International Leaders.* Each year, MIC coordinates tailored professional study programs for nearly 2,000 people such as elected officials, journalists, business leaders, agronomists, and manufacturers. Group and individual projects are conducted on topics such as the U.S. political process, economics, education, and the environment and take place in cities throughout the United States. Typical programs include Yugoslavians learning about commercial and investment banking, Brazilians learning about American trade policies, and Thais meeting with Americans to develop refugee policies.

- *World Affairs Seminars.* Every year ambassadors and high-level diplomatic officials from over 100 countries attend MIC seminars discussing topics on a variety of international political and economic issues. MIC also provides language training and recreational activities for diplomatic families.

SUMMARY

HRD has had a long and increasingly important history in the United States. Over $250 billion per year is spent on training, and some 200,000 people work in the HRD field. The need, however, far exceeds these resources as only 10 percent of the work force is trained each year.

Over the past few years, several major shifts have occurred in HRD, including (a) shift of emphasis from nice-to-know courses to needs-driven programs such as team productivity and quality, (b) shift of status with HRD enjoying more organizational respect, (c) shift of provider from internal to external HRD professionals, (d) shift of content to areas such as marketing, leadership, and technology, (e) shift of recipient to include people at both the higher and lower levels of the organizations, and (f) shift to more technology-based methods.

This chapter described the highly acclaimed HRD programs of Xerox Corporation, Aetna Life and Casualty, Federal Express, Business Council for International Understanding, and Meridian International Center.

REFERENCES

AMERICAN SOCIETY FOR TRAINING AND DEVELOPMENT. *Serving The New Corporation.* Alexandria, Va.: ASTD Press, 1986.

CARNEVALE, ANTHONY P. *Train America's Workforce.* Alexandria, Va.: ASTD, 1990.

GALAGAN, PATRICIA. "David T. Kearns: A CEO's View of Training." *Training and Development Journal* (May 1990), pp. 41–50.

GALAGAN, PATRICIA. "Training Delivers Results to Federal Express." *Training and Development Journal* (December 1991), pp. 27–33.

GALAGAN, PATRICIA. "Underwriting Business with Training." *Training and Development Journal* (October 1989), pp. 30–35.

KLIEMAN, CAROL. "Recession or Not, Training Remains an Essential Expense." *Washington Post* (January 19, 1992).

PETERS, TOM. *Thriving on Chaos.* New York: Alfred A. Knopf, 1987.

Entering the Global HRD Field

Today, tens of thousands of people around the world work in the field of global human resource development. They work as curriculum developers, consultants and researchers, training instructors, administrators, and career counselors. The work can be exhausting, frustrating, and often unsuccessful, but it can also be the most exciting, challenging, rewarding, and important work in the world.

In Chapter 21, we explore the career opportunities in global HRD. Career opportunities in five organizational categories are considered—corporations, consulting firms, public international, government, and private, nonprofit agencies. Sample international HRD positions as well as resources are provided in each category. In Chapter 22, we examine the competencies (attitudes, skills, and knowledge) essential for being successful in human resource development when working in global or multicultural settings.

Every year, millions of people from every country are sent abroad for short- and long-term work assignments. For many, it is not a productive or satisfying venture because they had not been prepared prior to departure, supported while abroad, or welcomed back to the home organization. In Chapter 23, we describe the types of HRD programs that effectively assist people in these cross-cultural experiences. The content, timing, and training techniques of effective global orientation programs are discussed and analyzed.

❦ ❦

CHAPTER 21

Career Opportunities in Global HRD

INTRODUCTION

Few employment arenas are as exciting, rewarding entrepreneurial, intriguing, mysterious, and fraught with mischief and misfits as is the international job market.

Ronald Krannich
The Complete Guide to International Jobs and Careers

A career in the field of global HRD is as exciting and challenging as any opportunity can be. While there are difficulties and frustrations exacerbated by operating in a cultural setting other than your own, thousands of HRD professionals are working successfully in over 170 countries around the world.

In this chapter, we will examine career opportunities by surveying five broad categories of institutions that employ global HRD professionals. In exploring each of these categories, we will identify the employment characteristics of representative organizations and the types of HRD jobs available. Resources for additional assistance and information will also be provided.

❦ Value

An understanding of HRD career opportunities, the organizations that are most likely to provide them, and the various types of jobs available will enable you to evaluate the field in terms of your own needs and desires. The resources that are identified as being able to provide additional information and assistance will form a good basis for research into any particular area that might be of interest.

❦ Learning Objectives

After studying this chapter, you should be able to:

1. Identify the categories of institutions that offer global HRD employment opportunities
2. Understand the employment characteristics of these various types of institutions
3. List the types of HRD jobs available in the global marketplace
4. Know where to obtain additional employment information and assistance through the resources listed

There are five major organizational categories for global HRD opportunities—multinational corporations, training and consulting firms, public international organizations, government agencies, and nonprofit organizations.

MULTINATIONAL CORPORATIONS

Over 100,000 U.S. firms are involved in international business, and 25 percent of them maintain offices abroad. Many U.S. multinationals earn 50 percent or more of their revenue from overseas operations. Hundreds of smaller U.S. firms are also involved in importing or exporting products and services. As a matter of fact, *USA Today* recently reported that 34 percent of firms with less than ten employees were operating internationally!

In addition to U.S. firms, there are thousands of foreign owned companies in the United States, most of them from Canada, Britain, France, Germany, the Netherlands, and Japan.

HRD positions in these U.S. and foreign multinationals are growing. Emphasis is placed on high performance individuals who are creative and results oriented. Management and language skills are highly valued. These global companies generally seek employees with experience in their particular industry.

Some growth areas in the corporate world include Eastern Europe, Japan, Indonesia, and Mexico. Southern Africa, Thailand, and Spain also appear to be expanding areas for U.S. corporations.

Computers, electronics, telecommunications, pharmaceutical, and petroleum are hiring in particularly large numbers. Banks and other financial institutions will continue to expand because of the interdependence bred by a global economy. As businesses grow globally, so does the travel industry. Hotels, airlines, restaurants, and tourist services are all places in which the number of international jobs are rapidly expanding.

Larger global corporations today tend to have fewer overseas assignments because of the growing costs of expatriates and the availability of talented local staff. Therefore, some of the best opportunities for working abroad may be with small companies just entering the international arena or expanding into new countries.

Human resource opportunities in large multinational corporations include positions in recruitment, compensation, relocations, staff relations, labor relations, organization development, staff planning, and training. The want ads for international corporate HRD jobs might look like this:

- *International Training Manager—Citibank.* Manage marketing, design, and delivery of international customer training programs to help participants from over sixty countries become more sophisticated investors. Maintain good cross-cultural relations among participants. Consult with senior line presenters and subject-matter experts on their presentations.
- *Regional Training Center Director—Union Oil Company.* Supervise series of technical training programs, sometimes including English-language training. Manage line supervisors and guarantee smooth supervisor-employee relationships.

Keep in mind that few multinational employers have strictly international career paths. A lot of trainers in these organizations alternate between domestic and foreign assignments.

The best source for identifying which U.S. corporations are operating in which countries is the *Directory of American Firms Operating in Foreign Countries.* The *Directory of Foreign Firms Operating in the U.S.* provides similar information on foreign firms operating in the United States. Another valuable resource is the International Division of the U.S. Chamber of Commerce which has lists of its organizational members in over forty countries.

TRAINING AND CONSULTING FIRMS

There are over 100,000 consultants worldwide earning over $10 billion per year. Recent figures from *Consultant News* suggest that the consulting business has been growing at 20 percent to 25 percent a year, ranging from 15 percent a year for strategy consulting to as much as 50 percent a year for instructional technology work.

Consulting firms are generally composed of three levels of employees: (1) a core of permanent managerial and technical staff; (2) associates who, although independent, work a high percentage of their time with this particular consulting firm; and (3) short-term consultants who are hired for specific projects ranging from a few days to several months. Occasionally a three-year or five-year contract designed to institutionalize change in a country's infrastructure will require a long-term consultant. Compensation is usually based on a daily rate ranging from $200 to $2,000 per day.

Many international consultants work independently for a number of different consulting firms. Consulting firms maintain computerized rosters and include these resumes in the project proposals they submit to contracting organizations.

Consulting firms generally look for people who can "hit the ground running," i.e., they have the technical and language skills necessary to immediately begin delivering the products or services requested. In addition to the technical skills needed overseas, these firms look for project managers, administrative staff, technical specialists, and proposal writers to work at their main offices.

Skill areas which are most in demand today include agriculture, entrepreneurship, economics, human resource development, health, and management training.

There are a number of ways to locate the consulting firms which are most successful in the international arena: (1) the weekly business section of major newspapers, (2) the "Contract Awards" section of the *Commerce Business Daily*, and (3) *Consultant News*.

The international consulting market is lucrative but volatile. To be a successful consultant, you must constantly sell yourself because you live from one contract to another. It's important to be on top of the geographical changes that transform this field. Five years ago, government-assistance consulting contracts focused on French-speaking West Africa. A couple of years ago, this focus shifted to the Caribbean Basin. Now it's on Central America and Eastern Europe.

Typical HRD jobs in international consulting firms include:

- *Health Specialist—Trade Tech International.* Six-month assignment. Work with counterparts on project team to design a program for Ministry of Health. At the end of six months, local government officials will take over project management.
- *Management Consultant—Booz Allen and Hamilton.* Provide management consultation to new or expanding organizations in small-business development. Consult with government agencies or multinational corporations on how to develop entrepreneurial activity in a particular country.

PUBLIC INTERNATIONAL ORGANIZATIONS

The Public International Organizations—the World Bank, International Monetary Fund, Organization of American States, Pan American Health Organization, United Nations Development Program, and the International Labor Office, and others—employ more than 100,000 people around the world.

Going the route of the public international organizations is one of the most difficult ways to enter the international HRD job scene. The United Nations describes its "typical recruit" as a thirty-six-year-old who has an advanced degree, high-level experience, and is fluent in at least two of the official languages of the UN—i.e., Arabic, Chinese, English, French, Russian, or Spanish.

Because of high salaries, excellent benefits, cross-cultural contacts, opportunities for causing macro changes, and job prestige, there is keen competition for jobs within these organizations. There are also general quotas for each nationality based upon the contribution of a government to the particular UN organization. Americans account for approximately 15 percent of the employees of public international organizations.

An excellent source of information and assistance regarding job opportunities with the UN are the UN information offices located throughout the world. Current positions available are contained in loose-leaf binders at these offices where one can also pick up UN application forms and other job resource materials.

Salaries are quite good in these organizations, ranging from $25,000 per year for a junior-level hire to $100,000 for senior overseas positions. Generous benefits—free housing, free tuition for school-age children, and duty-free importation of goods—make public international jobs very attractive.

These organizations tend to be hierarchical, bureaucratic, and slow moving. Decisions on HRD programs may involve a host of people, and innovation requires consensus across a wide range of cultural biases.

The following positions represent HRD assignments common in public multinationals:

- *Training Analyst—United Nations Institute for Training and Research (UNITAR)*. Analyze training needs for U.N. staff. Orient new delegates to General Assembly procedures. Research international training issues.
- *Technical Specialist—World Health Organization*. Conduct technical training for health-care counterparts in various overseas locations. Design, deliver, and evaluate the training.

GOVERNMENT AGENCIES

The federal government provides a large number of international job opportunities. Over 50,000 federal civilians work overseas for the U.S. government (in addition to the 500,000 in the U.S. military). Another 50,000 to 75,000 federal employees work in international-related jobs in the United States. Nearly every single federal agency has international interests and staffs its agency accordingly.

In addition, international opportunities with state and city governments are rapidly growing. These agencies are increasingly involved in trade, promotion, tourism, and shipping. The governors of several states have made extensive efforts to increase exports from their states, and numerous staff positions have been created to effect that effort.

The federal agencies with the largest number of international positions are:

- Department of Defense (with numerous types of civilian positions in over forty countries)
- Department of Commerce (International Trade Administration, Foreign Commercial Service)
- U.S. Information Agency (Voice of America)
- Department of State
- Peace Corps
- Department of the Treasury (U.S. Customs Service, Office of International Tax Affairs)
- U.S. Agency for International Development
- Department of Agriculture (Foreign Agricultural Service)

It is important to realize that federal agencies that are primarily international in scope (e.g., State Department, U.S. Agency for International Development) follow a different personnel system (Foreign Service Rank) than the domestic-focused agencies governed by the Office of Personnel Management.

There are a number of newsletters which focus on job vacancies in the U.S. government, with special sections on international jobs. Two of the best are *Federal Research Services* and *Federal Jobs Digest*.

Government employees posted overseas enjoy life styles similar to those of public international employees. Someone with a bachelor's degree can expect to start with a salary between $20,000 and $30,000. A master's degree warrants between $30,000 and $40,000.

The foreign service exam is the official passport to the government's international HRD positions. Offered every December at universities in the

United States and overseas, the exam asks multiple-choice questions about everything under the sun—politics, economics, art, music, literature, and more.

The Peace Corps stands out as a superb means of entering the international field—as a volunteer if you have little or no HRD experience or as a trainer if you have an extensive background. Many of the mid- and senior-level international HRD professionals in the U.S. government began their careers as Peace Corps volunteers.

Typical HRD jobs in the government include:

- *Program Administrator—Foreign Service Institute.* Manage staff of HRD professionals to deliver wide range of training courses. Responsible for recruitment of instructors and general administration.
- *Trade Consultant—State Office for International Trade.* Provide training and technical services to state-based corporations seeking to export products overseas.

NONPROFIT ORGANIZATIONS

This category of international jobs includes private voluntary organizations, educational and exchange institutions, and associations, foundations, and research organizations.

❦ *Private Voluntary Organizations*

Among the more well-known local private voluntary organizations (PVOs) are American Red Cross, CARE, Save the Children, Foster Parents International, Catholic Relief Service, YMCA, Christian Children's Fund, and the Salvation Army. Most PVOs are fairly small with staff sizes being generally less than fifty employees.

These organizations provide a variety of services to Third World countries such as feeding the hungry, caring for children, promoting health care, providing medical assistance, and conducting educational programs. People seeking to better the world rather than seeking high salaries gravitate to these organizations.

The PVOs recruit people who have grass-roots experience (like returned Peace Corps volunteers), a technical skill (health, agriculture, business, etc.), good management skills, and the ability to work effectively in another culture at the grass-roots level.

Pay for staff positions is usually low, with entry-level salaries in the neighborhood of $15,000. Executive directors may earn no more than

$60,000. To gain a staff position, it helps to network among board members and existing staff.

Private voluntary organizations offer HRD jobs like these:

- *Training Director—Save the Children Federation.* Train field staff in community-development skills. Periodically travel to overseas programs to conduct technical or management training. May supervise a small staff of two or three trainers.
- *Community Development Worker—World Education.* Help low-income women develop occupational skills. Design and conduct training in health, child care, and nutrition.

PVO overseas employees must often deal with host-country ministry officials, headquarters personnel in the United States, AID officials in Washington and in the host country, and local program participants. HRD positions in these organizations demand persistence and creativity.

There are a number of resources for locating international jobs in this category. The three best are:

1. *Interaction's Monday Developments*—a weekly update published by Interaction, a coalition of over 100 PVOs
2. *Access*—a monthly listing of job opportunities with voluntary organizations
3. *Job Opportunities Bulletin*—a bimonthly list of job vacancies available with international PVOs

❦ *Educational and Exchange Institutions*

According to the latest research done by the Institute for International Education, over 400,000 foreign students are studying at U.S. universities. More and more colleges and universities have a high percentage of foreign students, especially in the graduate schools of business and engineering. There are large numbers of students from Southeast Asia (Hong Kong, China, Philippines, Malaysia, India, Indonesia), as well as from Europe and the Middle East.

This large number of foreign students creates hundreds of international HRD jobs for English language training, student counseling, etc. These organizations provide greater opportunity for entry-level positions since overseas experience or a foreign language is not a necessity. The opportunity for cross-cultural experiences with peoples of many countries can be very rewarding.

Thousands of Americans teach overseas at the Department of Defense Dependent Schools; private American schools serving children of diplomats and executives of U.S. corporations (e.g., ARAMCO, Firestone, Mobil); and English-language schools—private or government. Japan, for example, recruits hundreds of Americans every year to teach English in schools and institutes throughout that country. Many embassies will provide pamphlets describing educational opportunities in their countries.

Organizations like the American Field Service, Experiment in International Living, the Institute of International Education, the Council on International Educational Exchange, and Youth for Understanding have extensive international HRD opportunities. So do various nonprofit foundations and institutions of higher learning.

Most of these groups feature lean and flat organizational structures with as few as three levels. So, while it may be easier to enter international HRD through this category than the ones we have already described, there is not much room to move. People in the education and cultural-exchange field often change employers frequently in an effort to gain more responsible and higher-paying positions.

Educational and cultural-exchange organizations prize two essential skills: the ability to design and conduct international education programs and the ability to raise funds. They depend on outside funding—the Agency for International Development (AID) and the U.S. Information Agency in particular—and their programs are susceptible to political and economic changes.

Typical HRD jobs in international educational and cultural exchange organizations include:

* *Foreign Student Adviser—Universities.* Manage cross-cultural orientation programs for foreign students. Direct foreign study programs for Americans. Counsel students on academic and personal adjustment problems.
* *Regional Director—Youth for Understanding.* Recruit host families for visiting foreign students. Train hosts and students. Design cross-cultural workshops for community groups.

❦ *Associations, Foundations, and Research Organizations*

Associations, most of which have an international division, not only offer job opportunities but also can be an excellent source for networking with people with your professional interests who can assist in identifying international HRD jobs. Most of these associations have job banks as well.

Many foundations and research organizations also focus on international development and global issues. While the major international foundations are in New York and the Midwest, scores of international research organizations are located throughout the United States.

SUMMARY

The opportunity for, and the challenge of, a career in international HRD is growing every day. Currently, thousands of HRD professionals are employed in various aspects of the field in more than 170 countries around the world.

The institutions that provide HRD employment opportunities can be classified into five categories:

- Multinational corporations
- Training and consulting firms
- Public international organizations
- Government agencies at the federal, state, and local levels
- Nonprofit organizations

Each of these categories has different employment characteristics, types of HRD jobs available, and resources for additional assistance and information.

Entering any profession can be a challenge, and global HRD is no exception. To be successful, you should: (a) research the HRD field by talking to global practitioners and reading professional journals and books on global HRD; (b) learn about organizations involved in global activities; and (c) develop the global competencies needed for international assignments. The excitement and rewards will be worth the long journey.

REFERENCES

CHANG, RICHARD. *An Introduction to Human Resource Development Careers.* Alexandria, Va.: ASTD Press, 1990.

KOCHER, ERIC. *International Jobs—Where They Are, How to Get Them.* Reading, Mass.: Addison-Wesley, 1989.

KRANNICH, RONALD, AND CARYL KRANNICH. *The Complete Guide to International Jobs and Careers.* Woodbridge, Va.: Impact Publications, 1990.

MARQUARDT, MICHAEL, AND HOWARD SCHUMAN. "Getting an HRD Job Abroad." *Training and Development Journal.* (February 1988), pp. 24–30.

POWELL, JAMES N. *The Prentice-Hall Global Employment Guide.* Englewood Cliffs, N.J.: Prentice-Hall, 1990.

POWERS, LINDA. *Career Opportunities in the International Field.* Washington, D.C.: Georgetown University Press, 1986.

SCHUMAN, HOWARD. *Making It Abroad: The International Job Hunting Guide.* New York: John Wiley and Sons, Inc., 1988.

❦ ❦

CHAPTER 22

Competencies for the Effective Global HRD Practitioner

INTRODUCTION

He who smiles rather than rages is always the stronger.

Japanese Proverb

The reality of this proverb is especially valid for HRD professionals wishing to implement successful programs in another culture. Almost all experienced global employers agree that one of the most important characteristics of workers in a crosscultural environment is their ability to be patient, to relax, and to accept and appreciate the differences and frustrations of life abroad. Clark calls this attitude the "most powerful" skill of the global trainer. A number of other attitudinal, technical, cognitive, and interpersonal skills essential for those implementing HRD activities abroad will also be discussed in this chapter.

❦ Value

An understanding of the competencies that underpin global HRD success will prepare the HRD professional for the challenges and difficulties of being effective in other cultures. A pre-assessment of individual areas of strength and weakness enables the HRD professional to focus on those competencies that need augmentation prior to the beginning of an international assignment.

❦ *Learning Objectives*

1. Describe the competencies that experts have deemed important for international professionals in general and for HRD practitioners in particular.
2. Explain the reasons for the importance of these competencies and provide examples of their day-to-day application in HRD practice.

CHARACTERISTICS AND SKILLS FOR OVERSEAS SUCCESS

A general consensus exists among those who have lived and worked abroad as to what characteristics a person should have to be successful in implementing international program activities (Schuman).

Kohls, in his classic *Survival Kit for Overseas Living*, developed the following list of personal skills that he judges to be important for anyone considering overseas employment:

- Tolerance for ambiguity
- Sense of humor
- Ability to fail
- Motivation
- Self-reliance
- Strong sense of self
- Tolerance for differences
- Communicativeness
- Curiosity
- Perceptiveness
- Warmth in human relations
- Low goal/task orientation
- Open-mindedness
- Non-judgmentalness
- Empathy
- Flexibility/adaptability

Konen arranges the attributes of success under five categories:

1. Job Factors
   (a) Technical skills
   (b) Acquaintance with host-country and headquarters operations
   (c) Managerial skills
   (d) Administrative competence
2. Relational Dimensions
   (a) Tolerance for ambiguity
   (b) Behavioral flexibility
   (c) Non-judgmentalism
   (d) Cultural empathy and low ethnocentrism
   (e) Interpersonal skills

3. Motivational State
   (a) Belief in the mission
   (b) Congruence with career path
   (c) Interest in overseas experience
   (d) Interest in the specific host-country culture
   (e) Willingness to acquire new patterns of behavior and attitudes
4. Family Situation
   (a) Willingness of spouse to live abroad
   (b) Adaptive and supportive spouse
   (c) Stable marriage
5. Language Skills
   (a) Host-country language
   (b) Nonverbal communication

Mendenhall and Oddou assert that success in overseas work assignments depends upon the possession of specific skills that they detail as follows:

❦ *Personal Skills*

Those techniques and attributes that facilitate the expatriate's mental and emotional well being are personal skills. They can include meditation, prayer, or other means of finding solitude, and physical exercise routines, any of which tend to decrease the individual's stress level. One's ability to manage time, delegate, and manage his or her responsibilities are also personal skills.

❦ *People Skills*

Effective interaction with others, particularly with foreigners, is another necessity for successful adaptation. The person who desires or needs to communicate with others, is willing to try to speak the foreign language (even when not necessary), and doesn't worry about making linguistic mistakes is much more likely to be successful than the person who is introverted, self-conscious, or otherwise not comfortable when interacting with foreigners.

❦ *Perception Skills*

These skills deal with the cognitive processes that help the individual understand why foreigners behave the way they do. The willingness to make tentative conclusions from the first observation of different actions and attitudes is an important cognitive dimension. Managers have been taught to size things up quickly to make an equally quick decision. Perception skills also relate to one's consciousness of social cues and behaviors, one's attentiveness to them, and one's ability to imitate what he or she perceives (p. 261).

MEASURING OVERSEAS EFFECTIVENESS

There are a number of instruments that can be used to help a person determine if he has the characteristics and skills to be successful overseas. One of the best instruments to measure potential overseas effectiveness is the Overseas Assignment Inventory developed by Tucker and Baier. It can forecast a person's capacity for crosscultural adjustment and performance by measuring his score on the following 14 success predictors:

1. *Expectations*—Those who are realistic about what it will be like to live and work in a foreign country—including its associated difficulties as well as the probable benefits—have a greater chance of success than those who have low expectations.
2. *Open-mindedness*—Open-minded individuals are those who are receptive to different values and ideas without feeling that their own are being threatened. Those who feel that their beliefs are superior will face greater difficulties.
3. *Respect for others' beliefs*—People who are nonjudgmental and demonstrate a willingness and ability to respect and be interested in the beliefs of others will be more likely to implement meaningful intercultural programs.
4. *Trust in people*—Those who can convey and encourage mutual trust will be more effective.
5. *Tolerance*—The ability to accept and interact with people with fundamentally different habits, life styles, and values is essential for adapting to a foreign environment.
6. *Personal control*—Individuals who believe they can, to some extent, shape or direct the course of their work will be more successful than those who believe that things happen because of luck or fate.
7. *Flexibility*—The ability to try new ideas and realize that there is more than one valid way of approaching a problem is crucial in overseas success.
8. *Patience*—Understanding and accepting delays, different perspectives of time and decision-making styles, bureaucracies, etc. is absolutely essential for global effectiveness.
9. *Adaptability*—Those who can socialize comfortably with new people in new surroundings will be more effective than the loner who feels comfortable only with familiar friends with similar values.
10. *Self-confidence/Initiative*—Self-starters who not only trust their own judgments but also are willing to accept the judgments and methods of others will be more successful than those who wait for direction and push from headquarters or from local people in country.

11. *Sense of humor*—A key crosscultural skill is the ability to bring humor into difficult situations, and to be able to laugh at and learn from one's own mistakes.

12. *Interpersonal interest*—Those who are truly interested in and concerned about others have a great advantage in working overseas.

13. *Interpersonal harmony*—Empathy, acceptance, and the ability to mediate disagreements can enhance organizational effectiveness.

14. *Spouse/family communication*—People with strong, open communication patterns will be better able to handle cultural difficulties than those experiencing stress and troubled family relationships.

COMPETENCIES FOR GLOBAL HRD EFFECTIVENESS

Over the past several years, the authors have interviewed scores of international professionals from all over the world to find out what they considered to be the most important competencies for individuals in the training and development field. Although similar to those mentioned above, there were some differences and additions. The sixteen global HRD competencies, (which we have classified according to attitudes, skills, and knowledge) most frequently and strongly supported were the following:

ATTITUDES

❦ Respect for the Values and Practices of Other Cultures

HRD practitioners, like everyone else, grow up learning what they believe is the best way of acting and behaving; to think or act otherwise would be foolish. Our mind is "programmed" to think in a certain way; society through religion, schools, politics, and other cultural factors reinforces this ethnocentric way of acting; we think that we are the best, that we have all the answers. Americans, in particular, have been taught that their way is the best, that other ways are inferior and need to be changed.

It is difficult, therefore, to accept the fact that other ways of thinking and opposite values should be respected. As Storti states, "One must accept the other culture, not that it is good or bad, but different" (p. 10). Learners easily recognize if they and their way of life are respected or rejected by the trainer. They value sensitivity to their different world view.

It is important to note that the learners do not usually expect you to adopt the practices of their culture. The authors remember one American trainer who dressed in the Saudi tradition, i.e., "went native," when training. This act was ridiculed by the trainees and harmed rather than helped the learning process.

❦ *Patience and Tolerance*

Coping with the unavoidable stress of an intercultural setting is difficult. Yet the ability to react to new, different, and, at times, unpredictable situations with little visible discomfort or irritation is important for the global HRD professionals.

The "jiitsu" of adapting to an unclear and differently programmed environment requires a tremendous amount of patience. Always allow plenty of time for laying the groundwork before beginning HRD activities.

That we can control time and the future are fundamental American beliefs, but they may be totally opposite to the beliefs of other cultures. Waiting for consensus is extremely difficult for Americans yet essential in developing HRD programs, negotiating contracts, and training participants.

❦ *Commitment to HRD*

A healthy respect for one's profession and a concern for one's image are important attitudes. Demonstrating a commitment toward high quality and believing that HRD is an important leverage for developing individuals, organizations, and nations sets apart the mediocre from the effective global HRD professionals.

This attitude leads one to seek to be thoroughly prepared for all HRD activities, to accept personal responsibility for efforts, and to always show concern for quality and improvement.

❦ *Initiative and Persistence*

Often global HRD practitioners find themselves far away from headquarters and in a cultural environment that may expect all initiative and direction to come from them. Sometimes the learners have no interest in working and want you to relax, enjoy the fine weather, and socialize. There are even times when the trainees may see you as imposing corporate values and work behavior (e.g., management by objectives, participative management) that is contrary to their cultural beliefs and practices. These are the occasions, and they are not infrequent, in which the initiative and persistence of the global HRD practitioner are all that stand between success and failure.

❦ *Sense of Humor*

Global HRD professionals should have a sense of humor, i.e., the humility and ability to laugh as you deal with the unexpected and the unknown.

Stress can be very high in intercultural situations where one is uncertain about what to expect and has less control over one's interactions or results. A sense of humor is, as Schuman writes, "indispensable for dealing with the cultural mistakes and faux pas you will certainly commit" (p. 11).

SKILLS

❦ *HRD Skills*

To implement HRD programs in other cultural environments, you must have a strong mastery of the HRD skill competencies. As was seen in Chapters 3 through 6, each of the major HRD roles must be adapted to the cultural environment. Developing a learning climate, designing training programs, transmitting information and experience, assessing results, providing career counseling, creating organizational change, and adapting learning materials are much more complicated in a culture other than our own. If a consultant or administrator does not already possess strong HRD skills and competencies in his own culture, those weaknesses will be magnified in other cultures.

❦ *Communication Skills*

Communications is the sine qua non skill in working across cultures. Even if the learner speaks English, the idiomatic expressions and examples used in the United States may be unintelligible in another cultural setting. Speaking more clearly and slowly is important.

Listening also becomes much more complex. Understanding nonverbal messages provided by a person from another culture may be difficult. Yet, as Clark states, "being aware of what others are feeling" is also critical in intercultural consultation and training. For example, in the United States we are encouraged to ask questions in order to assure good communications. In some cultures, this may be perceived as incompetent or even rude.

❦ *Creativity*

The global HRD environment requires a great deal of creativity and adaptability. Programs and procedures need to be modified or changed totally for the learners and the organization. Training styles must be adjusted. Even problem solving may require new approaches, since participative approaches may not be culturally appropriate.

❦ *Cultural Flexibility*

Adjusting to another culture is a skill which many people lack. As a result, they either return home before the assignment is completed or remain, but with a negative attitude toward all or most of the local culture and customs.

There are a number of ways that help the global HRD practitioner to gain a reasonable cultural adjustment level:

- Continue to learn more about the host country
- Attempt to find the cultural reason behind everything in the new environment
- Do not succumb to disparagement of the host culture
- Identify sympathetic host country people with whom to share confusion and frustration
- Have faith in yourself and in the positive outcome of the experience

❦ *Self-Management of Learning*

Globalization has made change ever faster and convulsive. Technology and information push the need for continuous learning of new knowledge and skills. To deal with this continuous chaos, the HRD professional must have the ability to correctly diagnose learning needs and to identify the sources necessary to provide such learning. The global HRD professional needs to update and expand technical, managerial, and interpersonal knowledge on an ongoing basis.

KNOWLEDGE

❦ *Knowledge of One's Own Culture*

Recently, a number of noted intercultural specialists were asked what information was most needed by people working in another culture. Ranked number one was "knowledge of one's own culture." Know thyself, therefore, is the first lesson for global HRD professionals since our behavior is influenced by our basic cultural values, beliefs, and assumptions. Unless we become conscious of these values and carefully examine them, we will not be able to understand why we react toward other cultures in the way that we do.

Before embarking on an international HRD career, one should consider attending a cross-cultural or cultural-awareness program. Examples of such cultural programs are described in Chapter 23.

❦ Knowledge of Other Culture

To fully appreciate the local culture and to achieve maximum benefit from the HRD experience, one must learn as much as one can about the culture. Having such information will provide the practitioner with reference points, case studies, resources, and cultural values—all of which will make the HRD program more relevant and effective.

Kohls recommends gathering information about these ten areas as valuable in working in another country:

1. Symbols
2. Human and Natural Resources
3. Family and Social Structure
4. Fine Arts and Cultural Achievements
5. Religion and Philosophy
6. Economics and Industry
7. Education
8. Politics and Government
9. Science
10. History

❦ HRD Field

As the technology of HRD advances rapidly, the global HRD practitioner must utilize this new information and capability to effectively work in other cultures. He should be aware of the key forces influencing HRD around the world, be able to tap into HRD data bases, and be familiar with computer-assisted-instruction (CAI). It is important for him to stay current with HRD literature and research.

❦ Language

More and more global HRD practitioners are stressing the importance of speaking or, as a minimum, understanding basic phrases and the structural content of the target language. Language is important because it reflects cultural nuances. For example, Mandarin provides a sense of hierarchy, place, and order. The Thai language shows great respect for elders. The Spanish language reflects the passive locus of control.

In addition to the verbal, spoken language, nonverbal language is critical in understanding a culture. The body language, gestures, and environment of a high-context culture often communicate more clearly and completely than the verbal language.

Almost everyone appreciates attempts by a nonnative speaker to communicate in the native language. Often the show of good will is much more important than the degree of proficiency in the utterance. One of the authors recalls a humorous situation on an Italian train in which he and another man stumbled through several minutes of halting French before they discovered they were both Americans.

❦ *Corporate Culture*

White and others stress the importance of knowing and understanding the strategic dimensions of the corporation or business that is your employer or your client. Too often HRD practitioners are not very knowledgeable about corporate culture—its history, rituals, structure, strategies, communication processes, symbols, etc. Increasingly, they will need to start up, lead and mobilize corporate teams to work on issues such as product development, marketing, and sourcing.

❦ *Global Perspective*

Globalization is the key dynamic as we enter the twenty-first century. Global telecommunications and international business competition have forced most industries into globalizing. Global HRD professionals must obviously understand the elements that have created globalization, including global political and economic issues, and the steps necessary for organizations to become functionally global. They need to know the standards and models of successful globalization and resources for guiding that process. They must understand the thinking and behavior of both customers and competitors around the world. An essential attribute will be their ability to analyze, join in, and create global networks for acquiring worldwide information and influencing people worldwide.

SUMMARY

Since practicing HRD in one's own culture is often difficult and challenging, it should come as no surprise that doing so in a foreign environment is even more so. Every HRD role and each culture demands specific competencies. Based upon interviews with scores of recognized successful HRD practitioners, the authors have identified sixteen competencies deemed important in all situations and classified them under the categories of attitudes, skills, and knowledge.

Of the three categories, attitudes are undoubtedly the most important and include respect for the values and practices of other cultures, patience with ambiguity, a commitment to HRD, initiative and persistence, and a sense of humor.

The HRD professional will also find it useful to have skills in HRD practice, communication, creativity, cultural adjustment, and self-managed learning. Finally, a knowledge of one's own culture, the target culture, the field of HRD, target language, client corporate culture, and the global perspective will contribute to an HRD practitioner's success in international assignments.

REFERENCES

CLARK, CLIFFORD. "East Meets West," *Training and Development Journal* (October 1990), pp. 43–47

KOHLS, ROBERT. L. *Overseas Survival Kit for Overseas Living*, 2nd ed. Yarmouth, Maine: Intercultural Press, 1984.

MENDENHALL, MARK AND GARY ODDOU. *International Human Resource Management*. Boston: Kent Publishing Company, 1991.

RONEN, S. "Training the International Assignee," in *Training and Career Development*, edited by I. Goldstein. San Francisco: Jossey-Bass, 1989.

SCHUMAN, HOWARD. *Making It Abroad: The International Job Hunting Guide*. New York: John Wiley & Sons, 1988.

STORTI, CRAIG. *The Art of Crossing Cultures*. Yarmouth, Maine: Intercultural Press, 1989.

CHAPTER 23

❦ ❦

Preparation for Global HRD Assignments

INTRODUCTION

People who go abroad to live and work do genuinely want to adapt to the local culture; most of them, however, do not.

Craig Stort:
The Art of Crossing Cultures

Until recently, multinationals and especially those based in the United States have often treated expatriate assignments as a sort of necessary nuisance and have sometimes selected candidates for them from among those who could be spared rather than those who might be most appropriate or effective. As geopolitical and economic changes sweep through the global business communities, strategic planners in these same companies are beginning to see foreign assignments as a necessary and desirable feature of both individual and company growth. As a result, the process of selecting, training, supporting, rewarding, and learning from expatriates has become an important upper-management concern in many global organizations.

277

❦ Value

Familiarity with the best practices of successful HRD departments in recruiting, preparing, and supporting expatriates will enable you to both employ these practices as an HRD professional and assess the process that is in place in a company where you might be considering an overseas assignment yourself. Experience and research have both shown that early returns of expatriates or failures to achieve goals in overseas assignments can be dramatically reduced if more care is given to HRD practices in expatriate selection, preparation, and support.

❦ Learning Objectives

After studying this chapter, you should be able to:

1. Identify the strategies that support the best possible personal and organizational results from expatriate assignments
2. Describe best practices in expatriate selection, preparation, support, and return
3. Recognize the value of merging long-term strategic planning with overseas assignment policy and process
4. Identify organizationwide benefits that can be gained through appropriate recognition and use of repatriate resources

NEED FOR HRD SUPPORT FOR OVERSEAS ASSIGNMENTS

Every year there are a high number of unsuccessful adjustments and early returns of American business expatriates. Well over 30 percent of U.S. corporate overseas assignments fail. Copeland and Griggs have estimated that the direct cost of these failed expatriate assignments is over $2 billion a year, not including loss of future business opportunities and damage to corporate reputations.

There are several causes for these failures. Number one is lack of preparation for the overseas assignment. Following close behind are careless and inefficient selection processes, lack of preparation and provision for the expatriate family, insufficient organizational support of the expatriate, and individual inability to adjust to the foreign culture or business environment. Since people don't usually go overseas for HRD assignments on their own, we need to focus here on the process that companies use in order to prepare individuals for overseas assignments, whether of an HRD or other nature.

If we take the causes for expatriate failure noted above, rearrange them chronologically, and look at them from a preventive point of view, we've created a good strategy for ensuring expatriate success:

1. Make overseas assignments both an integral part of managers' career development and a valued asset in future selection and promotion decisions.
2. Establish selection criteria and use them extensively and carefully in selecting candidates for overseas assignments.
3. Prepare expatriates, once they've been identified, by providing extensive education and training designed to give them the information and skills required for success.
4. Recognize the expatriate's family situation and provide practical and human support for the family.
5. Ensure communication with, and support of, the expatriate during the overseas assignment.
6. Plan for repatriation from the very beginning of the assignment and take advantage as an organization of the experience and knowledge brought back by expatriates.

It's immediately apparent from this list that many of the necessary conditions for expatriate success must be established by the company. These conditions alone will not be sufficient, but their absence imperils any overseas assignment.

ASSIGNING ORGANIZATIONAL VALUE TO OVERSEAS ASSIGNMENTS

U.S. companies have historically undervalued the importance of overseas assignments. They were seen, at the very least, as a temporary switching of personnel to a sidetrack while the express continued down the main line. At worst, they were a signal that a career peak had been reached and was unlikely to be surpassed. These days, however, the continuing shock waves of global competition felt by American business have jarred this perception considerably. Increasingly, overseas assignments are seen as an integral concern in strategic planning. The survival of the company in the global marketplace is at stake. Adler observes that assigning someone to an international project involves more than just getting the job done. It also involves selecting someone specifically for the benefit of the overall operation and for international career development—to get to know the worldwide networks and contacts for information and communication links and to help the firm itself to integrate and develop into a global organization.

At Xerox, for example, a heightened sense of global customer needs has resulted in an emphasis on overseas assignments. According to David Muxworthy, manager of Senior Management Education, at least 80 percent of Xerox's top 300 managers have had international assignments. "It's extremely important, not simply as an exercise. We think it's critical to really understanding the differences between business practices and markets in different countries. Most Americans, even if they've done a lot of reading about how the world has changed and what an international business really is, don't get a true feeling for that unless they've experienced it firsthand" (Callahan, p. 29).

In addition to placing recognizable value on expatriate assignments, organizations need to create clear career expectations and paths for those who go overseas. The international assignment should be seen by everyone as a first step in a process that, managed successfully, can lead to the top of the global organization. One way to make this perception real is to dedicate significant upper-management attention and company resources to developing international career paths.

An example can be seen in corporate sponsorship of the University of Michigan's Global Leadership program. The thirty-four corporate sponsors, including such global giants as NEC, Exxon, Philips, Sony, American Express, and Bull, not only send key executives to a five-week off-site program at the cost of $30,000 per participant but also commit to three years of action research on globalization within their own companies. Typical areas of research include assessing the company's progress in the globalization process as well as the degree of internal operational management success. The signal these companies are sending both internally and externally is that global experience and career success within the organization go hand in hand.

Boyacigiller, in a study of the international staffing practices of a major U.S. financial institution, concludes: "international staffing decisions need to be tied to other strategic decisions. The emphasis during staffing should be on long-term organizational development and management development and above all on long-term commitment to learning about international markets. The international education that future executives could acquire in these types of assignments cannot be replicated in any classroom" (p. 154).

ESTABLISHING AND EMPLOYING EXPATRIATE SELECTION CRITERIA

As awareness of the importance of overseas assignments and the cost of their failure has begun to grow, companies have started to pay closer attention to the selection process. Initially this resulted in an interim, unsuccessful strategy of sending the "best man." As Dunn points out, the best candidate based upon a domestic track record is often exactly the wrong person to send on an expatriate assignment. Success in the rough-and-tumble world of New York's financial community does not guarantee success in the world of Japanese finance. In fact, the skills and attitudes needed in New York are probably those that will lead to frustration and failure when applied in Tokyo.

In the "best man" approach, technical knowledge has often been emphasized to the exclusion of almost all other criteria. Of course, technical knowledge has always been a prerequisite for success in business assignments, and it should always be a factor in the selection process. However, lack of technical knowledge has rarely been the main reason for failure in overseas assignments, and it is usually safe to assume that the selection process will include an evaluation of technical skills.

What expatriates have often lacked are the people skills and cross-cultural understanding necessary to bring their technical savvy to bear in an effective manner. Candidates, no matter their native country, should never be selected on purely local criteria; in fact, quite the opposite should be the case. Importance must be given to the candidate's ability to see beyond the local national culture and to move into the cultural world of his or her assignment.

IBM's Laidlaw says that the corporation has become more selective over the years about the people it sends on international assignments. "We're trying to be more sensitive and careful. We're giving more consideration to the individual's potential. We're considering the value of the assignment, both to the individual and to the business" (Callahan, p. 32).

Those companies that have gone beyond the "best man" approach have established selection criteria for identifying the best candidates for each expatriate situation. Not surprisingly, they have found that many of the personal characteristics we identified in Chapter 22 are indicators of success in overseas assignments. These include characteristics such as cultural self-awareness, nonjudgmental perspective, self-support and motivation, tolerance of ambiguous situations, and commitment to professional behavior.

In the selection process, you're faced with the challenge of learning a great deal about a person under less than ideal circumstances. While each of these skills might be easily recognized over a long working relationship with an individual, they are difficult to assess in a relatively brief selection process. In the end, evaluations by colleagues, psychological appraisal, candidate self-evaluation, the impressions of interviewers, and even anecdotal material all become part of the mix in determining a candidate's personal skills and attributes.

PREPARING AND TRAINING EXPATRIATES FOR THEIR ASSIGNMENTS

Once a candidate has been selected for an expatriate assignment, there is usually a need for extensive orientation and training with regard to the target country and culture, as well as the particular features of the assignment. The exact nature of the preparation process depends upon the candidate profile and the degree of similarity between native and target cultures.

For most Americans, expatriation to any country other than Canada, and in some cases England, is a big step in terms of cultural and language adjustment. To a lesser degree, other foreign nationals face similar challenges when they move away from their immediate geographic area. Because of their history and geography, Europeans, perhaps more than other people, are likely to speak two or more languages and move relatively easily between or among their cultures. Educated natives of a country with a colonial history are also likely to be conversant with two cultures and move easily between them. For the rest of us, however, and especially Americans, expatriation is a formidable challenge that is best addressed early and extensively.

Most corporations make some attempt to prepare employees for overseas assignments; the question is one of degree. Efforts range from having the prospective expatriate talk with a couple of colleagues who have worked in the target country to providing on-site corporate training programs to sending candidates to seminars like the University of Michigan's intensive Global Leadership program or to consulting firms like Moran, Stahl, and Boyer, which specialize in intercultural skills training.

Such training programs, whether they are conducted by corporate training staff or outside consultants, are typically designed to address the participants' awareness, attitudes, knowledge, and skills with regard to the target culture. Goals include providing:

- Understanding and insight into global and regional geopolitical forces and changes and their relationship to business
- Awareness of the existence of cultural differences and an understanding of the basis of these differences, especially as they occur between the native and foreign cultures
- Tools and techniques for developing and practicing effective business strategies within the foreign culture
- Global business strategies for establishing joint ventures and alliances
- Skill building in areas such as language, interpersonal communication, adjustment, and adaptation
- Leadership and management skills needed in global companies

Methods for achieving these goals can include instruction and training by content experts, country and regional briefings by embassy personnel or others who are knowledgeable about the foreign culture, predeparture visits to the overseas location, and strategy sessions with regional managers and other expatriates with experience in the region.

Moran, Stahl, and Boyer, among the best-known American firms specializing in intercultural training, offers a four-phase training model. Contents and specifics will vary depending upon client needs and target cultures, but programs typically include these levels:

- Level 1 training raises participants' awareness of cultural differences and examines the effects they have on business situations.
- Level 2 focuses on cultural attitudes and how they are formed.
- Level 3 provides background knowledge and practical information about the target country.
- Level 4 concentrates on skill building in areas such as language, nonverbal communication, cultural stress management, and adjustment and adaptation.

Many corporations turn to consulting and training firms to provide specialized aspects of expatriate training and preparation. For example, East West Consulting Group, based in Lafayette, California, offers language and cross-cultural training that covers every region of the world. A typical East West cross-cultural program might last from two to five days and include video and other types of presentations, identification of the features and beliefs of the participants' own culture, cross-cultural simulations, and learning sessions with foreign informants from the target culture.

The goals of such a program are to enable participants to better:

1. Understand that their concepts of what's important in business (and in life) are culturally based and not universally shared
2. Recognize the key areas in business where the target culture and the native culture differ in priorities and beliefs
3. Apply verbal and nonverbal communication skills in job-related cross-cultural communications
4. Identify typical areas of cultural misunderstanding such as:

   - directness
   - willingness to commit
   - trust
   - people versus task orientation
   - authority and power structures
   - role of tradition and respect
   - time orientation
   - profit and other motivations

5. Understand and respond to target culture business practices, protocol, and management styles
6. Develop action plans designed to enhance cross-cultural communication and management skills

One of the East West Consulting Group's cross-cultural programs, tailored specifically for Americans going to Japan, includes the following areas of concentration:

1. Overview of Cross-Cultural Challenge
2. Successful Intercultural Adjustment
3. Culture: Definition, Components, Characteristics
4. Cultural Self-Awareness
5. The Role of Perception
6. Factors Creating and Influencing Cultural Environment
   - Religion
   - Education
   - Economics
   - Politics
   - Family
   - Class Structure
   - Language
   - History
   - Natural Resources
   - Geography

7. The American World View: Beliefs, Values, Norms, Attitudes, Assumptions, Expectations
8. The Japanese World View Compared and Contrasted with the American
9. Comparison of Key Elements of Japanese and American Cultures
   - Sense of self
   - Notions of Time
   - Norms and Values
   - Communications and Language
   - Dress and Appearance
   - Food and Eating Habits
   - Relationships
   - Beliefs and Attitudes
   - Mental Processes and Learning
   - Work Habits and Practices

10. The Japanese Business Context
    - Professional Behavior
    - Social Behavior in Business Situations
    - Relationship to Nation and the World
    - Corporate Organization

11. Doing Business with the Japanese
12. Strengths/Weaknesses of Each System
13. Japanese Business Etiquette
14. Establishing Working/Interpersonal Relationships
15. Flashpoints in Japanese/American Business Interactions
16. Debriefing and Participant Evaluation of Program

The East West Consulting Group program and others like it offer corporations the opportunity to bring expatriate training in-house immediately, evaluate the degree to which it meets their needs, and make long-term decisions on developing their own programs without sacrificing current training needs.

RECOGNIZING AND PROVIDING FOR THE FAMILY SITUATION

In a survey of expatriate assignments within eighty U.S. multinationals (Tung, 1987), respondents were asked to indicate the most important reasons for expatriate failure. The number one reason cited was "inability of the manager's spouse to adjust to a different physical or cultural environment"

(p. 206). Also high on the list (number three) was "other family-related problems." These findings are consistent with other studies that show that poor family adjustment is a key factor in expatriate failure. Theoretically, one could respond to this problem by selecting candidates who are single, but it's well known that the loneliness built into an overseas assignment is even more overwhelming if the expatriate, in fact, goes alone.

Instead, companies are beginning to take steps to ensure, first of all, that family members and especially spouses are prepared, trained, and supported in much the same way the expatriate is. In the selection stage, interviewers should talk to the spouse, who often stays at home and is more likely to be able to predict the impact of the overseas assignment on the family and identify any special situations that need to be addressed. His or her understanding of the challenge and willingness to meet it are also critical predictors of success. Preliminary trips to the host country for both the expatriate and the spouse are another good way to give both of them a chance to evaluate the life they might be choosing. Such a trip can also provide management with a realistic sense of expatriate and spouse interest in, and suitability for, the assignment. It also allows for their introduction to other members of the expatriate community and local nationals who would become part of their everyday lives.

During the preparation stage, companies are increasingly providing training and orientation programs, not only for the expatriate but also for the spouse and older children. Since the spouse is going to have to face the same cross-cultural adjustment challenges as the expatriate, there is equal reason to prepare and train both partners. These training programs are designed to make the employee, the spouse, and other family members more flexible and adaptive by providing them with information about, and insight into, the culture in which they're going to live.

Many European multinationals, for example, send their prospective expatriates and spouses to residential programs at the Center for International Briefing at Farnham Castle in the United Kingdom. The center offers two types of residential programs: a week-long cultural awareness program and a four-day regional program. The latter focuses on the historical, political, religious, and economic factors that shape the world view of the people of a particular region and contrasts that world view with those of the participants. Through lectures, audiovisual presentations, and discussions with outside speakers, the center tries to help individuals adjust in a practical way to the work and community environments. In contrast, the cultural awareness program does not focus on a specific region or country, but seeks to broaden individual understanding of, and appreciation for, other countries through lectures and experiential exercises.

Once the family arrives at the overseas location, company representatives or consultants should integrate them into the community as quickly as possible. Especially in those situations where there is no expatriate community, the company should contract with local firms to provide practical support during the initial stages of the relocation. These local sponsors should not only arrange social and professional introductions but also provide practical assistance in finding housing and schools, connecting utilities, identifying shopping and recreational locations, and so on. Relatively basic procedures like getting the telephone hooked up can be endlessly complex and frustrating in a foreign country. The means of establishing relations with schools and local businesses are liable to be formidable and bewildering and largely unknowable without local help. The sooner the family is able to get into new daily routines, the less likely the expatriate is to spend much of his or her time dealing with family crises.

Local orientation and language programs should also be made available soon after arrival. The degree to which the family can function within the community in the native language will, in large measure, affect its ability to adapt and adjust to its new surroundings. Their increased participation in the community will also provide the local people with an opportunity to observe and adapt to their visitors' appearance and behavior.

From beginning to end, the expatriate process must recognize and provide for the family if it is likely to succeed. Failure to do so will often result in expatriates who are ineffective in their jobs, unhappy in their social lives and marriages, and subject to bouts of depression, substance abuse, feelings of alienation from others, lack of motivation, and inappropriate behavior both at work and at home.

ENSURING OVERSEAS COMMUNICATION AND SUPPORT

Unless policies and practices are established to keep expatriates in the loop, once the expatriate and family are out of sight of headquarters, it is likely they will also be out of mind. In order to avoid this unhappy and unprofitable situation, global companies are beginning to link overseas assignments with long-term strategies and are devising ways to ensure that such assignments are part of their day-to-day operating concerns. These firms support and train their expatriates in a number of formal and informal ways.

Some encourage their expatriates to call corporate or division headquarters as often as needed to ask questions, seek guidance, gain from the experience of returned expatriates, or just to talk with someone about concerns and problems. Others make an organized effort to inform the expatriate of any in-country support systems and make introductions if desired. Local branches of clubs such as Rotary or Lions are identified. Religious congregations and alumni associations might also have local representation. Links can often be forged with expatriate communities of other home-based firms or subsidiaries.

In some companies, expatriates are linked to a "parent" or "mentor" at corporate headquarters who takes on responsibility for apprising the expatriate of the evolving headquarters situation and responding to his or her concerns and needs overseas. Where there is no one-to-one linking, many companies have a department or division that is responsible for coordinating and overseeing the well-being and career progress of expatriates. Other firms have a senior manager at each of their overseas locations who has a part-time responsibility as a career manager or sponsor for other expatriates. This person's responsibilities might include informal counseling, sponsorship of meetings to discuss problems and successes, communication of concerns back to the home office, and updating of local expatriates on new policies, strategies, and developments at corporate headquarters.

At least once a year, and more often as events dictate, expatriates should be brought back to headquarters for meetings and briefings that ensure communication in both directions. Truly global organizations should also rotate the location of major annual events so that expatriate locations can become better known and gain more credibility with home-based corporate management. Senior management visits and briefings held at regional locations throughout the company's sphere of influence also present opportunities for expatriates who are widely scattered within a region to meet, benefit from each other's experiences, and share resources.

Expatriates should also be included in ongoing training programs both for their own personal growth and to enhance their effectiveness on behalf of the company. Gerald Jones, vice-president in charge of international operations at the Forum Corporation, points out, for example, that managers who are closest to a country's customers are those who can most benefit from training in flexibility. "People in direct contact with the customer must be able to change quickly. They need training not in traditional topics, but in innovation, agility, and adaptability." Jones sees the link between global strategy and expatriate training as essential. He suggests that companies must "create the strategy and, through training, communicate it. What's happening now is that the linkage is taking place much closer to the marketplace, and both training and strategy are being developed closer to the customer" (Callahan, p. 32).

PLANNING FOR REPATRIATION

The repatriation process can be seen from two perspectives: that of the expatriate and that of the organization. From the expatriate's point of view, the transition back home should be orderly and supportive of personal and career needs. The organization should see it as an opportunity to gain additional benefit from the now-completed overseas assignment.

Ideally, the repatriation process should begin when expatriate candidates are being recruited. Clear career paths that both encourage and reward overseas experience need to be carved out. Probable next steps after repatriation need to be understood even before the expatriate embarks on the overseas assignment. And there has to be an organizational structure in place that attends to the process of repatriation at every step. James Harris puts it well when he observes, "We really need to take better care of what may be approaching two million expatriates who will someday be coming home" (p. 49).

❦ *Making the Best Use of Expatriates*

As we can see, repatriation is an important part of global strategy and needs to be carefully considered as such. From the company's point of view, returning expatriates offer a resource that should not be overlooked. They bring back considerable experience, information, and expertise that can be applied immediately and in the future. They can help in the expatriate selection and training process by providing insights into the realities that have to be faced by those on overseas assignments. They are likely to be in-house experts in the culture of the country and region of their own assignment and probably have invaluable contacts and tips that can be passed along. They can provide reality testing for candidates who are preparing to go overseas and give real-world credibility to the preparation and training process. They can be used to support the return of other repatriates and act as sponsors for expatriates still overseas. Finally, they can be a source of valuable input in both global and regional strategic planning.

For all of these reasons, a structured and carefully handled expatriation process provides an organization with considerable and ongoing returns on overseas assignments, and will lead to a greater expatriate success rate and reduced turnover of repatriates in the future.

SUMMARY

Numerous studies show that a high percentage of corporate overseas assignments fail. The estimated direct cost of these failures is over $2 billion a year, not including loss of future business opportunities and damage to corporate reputations.

The number one cause of these failed expatriate assignments is lack of preparation for the overseas assignment, and following close behind are careless and inefficient selection processes, lack of preparation and provision for the expatriate family, insufficient organizational support of the expatriate, and inability of the expatriate to adjust to the foreign culture or business environment.

Since individuals do not usually go overseas for HRD assignments on their own, it's important to try to improve the process that companies use in order to prepare individuals for overseas assignments, whether of an HRD or other nature. The authors have identified a six-step strategy for selecting, preparing, supporting, returning, and valuing expatriates, described some of the best HRD practices in the areas of overseas assignments, and emphasized the need to link strategic planning and globalization with expatriate policy and process.

Both the individual and company perspectives and benefits of providing training for overseas assignments have been examined in detail.

REFERENCES

ADLER, NANCY. "Globalization in Human Resource Management." In *Research in Global Strategic Management: A Canadian Perspective*, Vol. 1, edited by Alan M. Rugman. Greenwich, Conn.: JAI Press, 1989.

BOYACIGILLER, NAKIYE. "The International Assignment Reconsidered." In *International Human Resource Management*. Boston: PWS-Kent Publishing Company, 1991.

CALLAHAN, MADELYN R. "Preparing the New Global Manager." *Training and Development Journal* (March 1989), pp. 29–32.

COPELAND, LENNIE, AND LEWIS GRIGGS. *Going International: How to Make Friends and Deal Effectively in the Global Marketplace*. New York: Random House, 1985.

DUNN, FREDERICKA H. "The 'Best Man' Theory and Why It Fails." *Torch* (July 1991), pp. 5–6.

HARRIS, JAMES E. "Moving Managers Internationally: The Care and Feeding of Expatriates." *Human Resource Planning* (March 1989), pp. 49–54.

MENDENHALL, MARK E., AND GARY ODDOU. "The Overseas Assignment: A Practical Look." *Business Horizons* (September-October 1988), pp. 78–84.

STORTI, CRAIG. *The Art of Crossing Cultures*. Yarmouth, Maine: Intercultural Press, 1989.

TUNG, R. L. "Selection and Training of Personnel for Overseas Assignments." *Columbia Journal of World Business* (Vol. 16, No. 1, 1989), pp. 68–78.

❦ ❦

Future of Global HRD

We are rapidly approaching the twenty-first century. The "white water" of rapid(s) change around the world will continue ever more feverishly. What major forces will have an impact on global human resource development? What global issues will significantly affect the work of HRD professionals all over the world?

The authors have identified fourteen global HRD megatrends for the year 2000 and beyond:

1. Globalization
2. Learning Organizations
3. Global Technology
4. Ethics in the Workplace
5. Creativity
6. Emerging Roles of Women
7. Changing Global Work force
8. Pacific Rim
9. Entrepreneurship and Intrapreneurship
10. Quality and Service
11. Privatization
12. Spiritual Values and Religion
13. Work and Family Life
14. Environment

In Chapter 24, we examine each of these global HRD megatrends and discuss how some global leading-edge organizations and HRD professionals are already incorporating these trends into their work and propelling themselves and their companies into the twenty-first century.

Never before has the future so rapidly become the past. We need to open our minds to more distant futures, both probable and possible.

Alvin Toffler
Future Shock

John Naisbitt and Patricia Aburdene, in their best seller, *Megatrends 2000*, identified what they considered to be the top ten forces at work in the world as we approach the year 2000.

The authors' personal experiences in more than 100 countries as well as our research relative to HRD programs and literature throughout the world have led us to identify fourteen global megatrends (Figure 24.1) that we believe will have increasing impact on HRD and the workplace as we enter the twenty-first century. This chapter will examine each of the global HRD

1. Globalization	8. The Pacific Rim
2. Learning Organizations	9. Entrepreneurship and Intrapreneurship
3. Global Technology	10. Quality and Service
4. Ethics in the Workplace	11. Privatization
5. Creativity	12. Spiritual Values and Religion
6. The Emerging Roles of Women	13. Work and Family
7. The Changing Global Workforce	14. The Environment

FIGURE 24.1
Global HRD Megatrends

megatrends and identify the ways in which leading global "cutting edge" organizations have already begun to incorporate these trends.

❦ *Value*

Although it is clearly impossible to predict with certainty the future of HRD as we move into the age of globalization, an understanding of the areas that are likely to shape its evolution can supply a platform from which the HRD professional can embark on future education and career plans. The fourteen megatrends identified in this chapter provide a comprehensive sweep of the current environment for the profession and practice of HRD.

❦ *Learning Objectives*

After studying this chapter, you should be able to:

1. Identify the global HRD megatrends that are likely to have an impact on the evolution of the profession and its practices as we move into the twenty-first century
2. Recognize the importance of each of the megatrends in terms of its effect on HRD
3. Provide examples of the likely interplay between the fourteen global megatrends and HRD

GLOBALIZATION

As we have noted throughout this book, globalization has had and will continue to have a significant impact on the field of human resource development. We predict that the trend toward globalization will accelerate even more as we approach the year 2000. Tichy correctly calls globalization the "root cause" for change in the nineties and beyond. Globalization will continue to affect both *organizations* and their *employees* and, therefore, HRD.

Trade, travel, and television have laid the groundwork for a global life style for employees just as competition, telecommunications, and financial services laid the foundation for the global corporation. Companies, seeing the world as a single market, will strategize and structure accordingly. Companies that operate only domestically will think globally because global competitors will soon be operating in their backyard.

More and more employees around the world already share common tastes in food (McDonald's, pizza, spaghetti), fashion (denim jeans), and fun (Disney, rock music, television). The Tuareg, the largest tribe of nomads in the Sahara, delayed their migration for ten days one year in order to catch the last episode of "Dallas." People are reading the same magazines, watching the same movies, and dancing the same dances from Boston to Bangkok to Buenos Aires.

One of the most important factors accelerating globalization is the rapid proliferation of the English language. (Remember that language conveys culture as well as meaning.) There are over one billion English speakers in the world. In nearly 100 countries, English is the primary or a secondary language. English is the language of global media, of computers, of business.

Other signals demonstrating the degree to which corporations and individuals are beginning to "live and work in a global village" include:

- Over two billion passengers will fly the world's airways by the year 2000.
- Cable News Network (CNN) is seen simultaneously by millions of people around the world.
- Over three million Americans work overseas; foreign-owned companies employ another three million in the United States
- Computer software has been developed that automatically translates letters into Spanish, Italian, German, or French.
- Over 400,000 international students from 150 countries study in the United States each year.

More and more companies will seek globalization training, realizing that such training is the most critical, single element for global success. Corporations will realize that HRD is the primary tool for leveraging a single global vision as well as integrating local cultural differences.

LEARNING ORGANIZATIONS

There is an increasing concern among global corporations that individual learning will not be an adequate response to the learning needs of the twenty-first century, especially for corporations that must collect, analyze, and utilize information from hundreds of sources worldwide. This information is ever more easily accessed and transmitted; for example, the IBM "summit" can process 230 million instructions per second and optic fibers allow 8,000 conversations on a single fiber versus only forty-eight for copper wire. However, the information must still be learned by human beings in organizations.

The critical importance of organizationwide learning is highlighted by De Gues of Royal Dutch/Shell who writes that, for global corporations, "the ability to learn faster than your competitors is the only sustainable source of competitive advantage" (p. 70).

Senge states that work *must* become a continual process of learning how to create our future rather than react to our past. Successful learning organizations must possess the five disciplines of Systems Thinking, Personal Mastery, Mental Models, Shared Vision, and Team Learning. Learning organizations allow people to "continually expand their capacity to create the results they truly desire, where new and expansive patterns of thinking are nurtured, where collective aspiration is set free, and where people are continually learning how to learn together" (p. 3).

Morris listed the key characteristics of learning organizations:

- Individual learning/development is linked with organizational learning/development in an explicit/structured way.
- There is a focus on creativity and adaptability.
- Teams of all types are a part of the learning/working process.
- Networking—personal and aided by technology—is important to learning and to accomplishing work.
- The idea of the conscious evolution of self and organization prevails.
- Systems thinking—as expressed in deutero-learning concepts—and substantive learning are fundamental.
- Values and value creating are important drivers.

The future global organization will be like a brain, with the whole organization expected to think and then act directly on that thinking. There will need to be a collective learning environment that promotes a sharing of experience on a worldwide scale and that fosters an easy dialogue between the different countries and cultures within which a company functions.

To compete and survive in the global twenty-first century, Dixon notes that organizations need to:

- Learn more effectively from their mistakes
- Shorten the time required to implement strategic changes
- Anticipate and adapt more readily to environmental impacts
- Make greater organizational use of the knowledge of employees at all levels of the organization

- Expedite the transfer of knowledge from one part of the organization to another
- Become more adept at learning from competitors and collaborators
- Stimulate continuous improvement in all areas of the organization
- Accelerate the development of product and process innovation (p. 5)

Despite the critical need for learning organizations, there are as yet only a few good examples according to Kiechel. He identifies Honda, Ford, Analog Devices, and Quad Graphics as organizations that have begun developing as learning organizations. Other organizations consciously seeking to become learning organizations include Rover Group, AMP, and Motorola.

Although the focus of HRD professionals has traditionally been on individual learning (and that still is important), for the year 2000 and beyond, we will need to develop a macro view of learning and learn more about how the organization as a system learns. The economic future, according to Barham and Devine, is "not just about international competition or international collaboration. It is also about international learning. Managing across borders means learning across borders" (p. 37).

GLOBAL TECHNOLOGY

Toffler writes how the advanced global economy cannot run for thirty seconds without the technology of computers and the other new and rapidly improving complexities of production. And yet, today's best computers and CAD-CAM systems will be "stone-age primitive" in the near future.

The source of tomorrow's power will be the products of mind-work—scientific and technological research, sophisticated software, advanced telecommunications, electronic finance, and a better trained work force.

In the new millennium, every industrial country will have this same "hit parade" of technology—microelectronics, biotechnology, new materials (ceramics, plastics, and composites), telecommunications, robotics and machine tools, and computers and software. The result will be global head-to-head competition in every major market.

National corporations that will gain preeminence in the marketplace will be those that excel not in product technology—making better things—but those that excel in *process technology*—making existing things better. Excelling in process technology will depend not on having a small number of highly skilled scientists and engineers but on having a large number of highly skilled, productive workers who can read complex manuals, understand quality control statistics, and even run computers.

Examples of some of the technology affecting the workplace within the next decade include:

- Rapid advances in the field of biotechnology built upon the precise manipulation of organisms, which will revolutionize the fields of agriculture, medicine, and industry
- The emergence of nanotechnology in which nanomachines will possess the ability to "remake the whole physical universe"
- Satellite learning; e.g., Motorola, with its Iridium system, will place seventy-seven tiny satellites into low orbit, making it possible for millions in remote or sparsely populated regions like Siberia, the Chinese desert, and the interior of Africa to send and receive voice, data, and digitized images through hand-held telephones
- The rise of a new generation of small, automated factories
- Automatic translation telephones which allow trainers to communicate naturally in their own language to anyone in the world who has access to a telephone
- Artificial intelligence and embedded learning technology
- Silicon chips that can contain up to 100 million transistors allowing computing power that is now only in the hands of supercomputer users to be available on every desktop
- Supercomputers capable of one trillion calculations per second which will allow advances such as simulations of the human body for the testing of new drugs and computers that respond easily to spoken commands

ETHICS IN THE WORKPLACE

As business becomes more global, so do the ethical dilemmas and complexities facing global workers. Is it okay for American businessmen to pay off African custom officials, a practice some say is as accepted in that part of the world as tipping is in the United States? Is Eastern Europe a business opportunity or a social responsibility? Does one give Moslem workers time off during the Islamic holy month of Ramadan?

In addition to these and other international ethical issues, we have just emerged from the "greed is good" decade of the eighties and the gross scandals of BCCI, Pentagon waste, Japanese investment houses, Solomon Brothers Trading, and the Union Carbide disaster of Bhopal, India.

According to Blake and Carroll, corporations have begun to scramble to get on the ethics bandwagon. The Center for Business Ethics at Bentley College in Massachusetts has found 45 percent of the largest U.S. companies now have ethics programs or workshops. Over 350 universities now teach courses in business ethics. All courses at Georgetown's up-and-coming MBA program must include both a global and an ethical component.

Niagara Mohawk Power recently held full-day ethics workshops for all senior managers. Nynex and Pitney Bowes have training seminars for top officers. Hershey Foods has offered ethics awareness training for senior- and middle-level managers. GE has trained several hundred of its engineers in ethical reasoning and decision making. The Findhurst Community in Scotland hosts regular international conferences on ethics and business.

In a recent survey of 1,500 CEOs in twenty countries, ethics was rated as the most important personal characteristic for the global executive in the twenty-first century. The CEO must be above reproach, because impeccable ethical standards will be "indispensable to a firm's internal and external credibility." With ethical standards, the effective global executive will be better able "to inspire employees to realize their potential" (LePage, p. 63).

The American Society for Training and Development has also made ethics a high priority. In the *Models for HRD Practice*, thirteen areas of ethical challenge were identified:

1. Maintaining appropriate confidentiality
2. Saying no to inappropriate requests
3. Showing respect for copyrights, sources, and intellectual property
4. Ensuring truth in claims, data, and recommendations
5. Balancing organization and individual needs and interests
6. Ensuring customer and user involvement, participation, and ownership
7. Avoiding conflicts of interest
8. Managing personal biases
9. Showing respect for, interest in, and representation of individual and population differences
10. Making interventions appropriate to the customer's or user's needs
11. Being sensitive to the direct and indirect effects of intervention and acting to address negative consequences
12. Pricing or costing products or services fairly.
13. Using power appropriately

CREATIVITY

Einstein once wrote that "imagination is more important than information." And, as the technological revolution continues to phase out the lower end of the work scale, more creativity will be required of all workers.

Ohmae laments that people in business have forgotten how to invent. Corporations need to relearn the art of invention, especially for industries or businesses that are global, where one must achieve world-scale economies and yet tailor products to key markets. Global leaders need to *create* sustaining values for the customer which are far better than those of competitors.

White talks about the importance of world-class leaders who need to be "creative, to see possibilities globally, be open to learning, and possess an innovative spirit.... They need to prefer vision to numbers" (p. 51). Creativity training has been around for a long time, but the need and demand for it will grow rapidly all over the world as companies realize its importance in gaining a competitive edge.

Toffler, in his recent book *Powershift*, states that an "innovation imperative" will be essential since no existing market share will be safe, no product life will be indefinite. Companies will die unless they can create a continuous stream of new products. The corporate need for creativity will encourage worker autonomy, which implies a "totally different power relationship between employer and employee," one that tolerates error and encourages "a multitude of bad ideas to harvest a single good one" (p. 213).

A Global Intuition Network has been established to promote "the applied use of intuition in decision-making, share new knowledge on how to use this brain skill as it becomes known, and to promote ongoing research on intuitive processes for practical use in organizations."

Minnesota Mining and Manufacturing (3M), a successful global corporation, has recently undertaken specific actions to encourage creativity in their organization:

- Managers are rewarded for encouraging new, creative projects among their staff.
- Research and development people are allowed to spend up to 15 percent of their time working on their own ideas.
- Division managers have discretionary power to finance new, creative ventures.

Other companies are also pushing creativity and gaining from it. Maytag estimates that 20 percent of its productivity gains come from worker ideas. Ore-Ida runs a Fellows program for "good ideas" that uncovered $1 million worth of cost savings in one year.

EMERGING ROLES OF WOMEN

The changing roles of women and the impact of these changes on family and the organization will become ever more significant in the global arena as we enter the twenty-first century.

Already the entrance of women into the industrial work force is a worldwide phenomenon. In Japan, for example, 58 percent of females between the ages of 15 and 64 are in the work force. In Canada, one-third of all businesses are owned by women; in France, it is one-fifth. In Great Britain, women are establishing new businesses three times faster than men; in the United States, twice as fast. In the United States, women are taking two-thirds of the new jobs being created, most of them in the information/service industry (the primary industry of the twenty-first century).

Even developing countries, where, until recently, relatively few women had joined the work force, the percentage of females in the work force is now at nearly 50 percent. As cooking and cleaning technologies ease the burden at home, as agricultural jobs disappear, and as service jobs (which generally require less education) begin to proliferate, an even higher number of Third World women will enter the labor force. Even now China and Thailand have a higher percentage of female workers (75 percent) than any industrialized nation except for Sweden (79 percent). In those countries where female labor force participation remains low (e.g., Pakistan—12%), it is often for religious and cultural reasons.

Women have faced serious difficulties, however, as they have entered the labor market—the glass ceiling preventing few from emerging into senior management positions, sexual harassment, limited elder care and child care facilities, being placed on the "mommy track" and thereby limited in career opportunities, and the super woman ascription of being forced to do the impossible, i.e., full-time super mom and super employee. The new and growing responsibility of caring for their elder parents has added yet another difficulty requiring women to have more flexible hours and to demand more time away from their jobs.

As difficult as the corporate world has made it for women to move up the organization ladder, it is precisely the female style of leadership that may be most needed in the global corporation of the twenty-first century according to Naisbitt and Aburdene who see the "new corporate archetype" as being more like women than men. Why? Because the dominant principle within future global organization will have shifted from *management* in order to *control* an enterprise to *leadership* in order to *bring out the best* in people and to respond quickly to change. The leader in the twenty-first century global corporation will be more of a teacher, facilitator, coach who will encourage the new, better-educated worker to be more entrepreneurial, self-managing, and oriented toward lifelong learning.

Naisbitt and Aburdene suggest that HRD professionals look toward Sweden, a country which already provides such opportunities for women by, for example, allowing up to twelve months for maternity leave. Japan, which will desperately need all of its limited human resources, is building thousands of new child care and elder care facilities to allow women employees to retain their employment. Countries like Germany, Spain, and Greece are providing corporate subsidies to train women.

CHANGING GLOBAL WORK FORCE

The global work force in the year 2000 will be even more mobile, and corporations will increasingly reach across borders to find the skills they need. These movements of workers will be driven by the growing gap between the world's supplies of labor and the demands for it. While much of the world's skilled and unskilled human resources are being produced in the developing world, most of the well-paid jobs are being generated in the cities of the industrialized world.

Johnston, who recently completed an exhaustive study of global work patterns, has identified four major implications of this mismatch for HRD practitioners:

1. There will be a massive relocation of people including legal and illegal immigrants, temporary workers, retirees, and visitors. The greatest relocation will involve young, well-educated workers flocking to the cities of the developed world.

2. Some industrialized nations will reconsider their protectionist immigration policies, as they come to rely on, and compete for, foreign-born workers.

3. Labor-short, immigrant-poor countries like Japan and Sweden will be compelled to improve labor productivity dramatically to avoid slow economic growth. Increased training and outsourcing of jobs will become necessary.

4. There will be a gradual standardization of labor practices around the world in areas of vacation time, workplace safety, training, and employee rights.

Johnston goes on to state that the rapidly growing work force in developing regions, when combined with different rates of economic growth, will lead to a "major redefinition of labor markets" (p. 116). Nations that have slow-growing work forces but rapid growth in service-sector jobs (Japan, United States, Germany) will become magnets for immigrants. Nations whose educational systems produce prospective workers faster than their economies can absorb them (Argentina, Russia, Philippines, Poland, Egypt) will export people. *Business Week* (November 4, 1991) noted this phenomenon in the recent emigration of thousands of Soviet physicists, biologists, and engineers to fill jobs everywhere from Cambridge, Massachusetts, to Silicon Valley in California.

The result will be a workplace which will become more and more multicultural, at both the unskilled and skilled levels. Already, physicists of Bell Laboratories, for example, come from universities in England or India, as well as from Princeton or MIT. At Schering-Plough's research labs, the first language of the biochemists is as likely to be Hindi, Japanese, or German as English. It is routine for U.S. hospitals to advertise in Dublin and Manila for nurses. Engineers are recruited in England, India, and China to fill U.S. job openings. Hispanics and Asians will represent over 25 percent of the total U.S. work force by the year 2000.

The combination of a globalized work force and global corporations means that managers and employees must be able to work effectively with more and more people with differing cultures, customs, values, beliefs, and practices.

Cross-cultural training will become ever more important. Training firms which specialize in managing cultural diversity (already the number one training course within many corporations) will enjoy the prospect of even higher demands for their services.

PACIFIC RIM

Five hundred years ago the world's center of trade began moving from the Mediterranean to the Atlantic. Today it is shifting from the Atlantic to the Pacific. The cities of the Pacific Rim—Los Angeles, Jakarta, Tokyo, Sidney, Seattle—are taking over from the old established cities of the Atlantic—New York, London, Paris.

By the year 2000, Asia will have over half the world's population while Europe will contain less than 6 percent of the total. Already Asia is a $3 trillion a year market that is growing at $3 billion per week! The countries of the Pacific Rim speak more than 1,000 languages and have the most varied religious and cultural traditions in the world. Therefore, the impact of the Pacific Rim on corporations and HRD practice will be both cultural and economic.

The commitment of Asians to training and education is very high. This is evident among Asians in the United States where 44 percent hold college degrees compared to 25 percent of the general U.S. population. Korea has the highest number of Ph.D.'s per capita in the world. Japan has the world's highest ratio of engineers (24 per 1,000.) The Asian Region Training and Development Organization (ARTDO) remains the most active regional HRD association. National HRD associations are vitalizing the training communities in Japan, Philippines, Malaysia, and Thailand.

The size of the Pacific Rim's labor pool and growing economic power is causing more and more U.S. HRD organizations to refocus their mission and strategies to service organizations and people in this geographic area. More and more training firms are collaborating with Chinese, Japanese, Filipino, and Indonesian organizations.

ENTREPRENEURSHIP AND INTRAPRENEURSHIP

Entrepreneurship, whether in the large global corporations, in public enterprises, or in the failed socialist economies of Eastern Europe and China, will be a driving force for economic growth in the year 2000.

Communism has already been overthrown throughout Eastern Europe and the Soviet Union. In China, Vietnam, and Cuba, change is imminent. The socialism of Western Europe is also in decline as the failure of centralized planning and the high cost of welfare state programs has been realized. The public sector in the United States is being challenged to be more efficient, creative, and entrepreneurial with fewer resources.

Much of the training and development funds of the U.S. Agency for International Development, the Canadian Institute for Development Assistance, as well as the assistance agencies of Japan, Germany, U.K., and Sweden are being earmarked for the building of small businesses and the training of entrepreneurs in the developing nations of Asia, Africa, and Latin America, countries representing over half of the world's population.

HRD programs will be the critical tool to enable these countries to make the difficult transition to a competitive, free-market economy.

The larger corporations are also aware of the importance of entrepreneurship within their organization (or "intrapreneurship" as coined by Pinochet). They realize that, in a competitive global marketplace, they will need to recapture the entrepreneurial skills and attitudes that were part of their earlier success and growth.

GLOBAL QUALITY AND SERVICE

The ability to attract and retain customers with quality products and quality service will be the survival issue for global businesses in the twenty-first century. Global corporations realize that the focus on quality has turned Japan into an economic powerhouse. Even the public sector will be expected to be service and quality oriented or face privatization or loss of funding.

Business Week (October 25, 1991) devoted a special issue to this topic entitled "The Quality Imperative—What It Takes to Win in the Global Economy." In one country after another, quality has become a sort of mantra. In a global economy, those who provide quality products will survive and thrive; those who do not will wither and die.

Developing a quality product is only the beginning. How it is delivered is equally important in the global marketplace. Poor service sends more customers to your global competitors than price or quality. In a global study by

Forum Corporation, customers were asked to rate service quality. Lack of reliability and lack of cultural empathy were the top complaints.

The Forum study also found a direct correlation between employee turnover and service quality—companies with the lowest service quality ratings also had the highest employee turnover rates. In other words, quality lessens the need to continually train new workers.

Numerous global companies have begun to get on the total quality bandwagon. Fiat is retraining workers in all its plants in quality. Sulzer of Switzerland prides itself in providing better quality service and training than the Japanese. New GM workers in Mexico receive seven weeks of quality-focused training and now manufacture cars with the same or higher quality than U.S. models. Infiniti trains all of its car dealers on treating customers as *okyakusama*, or honored guests. IBM, Motorola, Milliken, and others offer quality training programs not only for their employees but also to business and engineering faculties throughout the United States.

PRIVATIZATION

State-owned enterprises are being sold in every part of the world. Amid the failure of communism and other command-economy models and the shortage of tax funds in free-market economies, governments are seeking to unload public companies.

The Washington Post (November 17, 1991) calls privatization the "biggest fire sale in history." From Australia to Argentina, Poland to Pakistan—all around the globe—countries are transferring their state-owned companies by selling them into private hands.

Over $90 billion worth of state-owned enterprises have been sold in the past three years. For sale are government-owned steel mills, once considered "a badge of nationhood" for less-developed countries; banks whose nationalization decades earlier was seen as a key to development; government-owned newspapers which had been used to maintain "government-think."

In a recent special report in *Business Week* (October 21, 1991), entitled "The Global Rush to Privatize," the authors describe the following actions:

- *Privatizatziya* is the rage in republics of the former USSR. Over the next three years, Russia wants to privatize 30 percent of its state-owned assets. ABB and Mitsui are planning investments in huge Siberian chemical plants; Coca-Cola is seeking a joint venture with a bottling plant in Kiev; new private companies plan to split up Aeroflot and create new airlines.
- 14,000 state-owned companies in Hungary, Poland, and Czechoslovakia are up for sale; Volkswagen has bought Czechoslovakia's Skoda; P & G purchased Czech detergent Rakona; Germany's Korf bought Hungary's OZD Steel.

- Mexico has sold its phone company, Banamex; Venezuela unloaded the state airline, VIASA; Brazil is preparing its steel company for privatization; Columbia is selling much of its coal business; Paraguay is auctioning off its cement plants and liquor distillery; Argentina sold its highways and even the Buenos Aires Zoo.

States and cities throughout the United States are privatizing services ranging from garbage collection to prisons to social services. Japan has sold its tobacco manufacturing and marketing company, as well as its railroad and telecommunications systems. Great Britain long ago sold British Steel and British Airways.

Roger Leeds, a former World Bank economist, calls privatization the "story of the 1990's." Joseph Linn, World Bank vice-president, calls it a "worldwide trend ... dominating what is going on economically in the 1990's and beyond" (*Washington Post*, Nov. 17, 1991, p. H9).

SPIRITUAL VALUES AND RELIGION

Naisbitt and Aburdene observed in *Megatrends 2000* that people around the world are turning toward religion and spiritual values in overwhelming numbers, that they are realizing that "science and technology do not tell us what life means. We learn that through literature, arts, and spirituality" (p. 293). By reaffirming the spiritual people experience a "more balanced quest" to better their lives.

James Autry's best seller among HRD professionals, *Love and Profit: The Art of Caring Leadership*, begins with the author's three basic beliefs:

1. Work can provide the opportunity for *spiritual* as well as financial growth.
2. The workplace is rapidly becoming the new *neighborhood*.
3. Good management is largely a matter of *love* (p. 13).

In the workplace, Autry believes, everyone should be treated with dignity and respect, honesty and trust, and with love. Such a workplace would be like "heaven" (p. 156).

Michael Ray, professor at Stanford University, sees the emergence of spiritual values as part of the new paradigm in business. Spirituality in this new paradigm does not refer to religion but rather "to the power of inner wisdom and authority and the connection and wholeness in humanity" (p. 37). It is a move to the spirit, to inner qualities such as intuition, will, strength, joy, and compassion.

William Miller, in the article "How Do We Put Spiritual Values to Work," describes how the director of Hewlett-Packard Laboratory, Frank

Carrubba, concluded that the most successful teams are built upon the "qualities and spirit and truth within themselves" (p. 80). According to Miller, an appreciation of deep, cultural values and a conscious development of those values is essential to corporate growth and the quality of life.

WORK AND FAMILY LIFE

Coping with conflicts between work and family will be one of the greatest employment challenges in the year 2000. Over the past two decades, the number of working women in the work force has nearly doubled on a worldwide basis. Single working mothers are becoming more common, and two-career families are becoming the norm in many countries. Recessions, mergers and acquisitions, relocations and corporate downsizing, as well as longer commutes to find affordable housing and the soaring costs of health care have all led to family pressures.

Companies will need to help employees deal with their family and work obligations. They will need to become "family-friendly."

The Families and Work Institute in New York recently created an index to measure work/family policies at companies. Among the family-friendly policies rated are:

- *Flexible work arrangements*—variable starting and quitting times, part-time work
- *Leaves*—length of parental leaves, who's eligible, job guarantees
- *Financial assistance*—flexible benefits, long-term-care insurance, child care discounts
- *Corporate giving/community service*—funding for community or national work/family initiatives
- *Dependent-care services*—child and elder care referral, on-site centers, sick-child programs
- *Management change*—work/family training for managers, work/family coordinators
- *Work/family stress management*—wellness programs, relocation services, work/family seminars

The institute recently conducted its first survey of 188 U.S. companies with the results showing that the average rating was a mere 68 out of a possible 610 points. Family-friendly corporate personnel policies are obviously still rare, but the pace of change is accelerating rapidly as corporate leaders realize their importance in retaining quality employees.

The top-rated corporation in the institute's survey was Johnson and Johnson, which provides flex-time, maternity leave, working at home after childbirth, part-time work, on-site day care, on-site aerobics, health care for part-timers, payment to employees who adopt, and, most important, a firm commitment by top management to change the corporate culture to be family-friendly.

Other companies offering solid work/family programs are IBM (employees have flex-time during meal breaks allowing workers on the second shift enough time to go home for dinner and tell the kids a bedtime story) and Stride Rite (which has converted a portion of its headquarters into an intergenerational day-care center for young children and elderly parents).

ENVIRONMENT

In this final decade of the twentieth century, many believe that this may be our last chance to avert environmental damage so severe that future generations will be unable to meet basic requirements for food and energy. Business leaders are increasingly aware that the earth operates as a single, unified ecosystem and that what occurs in one place will have repercussions in another. In a recent survey of over 200 global executives by Booz, Allen, and Hamilton, the proportion who believe environmental issues are extremely important tripled from that of two years earlier. *Fortune* magazine (February 12, 1992) stated that environmentalism is "not only the biggest business issue of the 1990's, but a mainstream movement of massive worldwide force. Companies are moving toward eco-responsibility."

Globe 92, an international trade fair and conference held in Vancouver, Canada, in March 1992, brought together thousands of corporate executives, environmental leaders, and government officials from eighty countries to "promote practical solutions to resolve the conflict between a healthy environment and a thriving economy." Participants were able to study leading-edge technology to protect and improve the environment. Conference speakers included Frank Popov, president and CEO of Dow Chemical, and Shridath Ramphal, president of the International Union for the Conservation of Nature.

Corporate and government leaders also gathered in Rio de Janeiro in June 1992 for the First Earth Summit to identify ways to achieve environmental protection as well as economic growth. The World Bank has committed $1.3 billion to demonstrate approaches in solving global environmental problems. The Japanese Committee for Global Environment represents a culmination of that country's efforts in building desalinization and denitrification installations that enable Japanese power plants to discharge 80 percent less pollutants than Western plants.

The forms and impact of future technologies will become more energy efficient, produce less waste, and contribute to the GNP with minimal consumption of natural resources. Shifts in these directions are already occurring in information technology, biotechnology, and advanced materials. Renewal energy sources—solar, wind, hydro, biomass, and photovoltaic—will become more competitive with conventional energy sources.

Human resource development professionals will need to provide the leadership in helping corporations develop environmental strategies that can become competitive, profitable, and secure and can lead to successful and ethical growth. Educating and training organizations on the uses and benefits of "green" technologies will be a crucial role in the next decade.

SUMMARY

Naisbitt and Aburdene, in their recent best seller *Megatrends 2000*, identified what they considered the top ten forces which will be impacting our society in the year 2000. The authors' personal experiences in over 100 countries as well as our research relative to HRD programs and literature throughout the world have led us to identify fourteen global megatrends that will significantly impact HRD and the workplace as we enter the twenty-first century. They are:

- Globalization
- Learning Organizations
- Global Technology
- Ethics in the Workplace
- Creativity
- Emerging Roles of Women
- Changing Global Work Force
- Pacific Rim

- Entrepreneurship and Intrapreneurship
- Quality and Service
- Privatization
- Spiritual Values and Religion
- Work and Family Life
- Environment

Many leading global organizations have already begun incorporating these trends into their HRD planning and practices. There is little doubt that these fourteen megatrends will have a large impact on the world of work and roles of the global HRD professional. HRD and the contributions made by global HRD professionals in the next century will be extremely important to economic success and global well-being.

REFERENCES

AMERICAN SOCIETY FOR TRAINING AND DEVELOPMENT. *Models for HRD Practice.* Alexandria, Va.: ASTD Press, 1988.

AUERBACK, STUART. "Around the Globe, the Sale of a Century." *Washington Post* (November 17, 1991), pp. H1, H9.

AUTRY, JAMES. *Love and Profit: The Art of Caring Leadership.* New York: William Morrow and Company, 1991.

BLAKE, ROBERT B., AND DEBORAH ANNE CARROLL. "Ethical Reasoning in Business." *Training and Development Journal* (June 1989), pp. 99–104.

CARNEVALE, ANTHONY. "Learning: The Critical Technology." *Training and Development Journal* (February 1992), S1–S14.

DE GEUS, ARIE. "Planning as Learning." *Harvard Business Review* (March-April 1998), pp. 70–74.

DIXON, NANCY. "Spotlight on Organizational Learning." *Torch* (March 1991), p. 5.

GALAGAN, PATRICIA. "Creativity and Work." *Training and Development Journal* (June 1989), pp. 23–32.

GALAGAN, PATRICIA. "The Learning Organization Made Easy." *Training and Development Journal* (October 1991), pp. 37–44.

GLOSGALL, WILLIAM ET AL. *"The Global Rush to Privatize."* Business Week (October 21, 1991), pp. 49–54.

JOHNSTON, WILLIAM. "Global Workforce 2000: The New World Labor Market." *Harvard Business Review* (March-April 1991), pp. 115–27.

KIECHEL, WALTER. "The Organization That Learns." *Fortune* (March 12, 1990), pp. 133–36.

LAMBERT, KATHERINE. "The Soviet Brain Drain Is the U.S. Brain Gain." *Business Week* (November 4, 1991), pp. 94–95.

LEPAGE, ROBERT. "The Global Executive of the Twenty-First Century." *Journal of European Business* (May-June 1990), pp. 62–64.

MORRIS, LINDA. "Learning Organizations: An Exploration." Unpublished, 1991.

NAISBITT, JOHN, AND PATRICIA ABURDENE. *Megatrends 2000.* New York: Avon, 1990.

OHMAE, KENICHI. The Borderless World. *New York: Harper Business*, 1990.

RAY, MICHAEL. "The Emerging New Paradigms in Business." In *New Traditions in Business.* San Francisco: New Leaders Press, 1991, pp. 33–45.

SENGE, PETER M. *The Fifth Discipline.* New York: Doubleday, 1990.

SHEPHERD, STEPHEN B. "The Quality Imperative." *Business Week* (October 25, 1991), p. 4.

TICHY, NOEL. Global Leadership Symposium, Ann Arbor, MI., 1990.

TOFFLER, ALVIN. *Future Shock.* New York: Bantam, 1971.

TOFFLER, ALVIN. *Powershift.* New York: Bantam, 1990.

WHITE, BREN. *World Class Training.* Dallas: Odenwald, 1992.

Author Index

309

Subject Index